Operating AI

Bridging the Gap Between Technology and Business

Ulrika Jägare

To my mother Ulla, who inspired me at a very young age to love writing and reading books, and to my two wonderful sons, Rasmus and Emil, who always supports my writing.

About the Author

Ulrika Jägare is an M.Sc. director at the global telecommunications company Ericsson AB. She has 22 years of experience in telecommunications in various leadership positions across research & development, product management, services, and sales. During the last 12 years, Ulrika has specialized in AI and data science, with a focus on bridging the gap between technology and business to enable business realization in practice. Ulrika established the first AI strategy for Ericsson and has been instrumental in implementing a data-driven approach across Ericsson through various major global initiatives. She was responsible for initiating Ericsson's first AI-based commercial offerings. Currently she leads a global AI and automation initiative in the area of Internet of Things (IoT).

Ulrika is also passionate about helping other companies leverage data science and AI in practice. She is a speaker and author in data science and in 2019 published *Data Science Strategy for Dummies* (Wiley), which is used in university courses in various countries. In addition, she has written several other books in data science since 2018 (Wiley) in collaboration with companies such as Databricks, Trifacta, Arm, Nice, and Cloudera.

About the Technical Editor

Mattias Lidström is a director of data science and machine learning at the telecommunications company Ericsson AB, where he defines and drives the adoption of AI within the company's products and services. Mattias has an extensive background in research in the fields of AI and machine learning, with more than 15 years' experience developing new concepts for AI, machine learning, policy control, user knowledge management, and context-aware services. His main area of interest is data science, particularly complex systems with big data and real-time communication. He holds an M.Sc. in computer science from KTH, Royal Technical Institute in Stockholm.

Acknowledgments

I have been fortunate to work again with professionals from Wiley to create this book.

I would like to thank Jim Minatel, associate publisher at John Wiley & Sons, and John Sleeva, project editor, who managed the process that got us from outline to a finished manuscript. Thanks to Christine O'Connor, managing editor, for making the last stages of book development go as smoothly as they did.

I am especially grateful for the expert support from my technical editor, Mattias Lidström, who is also a colleague at Ericsson AB.

Thank you to Mazin Gilbert, PhD and director at Google, for your support and for writing a relevant and engaging foreword to this book. I truly appreciate your view on applying AI in practice and the experiences you bring with you from your time at AT&T.

Finally, I would like to thank Kirk Borne, PhD and chief science officer at DataPrime, for taking the time to read my book and for your strong endorsement.

—Ulrika Jägare

Contents at a Glance

Contents

Foreword

The first time I met Ulrika, I knew she was a passionate and enthusiastic leader who cared immensely about operationalizing and productizing AI systems at scale. Although many books do a superb job of describing the wealth of AI technologies and parallelized algorithms, only a few describe the challenges of MLOps and the life cycle management of AI systems end to end. Widespread adoption of AI is not hindered today by any specific technology, but by the lack of understanding, trust, explainability, and experience in deploying these systems in the field. Many companies claim today to be using AI systems, but in reality, only a few of those systems are completely deployed and unleashing real business value.

I spent 30 years of my career in telecommunications on research & development of machine learning and AI systems, and I experienced firsthand multiple challenges that have hindered the massive deployments of AI. Let me state a few:

- Significant investment and multiple skill sets are required to build the underlying AI software and compute infrastructure, to create and test machine learning models, and to deploy and operationalize those models in the field. In a typical large company, this is an investment in the hundreds of employees across multiple organizations (operation engineers, architects, software developers, data scientists, researchers, product managers, marketers, to name a few), and millions of dollars in licensing, building, and operating the software and the underlying infrastructure. Saying it differently, the barrier to entry is significant in terms of investment.

- There is a lack of knowledge of the value AI brings to businesses today. In many forums, the power and scope of AI are misunderstood, and AI is perceived as a magic wand that can solve all problems. In reality, that is not true. AI systems are superb at solving repeatable tasks that humans take for granted. Examples include speech or pattern recognition. However, AI systems are miserable at generalizing across tasks and are incapable of making high-level inferences that employ knowledge of the environment and the world. That high-level knowledge is translated today in the form of deterministic policies and rules that are set by humans. That close collaboration between humans and AI systems is necessary for the successful outcome of any business challenge.

- AI systems feed on data. However, companies treat data as a liability and a cost rather than a key asset for running their business to compete in the marketplace. Good data is a powerful weapon that leads to competitive intelligence, and accordingly, it must be treated as a first-class asset. This includes all aspects of the data life cycle, from collection and quality assessment to addressing data privacy, access management, security, sovereignty, and transparency.

But deploying AI systems does not need to be that challenging and costly. Let me summarize a few key recommendations:

- Approach AI holistically by examining the process from end to end. This requires building and empowering one cohesive team and not vertical silo groups who carry out independent tasks across the AI development life cycle.

- Invest in a complete data and AI pipeline and infrastructure from the point data is collected to the point an action is taken and a closed loop is operational. This is one big giant step beyond performing data exploration and analytics research that is done today in many companies. Hyperscalers provide a wealth of infrastructure and tools that make this task pretty straightforward today.

- Define and track clear business metrics (e.g., the percentage of failures that are resolved automatically within 5 minutes), and not just fine-tuning metrics of the performance of machine learning models. The lack of clear and objective business metrics can waste time and resources.

- Transform your organizational culture from that of "fearing AI" to that of "embracing AI." "Legacy culture" is a hurdle for massive adoption of AI systems. Transforming the culture requires new training at all layers of the organization, and a coupling of performance in deploying successful AI systems with employees' financial merits.

I am excited about Ulrika's book as it addresses many of these issues and provides the blueprint enterprises need to adopt AI at scale. Enjoy reading!

—Mazin Gilbert, Director of Engineering, Telecommunications Orchestration, Analytics, and Automation at Google

Introduction

Artificial intelligence (AI) plays a critical role in optimizing the value gained from digital transformation. Across different business segments, companies seek to leverage new technologies for increased revenue or lower cost. But AI is much more than an accelerator for taking the digital transformation journey to another level and making it possible for teams to work smarter, do things faster, and turn previously impossible tasks into routine.

Artificial intelligence has started to be seen as a key business enabler across more and more industries. Corporations are starting to view AI as a technology for future-proofing their business way beyond organizational efficiency. It's a revolutionary approach where AI becomes the foundation of the commercial portfolio, whether it's products, services, or some type of "as a service" setup. By embracing the full potential of AI, every company and organization in some sense becomes a technology company, whether or not that is the goal. But are companies in general ready for this massive transformation?

I would argue that most companies are not ready for this massive transformation, but it's important to remember that neither are their customers. Remember that major technology shifts like the one that AI imposes hold a lot of promise but require a fundamental transformation to take place in order to gain the expected return on investment (ROI). This fundamental shift will not happen overnight and will definitely not proceed in a synchronized manner across different markets and business segments, nor across the public sector with all its various service functions.

However, it's worth noting that the COVID-19 pandemic has accelerated the need for, and understanding of, the benefits of a fully digitalized workplace and society. However, keep in mind that just because the digitalization journey is speeding up, that doesn't necessarily mean that adding AI capabilities will be the next natural step to take.

It's not as easy as it may seem to effectively deploy and leverage AI in the enterprise. To be successful, you can't only focus on the technical pieces—you need to also address aspects such as strategy, people, and ways of working as well as how your AI solution is intended to run in production. This is crucial to break down barriers between AI in development and AI in production, and to quickly and seamlessly be able to move AI models and operate increasing numbers of models on a continuous basis in a live setting.

There is no easy fix for this, but by learning how to balance your AI investment while keeping an operational mind-set throughout, you will be more likely to succeed.

This book is centered on the fact that operating AI is not the same as operating software. That is not just a statement, but a principle that has many implications for what it means to embrace AI in your company or organization. By reading this book, you will gain insights on how to approach AI in your enterprise with operations in mind, and by doing so you are much more likely to succeed with your objectives. An operational approach should be taken directly from the start when you build your AI foundation with reproducible model pipelines. In the development phase, consider potential operational factors such as modeling the target environment or the actual use case, and you will be better positioned to build a solution that will meet its objective when it's running in live operations.

Another important aspect in this book involves truly addressing the data perspective as part of your strategic investments in AI. Remember that without the data, your AI solution cannot run. Understanding and caring for your data is vital, as well as making sure you have the data rights needed, which can sometimes be the hardest thing to manage as part of an operational setting. What you don't want to do is find out too late that the data you need isn't accessible or is owned by another party, or perhaps that the data pipeline you have invested in will not scale in production.

This book will also focus on how to successfully deploy your models as well as operate your AI solution in live environments. You will learn how different model target environments can influence aspects through the whole AI life cycle, not only which deployment options you have but which data you need to train your model on, which AI technique you will benefit most from using, how to scale your solution over time, and how and why you need to monitor and maintain your model when it's operating in production.

Finally, it's important to remember that AI is all about trust. In order for a company to rely on the AI solution to take over parts of its operations, make decisions, and let the AI system take action based on identified insights, both management and employees must trust the AI solution enough. To ensure that trust, from the start you need to think about the operational context, legal rights, and transparency and reliability aspects. This is especially valid for commercial usage of AI. In order for your customers to trust your AI-based products and/or services, you must be able to explain how your AI solution works and what is actually going on. The less your customers understand of how an AI-based solution works, the more insecure they will feel about trusting it. Customers hate to buy a black box solution. Although more complex AI techniques like deep learning can be hard to explain even for the data scientists who are building the solutions, there are ways to work with explainable AI (XAI), which will be further explored in this book.

Since the main objective of your AI investment is to realize a business value, internal or commercial, it's fundamental to understand what can be expected from your AI investment. Most companies understand the difficulties involved in reaching their objectives, but they may not fully grasp how to best navigate these challenges given a specific industry or for a specific business model. The book helps you connect these pieces, apply an operational mind-set to the business perspective, and set you on the path to success.

What Does This Book Cover?

This book covers the following topics:

Chapter 1: Balancing the AI Investment   There is no simple answer to how to succeed with your AI investment, but there are some fundamental aspects that should be driving your objectives and realization plans, and that includes a balanced approach to AI. In this chapter you will find out what that means and why it is important for your business. The chapter will start by defining AI and by sorting out what AI is in relation to other related concepts such as machine learning (ML), automation, and robotics, just to name a few. This chapter will also address why you need to put more effort into making your AI model operational than you put into developing your AI model and how to embrace an operational mind-set for AI.

Chapter 2: Data Engineering Focused on AI Treating data as a valuable business asset should be the main priority in any company, and it's the key to staying on top of what is going on in your company. Leveraging data will help you understand what is not working and why, as well as enable you to see what is coming. This chapter will present a structured way for you to get to know your data and focuses on the importance of working with production. Furthermore, you will learn which data quality metrics are important and how to scale your data to succeed with your AI investment, as well as key competences in data engineering.

Chapter 3: Embracing MLOps In ML development the problem is seldom to technically develop, train, or implement ML models; instead, the main problem is mostly related to poor communication and lack of efficient cross-functional team collaboration. It might sound like an easy task to correct, but the fact remains that most AI projects do not make it to production due to this communication gap between the data scientists and the business. This chapter will introduce the most successful approach to tackle these problems: MLOps practices. You will learn that shifting the focus from building individual ML models to building ML pipelines is a game-changer. The chapter will also explain the importance of adopting a continuous learning approach. This chapter will also describe how to approach your AI/ML functional technology stack and ensure you have the right competences and toolsets for successful MLOps practices.

Chapter 4: Deployment with AI Operations in Mind It's important to remember that it's not until you deploy your models in a production setting that the value of AI can fully be realized. However, moving your models from the lab to production is far from an easy task. Successful model deployment is about a lot more than just running your model in another execution environment. When deploying AI models in production, you need to consider various areas spanning from legal rights and data access to managing retraining and redeployment of models in a live production setting. In this chapter you will learn how to handle model serving in practice and the role of the ML inference pipeline in this process. Furthermore, key success factors for industrializing

AI will be outlined, as well as why it's equally important to focus attention on the cultural shift that needs to happen.

Chapter 5: Operating AI Is Different from Operating Software
Observing and monitoring AI models in production is often an overlooked part of the ML life cycle, almost like an afterthought, when it should be seen as critical to a model's viability in the post-deployment phase. Because AI is built on continuous learning principles, it requires more operational support than traditional software. The feedback loop becomes fundamental, along with highly automated monitoring of model performance and data quality. This chapter will address the cornerstones of AI model monitoring and model scoring in production. Retraining in production using continuous training (CT) will be addressed, as well as how to efficiently handle model performance issues.

Finally, the chapter includes reflections on why different model monitoring is needed for different stakeholders, as well as considerations regarding model monitoring toolsets.

Chapter 6: AI Is All About Trust   Despite substantial investments in governance, many organizations still lack visibility into the risks that AI models pose and what, if any, steps have been taken to mitigate them. This is a serious problem, given the increasingly critical role AI models now play in supporting daily decision making. But there are also major reputational, operational, and financial damage that companies face when AI systems malfunction, expose personal data, or contain inherent biases. This chapter will address how to anonymize data and what that means for businesses. To gain trust in an AI solution, you also need to reduce the impact of bias, as well as be able to explain how a model arrived at a certain decision, which is further explored in this chapter. Finally, legal aspects on data rights and AI model rights are explored, including operational governance considerations related to data and AI.

Chapter 7: Achieving Business Value from AI   As businesses from every sector start ramping up their efforts to integrate AI into their operational model, companies must invest immediately in AI solutions or risk falling behind. The question addressed in this chapter is how to do that successfully. The chapter starts by explaining the challenge of leveraging value from AI and then describes the key aspects of achieving and measuring successful AI business realization. The chapter concludes by explaining the business operational differences for various AI business models.

How to Contact the Publisher

If you believe you've found a mistake in this book, please bring it to our attention. At John Wiley & Sons, we understand how important it is to provide our customers with accurate content, but even with our best efforts an error may occur.

In order to submit your possible errata, please email it to our Customer Service Team at wileysupport@wiley.com with the subject line "Possible Book Errata Submission."

How to Contact the Author

We appreciate your input and questions about this book! DM me on LinkedIn @ulrika-jagare, on Twitter at @jagare_ulrika, or on Instagram @datarush.

Balancing the AI Investment

Making a strategic decision to invest in AI is not just like any other decision. It's not only the financial aspect of the investment you must consider but the transformational power of AI for your company that needs to be understood. AI has the potential to fundamentally transform the business you are doing, and for some businesses it's even a question of survival to embrace this technology as fast as possible. Few examples in the market today have shown that businesses can achieve the expected values by just "doing some AI experimentation on the side." However, a surprisingly large number of companies either don't know what investing in AI means or truly believe that investing in AI means hiring a bunch of data scientists to build AI models. This attitude needs to change for more companies to gain the expected return on investment (ROI) from their investments.

The reality of today is that AI is reshaping entire industries, making it possible to achieve previously impossible levels of scale through operational efficiencies and continuous learning as well as innovation. The reason for this is that AI automates the extraction of insights from data, detecting patterns in a way that would take weeks, months, or even years for humans to do—if at all.

AI can be used to automate internal business processes and make them more efficient, as well as develop new and enhanced products and services in the commercial dimension. It can be used to predict what a customer is most likely to buy and to automatically detect manufacturing inefficiencies or fraudulent behavior. A retailer can use AI to predict the volume of traffic in a store on a given day and use that prediction to optimize its staffing. A bank can use AI to infer the market value of a home, based on its size, characteristics, and neighborhood, which, in turn, lowers the cost of appraisals and expedites mortgage processing. Autonomous vehicles are another interesting area of applied AI. There are not only AI capabilities built into an autonomous vehicle, but the vehicle also includes sensors that capture and encode data about the world. This could be seen as a "brain" that reasons and makes decisions. It seems that the more use cases and business segments AI is applied to, the more ideas arise in terms of where and how it can be used.

And we're just getting started with AI.

The fact is that modern data management and software capabilities have progressed far enough to allow any organization to capture and use its data to build, train, and validate even the most complex predictive AI models. Many companies have successfully embedded predictive models in their core business capabilities, which has empowered them to build game-changing products and services that would otherwise have been unachievable. And in doing so, they've proven that artificial intelligence is changing the business landscape forever.

However, although most of the business opportunity comes from adopting AI at scale, only a minor part of the enterprises tends to invest in AI across multiple business areas. One possible explanation for this could be that many business leaders are still exploring AI to better understand its benefits in their specific context. Just knowing that AI can solve problems that were previously unsolvable, and that AI can answer questions enterprises didn't even know to ask, isn't enough to go all in. On top of that, there are also misguided delusions that AI can solve anything, and when it becomes apparent that it can't, confusion arises about the true business value of AI. Hence, experience shows that achieving business success from AI requires experimental and incremental approaches to adoption, but it should also be acknowledged that introducing AI at scale is a transformational and challenging task for most large enterprises.

There is no silver bullet to succeed with your AI investment, but there are some fundamental aspects that should be driving your objectives and realization plans, and that includes a balanced approach to AI. In this chapter you will find out what that means and why it is important for your business. You'll learn why it's vital to approach your AI solution from an operational perspective from the get-go. The chapter will begin by defining AI and by sorting out what AI is in relation to other related concepts such as machine learning (ML), automation, and robotics, just to mention a few.

Understanding the AI life cycle is key and will be sorted out in relation to defining some of the operational fundamentals you need to address in order to succeed with your AI investment. I'll also clarify the importance of operating AI in the context of the AI life cycle.

Finally, this chapter will address why you need to put more effort on making your AI model *operational* than you put on *developing* your AI model. Understanding and accepting this is a first major step toward embracing an *operational mind-set* to AI, which is vital in order to succeed with your AI investment.

Defining AI and Related Concepts

Artificial intelligence (AI) refers to the ability in a computer program and in robots to emulate humans' and animals' natural intelligence. This refers primarily to cognitive functions such as the ability to learn from experience, to understand natural languages, and to solve problems, but also to tasks such as planning a sequence of activities and generalizing between situations. As more and more companies start to realize how AI can benefit their specific business, the uses of AI expand by the minute. Some examples of areas where AI is currently being applied are:

- Voice and face recognition
- Language translation
- Chat bots
- Digital assistants
- Image recognition
- Recommendation engines
- Self-driving cars

In relation to AI, it's worth mentioning the term *data science*. Data science can be defined as an interdisciplinary field that uses scientific methods, processes, algorithms, and systems to extract knowledge and insights from structured and unstructured data and that applies knowledge and actionable insights from data across a broad range of application domains.

Artificial intelligence and data science are unfortunately often used interchangeably in the industry, which sometimes causes confusion since there are some differences between the concepts. Whereas data science is a broader term than AI and should be seen as a comprehensive procedure, AI is instead a set of modeling techniques that a data scientist uses to develop models. It's also worth noting that contemporary AI used in the world today is *artificial narrow intelligence*. Under this form of intelligence, computer systems do not have full autonomy and consciousness like human beings; rather, they are only able to perform tasks that they are trained for. However, some prioritized objectives within AI research include machine reasoning, knowledge representation, machine planning and learning, natural language processing for communication, computer vision, and the ability to move and manipulate objects. Keep in mind, though, that *artificial general intelligence* (AGI) and artificial consciousness (or *singularity*, as it is also referred to) are still in a conceptual stage, and their real-world use is far from mature. The theory of technological singularity refers to a hypothetical point in time at which technological growth becomes uncontrollable and irreversible, resulting in unforeseeable changes to human civilization. However, most researchers in the industry can't agree on when AGI will be ready. Some estimate somewhere between 2040 and 2050 at the earliest.

Machine learning (ML) is the use of computer algorithms that improve automatically through experience based on patterns and deviations in data. ML is seen as a subset of AI. Machine learning algorithms build a mathematical model based on sample data known as *training data* to make predictions or decisions without being explicitly programmed to do so. Machine learning algorithms are used in a wide variety of applications where it's difficult or insufficient to develop conventional algorithms to perform the needed tasks.

These basic algorithms for teaching a machine to complete tasks and classify like a human date back several decades. But if ML isn't new, why is there so much interest today? Well, the fact is that complex ML algorithms—for example, using neural network techniques—need a lot of data and computing power to produce useful results. Today, we have more data than ever, and computing power is pervasive and cheap. The past few decades have seen massive scalability of data and information, allowing for much more accurate predictions than were ever possible in the long history of ML. Machine learning algorithms are therefore now better than ever and widely available in open source software. However, for more simple ML models the big-data revolution was more important than easy access to computational power.

Here are some common usage scenarios for ML:

- Predicting a potential value
- Estimating a probability
- Classifying an object
- Grouping similar objects together
- Detecting relations
- Finding outliers

There are many different types of ML algorithms, and each class works differently. In general, ML algorithms begin with an initial hypothetical model, determine how well this model fits a set of data, and improve the model iteratively. This training process continues until the algorithm learning is optimized or the user stops the process. Learning can be *supervised*, *unsupervised*, or *semi-supervised* (see Figure 1.1).

ML category	Scope	Used for
Supervised Learning (SL)	• Structured and labeled data • Gain direct feedback • Predict outcome/future	• Regression analysis • Classification of data
Unsupervised Learning (UL)	• Unstructured data and no labels • No feedback • Find hidden structure through patterns and deviations	• Clustering • Anomaly detection
Semi-Supervised Learning	• Uses a training dataset with both labeled and unlabeled data	• Uses a small amount of labeled data to improve the accuracy of a larger set of unlabeled data

Figure 1.1: Overview of supervised, unsupervised, and semi-supervised learning

Supervised learning (SL) needs structured and labeled data to run and is best used for classification of data or for regression analysis, or both. *Classification* refers to the problem of identifying in which category (subpopulation) an observation (or observations) belongs to. *Regression analysis* in the context of ML usually refers to building a prediction model.

Unsupervised learning (UL), in contrast, uses unlabeled data that the algorithm tries to make sense of by extracting features and patterns on its own. This technique is mostly used for clustering and anomaly detection. *Clustering* in this context refers to the task of grouping a set of objects in such a way that objects in the same group (called a *cluster*) are more similar to each other than to those in other groups (clusters). *Anomaly detection* is the identification of rare items, events, or observations that raise suspicion by differing significantly from the majority of the data. Typically, the anomalies translate to some kind of problem, such as bank fraud, network problems, medical problems, or even errors in a text. Anomalies are also referred to as *outliers, novelties, noise, deviations,* and *exceptions*.

Semi-supervised learning takes a middle ground. It uses a small amount of labeled data to strengthen a larger set of unlabeled data. Semi-supervised learning is especially useful for medical images, where a small amount of labeled data can lead to a significant improvement in accuracy.

Reinforcement learning (RL) is another technique that's turned out to be valuable for certain use cases. Reinforcement learning is an area of ML focused on how intelligent agents ought to take actions in an environment in order to maximize reward (see Figure 1.2). Reinforcement learning focuses on finding a balance between exploration (of uncharted territory) and exploitation (of current knowledge).

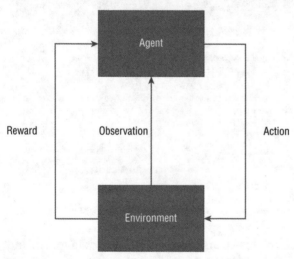

Figure 1.2: Reinforcement learning uses intelligent agents to make decisions.

The RL training environment is typically stated in the form of a Markov decision process (MDP), because many RL algorithms for this context use dynamic programming techniques. In mathematics, an MDP is a discrete-time stochastic control process. It provides a mathematical framework for modeling decision making in situations where outcomes are partly random and partly under the control of a decision maker. MDPs are useful for studying optimization problems solved via dynamic programming.

The typical framing of an RL scenario is that a basic RL agent AI interacts with its environment in discrete-time steps. At each time the agent receives the current state and reward. The agent then chooses an action from the set of available actions, which is subsequently sent to the environment. The environment moves to a new state, and the reward associated with the transition is determined. The goal of an RL agent is to learn a policy that maximizes the expected cumulative reward.

So, how does *deep learning* (DL) relate to ML? Deep learning is defined as a subset of ML where artificial neural networks—algorithms built around the neural structure of the human brain—learn from data. The same way human beings learn from day-to-day events over time, a DL algorithm executes functions repeatedly and continuously learns and adjusts itself to improve accuracy. They are called "DL algorithms" because the neural networks have various (deep) hidden layers that enable learning of complex patterns in large amounts of data, as shown in Figure 1.3.

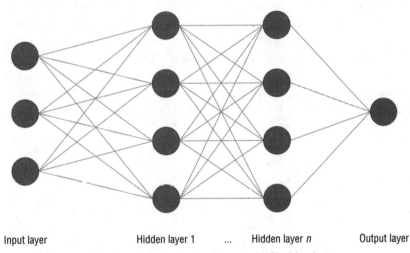

| Input layer | Hidden layer 1 | ... | Hidden layer *n* | Output layer |

Figure 1.3: Deep learning includes a neural network of hidden layers.

Deep learning is useful because it performs well on tasks such as image and speech recognition, whereas other ML techniques perform poorly.

Another concept closely related to AI is *automation*. AI is often confused with automation, yet the two are fundamentally different. Whereas AI aims to mimic human intelligence decisions and actions, automation focuses on streamlining repetitive, instructive tasks, usually with the objective to save time and money, and gives employees an opportunity to move on and upskill themselves to be able to handle more complex tasks.

So, what about *robotics*? A lot of people wonder if robotics is a subset of AI or if they are the same thing. Robotics is an interdisciplinary field that integrates computer science and engineering. It involves design, construction, operation, and use of robots. The goal of robotics is to design machines that can help humans. Robotics develops machines that can substitute for humans and replicate human actions. Robots can be used in many situations and for many purposes, but today many are used in dangerous environments, in manufacturing processes, or where humans cannot survive—for example, in space, under water, in high heat, and in the cleanup and containment of hazardous materials and radiation.

Robots can take on any shape and form, but some are made to resemble humans in appearance. This is said to help in the acceptance of a robot for behaviors and tasks that are usually performed by people. Such robots attempt to replicate walking, lifting, speech, cognition, or any other human activity.

So, does that mean robotics is a branch of AI? Well, it's surprisingly difficult to get experts to agree exactly what actually constitutes a "robot." Some people say that a robot must be able to "think" and make decisions. However, there is no standard definition of "robot thinking." Requiring a robot to "think" suggests that it has some level of AI, and however you choose to define a robot, the fact is that robotics mostly involves designing, building, and programming physical robots. As shown in Figure 1.4, only a small part of it actually involves AI.

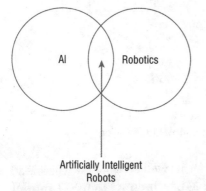

Figure 1.4: How AI and robotics interrelate

Operational Readiness and Why It Matters

The focus of the AI industry today is on identifying new AI use cases and the creation of new AI/ML models (see Figure 1.5). This is perfectly reasonable, as these models solve various business and technical problems and enable value creation, and are also what data scientists want to work with. Of course, building algorithms that can solve unsolvable problems is attracting more attention than building a solid data pipeline to feed the AI models with data and securing needed data quality. However, leading industry players are starting to realize that the key to a sustainable AI business lies not only in the number of AI models that are being developed, but also in the ability to successfully deploy those AI models, as well as to run them in a live production environment. Not until then can ROI be achieved.

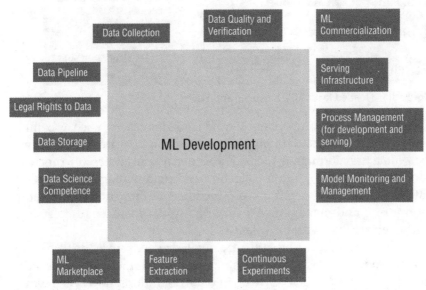

Figure 1.5: Current industry focus

Without a robust enabling system for the AI models, there is risk of suboptimal execution of the company's AI business, leading to increased development, delivery, maintenance, and operational costs and delayed or lost sales opportunities.

Therefore, in order to successfully achieve ROI from the AI investment, companies must carefully consider the context of their AI model development and better balance its focus (see Figure 1.6). Companies should rely on the fact that balancing the overall AI focus and embracing a robust enabling system for their AI development are the most important steps toward a successful AI realization.

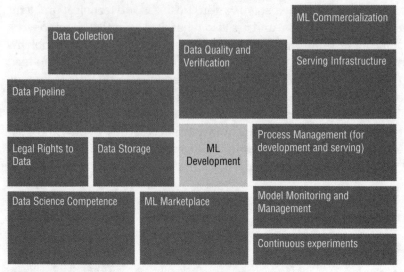

Figure 1.6: Needed focus for a balanced approach

This type of enabling system should consider aspects such as components and platforms (data pipeline, data infrastructure, data storage), tools (data transformation, model repository, model audit tool), processes and ways of working (data collection and data management process, data rights), live AI operations (production environment, support setup, monitoring and management), and finally, competence (data science competence across various roles).

Because the area of AI is still very much driven from a "de facto standardization" perspective, there is no one fully defined way to describe the *AI life cycle*—yet. Before we go into the definitions, however, I would like to draw your attention to the importance of knowing and understanding the production target environment as part of addressing the AI life cycle. This is critical for several reasons, but mainly because of the fact that designing and developing your AI model without understanding or considering how the model will need to operate in reality has proven to be a sure path to failure for many companies.

It's a fact that most companies tend to put most of the effort and financial means into developing AI but less so on bringing the AI models to production. Making sure that the environment that the models operate in is seen as part of the AI life cycle is key. So, what are those aspects that you also need to consider?

As shown in Figure 1.7, there are three main parts to the AI life cycle if you balance your view with less focus on AI development and allow yourself to appreciate the data and operational perspective, too. *Data engineering* refers to all aspects related to the data you need to develop, train, and run your AI models. It includes the practice of designing and building systems for collecting, storing, preparing, and analyzing data at scale. *Model development* refers to the actual development and training of models. *Deployment* and *Operations* refer to the deployment steps of the life cycle and the process of delivering and governing AI models in live production settings to secure expected business outcomes, such as better efficiency, predictions, innovations, and so on.

In parallel to these three fundamental steps, it's also vital to consider the correspondence between the training infrastructure in the lab and the *serving infrastructure* and technical architecture needed to realize your AI solution beyond the lab environment. Furthermore, the importance of underpinning your balanced approach using machine learning operations, or MLOps, practices for streamlining your AI teams has proven to be a key success factor for AI productivity. (This is addressed further in Chapter 3, "Embracing MLOps.") However, at the end of the day, acquiring and retaining the right competence to manage all needed aspects of the AI life cycle is fundamental. The people aspects will be covered in greater detail later in this chapter.

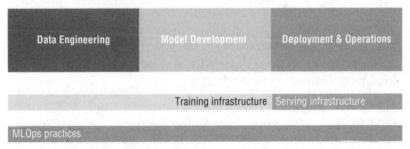

Figure 1.7: Operational readiness

The fact is that you can invest an enormous amount of money into AI development, but if you lack data rights to the data you need, or if you have an unstable data pipeline in production that keeps breaking down, your models won't run and won't be able to deliver the outcome you are expecting. So, where do you start to achieve this balance?

The following sections provide a set of examples of how to achieve this balance by embracing an operational mind-set from the start. Remember that it's not sufficient to just check off these areas by themselves; the key is to collaborate and execute across these three areas.

Applying an Operational Mind-set from the Start

What does it mean to apply an operational mind-set to your AI initiative? Let's start with some examples of data aspects to explain how an operational mind-set might impact development choices that you need to make early. (You can find more details about data engineering in Chapter 3.)

- **Data pipeline**—How should the *data pipeline* be approached to support AI development, AI deployment, and AI in production? *Data pipeline* in this context refers to moving data from a source location to a target environment. This includes aspects such as not only acquiring the data for development and training purposes but also considering how the data will be collected and pushed to your model in live operations.

- **Model target environment**—Is your data pipeline ready to serve models in production across various target environments? Have you decided where the model will run in production? Is it in the cloud or in an edge device, or do you have multiple execution environments to account for? How data will need to be acquired and secured for different production environments might impact your technology choices and platform approach significantly. If your model will run in a cloud environment—which is perhaps at another location than where the data is generated or collected—consider how you need to transfer and store your data. Will this in any way impact your AI design?

- **Data preparation**—Will your model run on raw and unstructured data, or does it require data preparation and certain data quality levels? If so, how will data preparation be addressed in an operational setting? Will the model need live data feeds, or is it more of an offline production environment? How will that impact the data pipeline's reliability, and does that constrain the choice of target environment, modeling technique used, or similar aspects? How will data preparation be handled in a live setting? Can you automate all steps to secure sufficient data quality? And how do you handle the support of the data pipeline in live operations so that a data issue doesn't stop your model from working?

- **Legal aspects of data**—Do you own and have access to the data needed to train your model on and to run it in production? If not, how can that be secured? Can you buy the data needed, or is it a question of legal and contractual negotiation? It's worth noting that *securing legal data rights*, even with customers who are willing to share their data, takes time and is not an easy task, with increasing data regulations like the General Data Protection Regulation (GDPR) in the European Union (EU) and the California Consumer Privacy Act (CCPA) in the United States. The difference between GDPR and CCPA is that the CCPA's definition is extra-personal, meaning that it includes data that is not specific to an individual but is categorized as household data, whereas the GDPR remains exclusively individual. However, to be sure that these types of regulations do not prevent your AI investment from being launched, it's worth spending time on early in development. If the access is limited, how does that potentially impact the ML techniques used? For example, do you need computer-generated "dummy data" for initial model training in the lab, and then deploy and run your models using distributed ML where the data can stay where it is? For more details on legal constraints on data, see chapter 6.

■ **Data quality**—How are you approaching needed *data quality*? It's one thing to prepare the data for the lab environment, but how will data management be handled in an operational setting? What are the mandatory quality operational requirements that the data architect or data engineer must know early? What about *biased datasets*? Are you considering how to avoid bias when selecting your training dataset, securing representative data for your operational setting?

Now let's consider some operational aspects related to AI model development:

■ **Model training**—Is your model development and training environment closely interlinked with your production and operational environment to secure seamless handovers to operation as well as involvement by development teams during operation?

■ **Output frequency**—How frequently are you expecting predictions and other insights to be generated, and should predictions be generated for a single instance at a time or for a batch of instances?

■ **Target environment**—In the model target environment, how many applications will access the model? And are the latency requirements of these applications understood and accounted for?

■ **Model monitoring**—Are you planning to monitor model performance during operation? If so, remember to consider this at the start of the model development. This is important because, depending on how a certain model will need to be monitored in production, it might impact development choices and priorities. In some cases, even the receiver or customer of the model demands transparency of model performance, so there must be a plan for this. This is especially true for AI models used for critical use cases like self-driving cars, where the model performance *must* be reliable.

- **Model retraining**—Another important aspect is how you plan to retrain or update your models once they are in production. This is vital because even the best models will need to be retrained sooner or later due to changing needs, priorities, or other changed preferences. Remember that the complexity of retraining your models will differ depending on which production environment they will run in. For example, in a cloud environment it's easier to access and retrain your models than if they were embedded in an application running on a device.

- **Model in production**—Finally, is your production environment and operational support setup ready to manage dynamic ML models in a live setting? Although the main job of a data scientist is to develop AI models, the job is ultimately not done until there is a working model in production helping the company or organization produce the ROI it's expected to achieve. So, in order to get to that point, a data scientist must see the role as part of a cross-functional team. An especially good working relationship is needed among the data engineers and the model deployment and model monitoring and support teams.

Let's say you're a data scientist for your company. You will become better at what you do if you truly care about how your model performs in production. That includes a better understanding of the data itself, but also balancing your attention between how your model performs in development and in production and its need for management and monitoring. Yes, it's true that a new model needs a lot of attention in the beginning before it has been properly trained and has stabilized, but even at that stage it's important to consider the future production environment it will run in.

NOTE   Remember that a data scientist who pays attention to the knowledge gained from the production environment will achieve a better overall business understanding of the target environment to help drive AI life-cycle improvements and new model innovations going forward.

Furthermore, depending on the AI model's purpose, another important aspect to consider is the customer relationship. For models that will be used for commercial purposes, as a data scientist you should have the opportunity to learn about customer needs and feedback on previous AI-based solutions. That will help you build better models and also gain a genuine understanding of the customer expectations, limitations, and opportunities in the next AI solution.

You should know that when you as a data scientist attend a customer meeting it brings more credibility and trust in your company's data science capabilities. However, remember to familiarize yourself with the business and customer context so that the meeting runs on the level appreciated by the customer and doesn't turn into a situation where your technical expertise is mismatched with customer expectations.

The Operational Challenge

By nature, data science and AI have been approached from an experimental and scientific perspective. However, the great and rapid advances in the various fields of research related to AI have resulted in unexpected potential to solve complex real-life problems, transform industries, and offer exponential commercial value. As companies start to rely increasingly on AI systems for critical business functions as well as business offerings, the industry must bridge the gap between technology experimentation and a stable and reliable foundation for delivering expected business results.

Achieving a reliable foundation for leveraging the value of AI requires a change of focus both in the traditional way in which data science projects are run and in the application of the scientific method. The purpose is to make AI systems and AI application in the business environment more easily accessible, scalable, reproducible, and collaborative—and, of course, focused on business results.

Deploying and scaling AI/ML across an enterprise requires implementing complex, iterative workflows end to end, from capturing data to developing ML models to running and managing models in live production environments. On top of that, it includes establishing efficient and cross-functional data science teams that span from development through deployment and operational support and feedback. Achieving this is not an easy task.

In addition, as the number of AI/ML solutions and models multiply in the organization or in the commercial portfolio, managing potential dependencies between AI-driven applications or functions as individual parts of a bigger "use case" could counteract another application/function. In that context, getting the AI solutions to production and establishing efficient operations can be slow, cumbersome, and fraught with "false starts" that make it even more difficult and expensive.

Although the end-to-end AI life cycle has been pitched as an actual "cycle," to date there has been limited success in managing this end-to-end process at an enterprise-level scale. Some of the reasons could be:

- Data scientists sometimes lack computer science skills and might not always follow good development operations (DevOps) practices.

- Data engineers, data scientists, and the engineers responsible for managing AI models in operations are acting in silos that create friction between the teams.

- The various ML tools and frameworks foster a lack of standardization across the whole industry.

The realization of AI from an enterprise perspective is still very slow and tough to scale. Many companies get stuck on data quality problems and find it difficult to truly automate processes end to end, collaboration across teams turns out to be more difficult than anticipated, and the actual operationalized AI models delivering business value are few.

Unfortunately, many AI use cases don't make it into production. There are many reasons for this, one of which is model inefficiencies that slow down or halt the entire process. In many cases, however, organizations simply fail to adequately adopt production models to the AI model's needs because of a lack of internal knowledge of how the AI solutions work or interoperate with other traditional software (SW) capabilities. Apart from technical challenges, there is also a long list of other cultural or business impediments.

As organizations start to see AI as a fundamental and vital piece of the company, they are usually wrestling with growing organizational pain. Isolated projects exist in silos across the enterprise, putting quality, security, governance, and compliance at risk. When applying an "AI factory" approach to turning data into decisions, you can make the process of building, scaling, and deploying enterprise ML solutions automated, repeatable, and predictable, but you lose the business value along the way.

Only through the industrialization of AI can you shift focus from technology solutions to business outcomes, empower continuous optimization, and encourage a learning culture across the enterprise.

Truly excellent industrial-grade AI requires transformation in almost every part of an organization, and as a result, it's easier to see that hurdles to adopting AI in your company are often actually organizationwide hurdles. Some of these hurdles are as follows:

Unorganized Machine Learning Experiments   Machine learning is an iterative process where you need to experiment with multiple combinations of data, learning algorithms, and model parameters, and keep track of the impact these changes have on predictive performance. Over time this iterative experimentation can result in thousands of model training runs and model versions, making it hard to track the best-performing models and their input configurations. There's also a competency-related risk. If you don't truly understand what your method does or why things change, you will never know what works and what doesn't—especially if it works fine at first but then something changes and you don't know why it's not working anymore.

Inefficient Deployment   Data scientists today use a variety of tools to solve many critical business problems. This often results in models being recoded into different programming languages, as the initial language may not be used in the production environment. This leads to longer cycle times and potential inconsistencies in the translated model, and it makes the operational feedback loop for issues or improvement proposals from operations to development inefficient.

Insufficient AI Model Monitoring in Operations   Efficient monitoring of models in operations is an essential element of the production environment, since it provides visibility into its various phases. Poor visibility into performance metrics and to the external tools used for monitoring is a major challenge. Custom tooling to monitor the technical health of models scales poorly, mathematical monitoring is hard and customized, and little to no tooling exists yet. On the other hand, standard monitoring tools tend to be too generic for identifying model drift, such as identifying whether the model execution is deviating from its objective. The truth is that what really happened based on the prediction is usually understood only well after the fact. This means that determining whether a model is functioning as it should needs to be customized on a per-model basis, which is both time consuming and reactive.

Fragmented Governance Model   As AI/ML moves to production, the need to govern assets like data, models, and infrastructure increases. That governance needs to include ensuring security, privacy, and regulatory compliance. Defining standards for AI in operations is essential for deploying and governing models at scale for enterprises. This includes visibility of models within teams and across organizations. It enables teams to understand how AI is being applied in their organizations and requires an official catalog of models. In the absence of such a model catalog, however, many organizations are unaware of their models and features, such as where they are deployed, what they are doing, and even how they are performing. This leads to substantial rework, model inconsistency, recomputing features, and other inefficiencies.

Inadequate Security Measures   There is a need for end-to-end enterprise security, from data capture to the production environment. The chosen platform must be capable of delivering models into production with inherited security, unified authorization, and access tracking.

Lack of Scalability   As the model moves from development to production, it's typically exposed to larger volumes of data. The platform must have the ability to scale from small to large volumes of data and automate model creation. Applied ML at enterprise scale requires a particular combination of cutting-edge technology and enterprise expectations. From a model perspective, where models have been deployed to endpoints (users) and your solution starts to serve many more users, this increased demand can bring down your ML services. The number of compute instances serving your models should increase when requests rise. But it's equally important to secure that when workload decreases, compute instances should be removed so that you don't pay for instances you aren't using.

Additionally, it's not only about scale of data and users but the number of actual models in production. Operating and monitoring a few models may be fine, but when you scale up to hundreds of models, it's difficult to make sure they are maintaining their reliability and not drifting. This is a common concern for customers in the banking sector, where entire teams of ML engineers are dedicated to just keeping their models accurate in the long term.

To add to the complexity, consider the fact that as your company matures in its AI utilization, operating individual AI models is not going to be the primary task. Instead, as the use case complexity grows where AI is applied, so will the complexity of the AI solutions. AI models will be dependent on each other, and you will need to manage AI solutions with many AI agents built into the same solution. This is referred to as ensemble modeling. You can think of *ensemble modeling* as a process where multiple diverse models are created to predict an outcome. This can be done either by using many different modeling algorithms or by using different training datasets. The final prediction is done through aggregating the predictions of each base model.

The reason for using ensemble models is that they combine multiple individual (diverse) models together, which creates a deeper understanding of the data, lower variance, and lower bias. The upside is that using ensemble modeling can give you superior prediction power, whereas the downside is increased operational complexity. Again, remember that this is a balance between what is technically and businesswise needed versus the potentially increased operational complexity it would drive.

Strategy, People, and Technology Considerations

Artificial intelligence has become one of the most critical capabilities for modern businesses to grow and stay competitive today. From automating internal processes to optimizing the design, creation, and marketing processes behind virtually every product consumed, AI models have flooded almost every aspect of our work and personal lives. And for businesses, the stakes have never been higher. Failing to adopt AI as a core competency will result in major competitive disadvantages.

Therefore, business and technology leaders need to implement AI across their entire organization, spanning a large spectrum of use cases. However, this sense of urgency, combined with growing regulatory scrutiny, creates new and unique governance challenges that are currently difficult to manage. Questions related to how AI models should run and stay in control after they're deployed are becoming important to understand and manage. This includes questions such as: How are my models impacting services provided to end customers? Am I still compliant with both governmental and internal regulations? How will my security rules translate to models in live operations?

The fact is that the whole industry has begun to hit its breaking point, and technology is evolving fast to try to handle the expectations on an AI production environment, although standardization is lacking. The same way good DevOps practices ensure that software development is efficient, well documented, and easy to troubleshoot, a similar set of standards for operating AI in production is needed—standards for MLOps.

This chapter discusses not only key success factors for MLOps but also explains the importance of the people perspective. Technology considerations that need to be considered early are also described.

Strategic Success Factors in Operating AI

Artificial intelligence holds great promise, but like most great things, it doesn't happen by itself. To succeed with your AI investment, you need to read up on AI and follow the technological advances and learnings in the industry on a continuous basis. This is not an area that stays the same for very long. What was seen as a "truth" yesterday is discarded tomorrow. This is a challenging task for any company to manage but a necessary aspect to understand in order to succeed. Therefore, AI should always be approached with an open mind and a willingness to persevere when apparent small wins turn out to be elusive.

So, what characterizes good MLOps? Actually, good MLOps practices are very similar to good DevOps practices and include:

- Reducing the time and complexity of pushing models into production
- Removing silos between teams and enhancing collaboration
- Bridging the gap between development and production with regard to model tracking, versioning, monitoring, and overall model management
- Establishing a truly cyclical life cycle for your ML pipeline
- Standardizing your ML workflow in preparation for increased regulation and policies

It's easy enough to make a list like this, but how you turn that into a practical implementation is an entirely different thing. At this point you might have launched a couple of experimental AI projects in your company, but has your organization actually delivered any tangible business results yet? If not, you're not alone. Most companies are still struggling to get the expected benefits realized in monetary terms.

As an example, many companies start an AI project by setting up a lab environment, just to realize later that they aren't able to operationalize their AI solution in a live setting. It simply doesn't fit into the existing business processes. On top of creating business transformative solutions that require much larger, structural changes in their company to deliver the expected results, they might have developed innovative and ground-breaking AI models without considering the requirements that the target environment puts on the models with regard to data aspects, governance concerns, or just operational performance. Monitoring might be diffi-cult to impossible. Hence, you might have to discard your model and start again, losing out on both time spent and money invested.

So, how do you avoid the most common pitfalls and get the right strategic approach to your AI initiative? Let's look at some important aspects to consider when embarking on the AI journey:

Realistic Business Objectives   A common problem with AI initia-tives is that the lack of AI understanding in a company can result in exaggerated expectations on what AI can do and how fast it can be done. Inflated expectations can also lead to dismissing AI alto-gether. The fact that it is extremely useful is then rejected when it turns out not to be magic. A vital part of your AI initiative, there-fore, must be to identify and understand company expectations and business objectives. If these expectations don't match up, this must be communicated clearly to lay the best foundation for your AI investment.

Remember, unrealistic expectations usually derive from a lack of understanding, not that anyone is intentionally trying to hinder progress. Once that is settled, you can move on to creating a clear business objective, with prioritized use cases. Remember to define measurable goals, benchmark current performance as a baseline, and then set clearly defined and realistic success criteria.

Right Stakeholders   In order to understand who your real stake-holders are, you must detail your use cases all the way into the operational setting. You need to figure out how the model output will be used and who will use it. This is important, because if you stop the scenario halfway, thinking that it will be resolved later, you might end up with an AI solution that crunches numbers and makes predictions but the outcome is unusable, is inaccessible, or doesn't fit into your company's business context and decision-making process. Therefore, it's vital to fully comprehend how the business expects that the output will be made available to the downstream receivers in terms of people and tool environments and become part of your business processes. At that point, you can gain a better understanding of what opportunities or constraints that will put on your AI operational environment.

Relevant Competence   It's well known that there is a shortage of data science talent on the market. Although more students are realizing that data scientist is "the role of the future" and more people across various industries are investing in upskilling and reskilling of their employees to be part of the AI journey, the truth is that becoming really good in data science takes time. It's also a fact that a data scientist who has the business understanding of the area is essentially more valuable to a company than one who has difficulties in relating to the business situation and the customer perspectives. To be successful, you also need to think about the staffing from an end-to-end perspective, including data engineering, model development and deployment, and operations. Data science is truly a team sport that requires different roles such as data engineers, ML engineers, and operational support engineers. And it requires these roles to work closely together.

Another key aspect in securing the right AI competence is the fact that it's often overlooked that management should also be knowledgeable in the area. Good, experienced AI managers are as rare as or even rarer than knowledgeable data scientists and data engineers.

A Sustainable Technology Stack   Unfortunately, it's not unusual for AI initiatives to fail due to a lack of planning on the technology front. To be more precise, it's not so much about having the right technology and tools for building and developing AI models as it is about not understanding how the operationalization of the AI solution must be thought of from the beginning. That's the toughest nut to crack! Remember, it's not about finding "the one application or tool that solves it all." A multitude of tools are in the AI ecosystem, and there's a reason for that. Which tool or application to use depends on what you are trying to do, which use case you are addressing, and what the operational setting needs to serve. A tool that might be perfect for a certain use case or ML technique might not be most suitable for another problem. The AI space is constantly evolving, and your technology stack needs to account for that. Additional details about the technology stack can be found in Chapter 3.

Holistic Governance   If anyone offers you an out-of-the-box "AI solution," you know you're being played. You cannot purchase a truly effective AI solution off the shelf, attach it to an existing application or process, and obtain the benefits. AI is not a single tool, platform, or solution whose capability can be mastered over time like you can with a traditional software (SW) solution. The fact is that AI thrives best when supported by an organizational ecosystem, where the right data governance, data engineering tools, and standards must be in place for you to develop your AI models at their core. And beyond development you need data governance, model reliability, and integration capabilities built into your architecture to achieve a successful AI model in operation. How well you continuously govern data across the entire organization plays a major role in the success and sustainability of your AI initiatives. While automation, business predictions, and product innovations might be the objectives of your AI investment, those goals can be achieved only by developing and maintaining models, and the models can only be as accurate as the data that trains them and feeds them in live operations. Remember that data fuels the model, which in turn drives a given set of AI capabilities. The data will change over time. New data sources become available, and data patterns change, and how well you govern your data may fluctuate over time. All these things impact how a model performs.

Some companies try to force AI into a rigid organizational structure where it doesn't fit. Others isolate the initiative where it can't benefit anyone or anything. But solving the problem isn't really about trying to fit AI into your existing organizational setting; it's about making the structure of your organization more flexible so that AI can be embraced.

Investing in proper AI governance also assists you in controlling and maintaining models across many different business lines. It ensures that business-critical applications are doing what they're intended to do or finding those that aren't. With the right AI governance, you will also have better access to the organizational history of models and predictions, including deprecated assets.

People and Mind-sets

Unfortunately, organizational issues often have more impact on AI initiatives and their chance of success than we might think. It's true that an AI project is different from a traditional SW project, since it requires different skillsets, platforms, programming languages, toolsets, and workflows. However, as a "development project," it should be managed as any other project. Still, because AI projects tend to blend scientific methodology with business-focused outcomes, traditional enterprise decision support tools are often ineffective. In addition to that, AI work is highly iterative, and even well-defined criteria might need to shift throughout different phases of the project as data scientists and business stakeholders explore what is possible, ethical, and profitable.

Furthermore, when it comes to the production phase of AI, it's also easy for the development organizations to hand over the solution and think of the operational aspects of the AI solution as somebody else's problem. Operational elements such as a well-performing data pipeline, data management of live data feeds, model monitoring and alerts, and other similar production activities may not be the most exciting areas to consider—and could be questioned since they increase the overall cost of doing AI—but they are very much needed. Remember that failure in any of these parts can crush even the most promising AI efforts.

So, what can be done to minimize the organizational impact and turn your AI initiative into a success story? Here are some suggestions for how to strategically approach this issue:

An Operational Mind-set   Without exaggerating, it's safe to say that AI has the potential to transform your entire business. AI can make your internal operations more efficient, it can uncover new insights, it can enhance your product and service portfolio, and it can enable new capabilities previously not attainable. However, integrating AI into your organization requires full operational transformation and a real experimentation-based approach. In order to achieve that, it's important to keep an open mind. Keeping an open mind is something you must do early on and reinforce often on the path to making AI operational.

To succeed with your AI initiative, you should be extremely intentional about the problems or opportunities you want to tackle. If you start by solving a problem that is realistic and achievable, you can prove the value of AI fast and make it real for your organization. The opposite of that is when AI becomes obscure and almost magic-like to people who don't fully understand the area. This fear or skepticism of AI can be tackled by delivering a tangible value early on.

To identify this objective, think big but in increments. Try to identify what opportunities you could go after with a certain capability. A good way to approach this is to first focus on capabilities that are assisting, rather than completely replacing and fully automating, an existing task right from the start. That can be perceived as too intrusive for people and get the opposite effect of what you are after.

The Right Culture   To succeed with building the right data-driven culture with an AI operational mind-set in your organization, it's important to be able to anticipate and identify unique barriers to change.

Some obstacles, such as employees' fear of becoming obsolete, are common across organizations and are easy to anticipate and can to some extent be countered with upskilling and reskilling efforts. But a company's culture may also have distinctive characteristics that contribute to resistance. For example, if a company has relationship managers who pride themselves on being attuned to customer needs, they may reject the notion that a machine could have better ideas about what customers want and therefore ignore an AI tool's tailored product recommendations. And managers in large organizations who believe their status is based on the number of people they oversee might object to decentralized decision making or reduction in number of direct reports that AI capabilities could allow.

In other cases, siloed processes can prevent the broad adoption of AI that is wanted and expected. Organizations that assign budgets by function or by business unit may struggle to assemble interdisciplinary agile teams, for example.

Understanding and trusting that AI/ML capabilities are good for both the company and the people in it is fundamental for a cultural change to happen. The data science teams in your company play a very important role in this. From a data science team perspective, any team member must be able to understand and articulate what a certain model can do and why a model is producing the results that it is. Your data scientists need to take the time to explain the outcomes of ML models to your business teams, who in turn need to be able to explain the resulting predictions and business decisions to your customers or shareholders. Succeeding with this is key to getting the right culture in your organization.

Different Recruitment Strategies   As the uses of AI technology expand into every industry, AI talent is coming from a very small pool of available candidates, even from an international perspective. But how can you find, attract, recruit, and retain AI talent when you're competing with acknowledged data companies like Google, Amazon, Tesla, and Apple? The answer lies in getting creative with your recruitment and hiring strategy.

Building the right team structure with the right competence up front is important, but it can be a challenging task because the very nature of AI tends to blur organizational lines and breaks down the barriers between traditional roles. That data knows no organizational boundaries is probably true, considering how different user scenarios for a single data type can spread all across a company.

The starting point for your recruitment strategy should be to adapt it based on the experience level you are looking for. You can't assume that the recruitment strategy should be the same for a junior versus a senior data scientist. Furthermore, don't forget the operational support roles. Usually, those type of roles require a good understanding of the AI product and service solution and its environment, but it's also good if the operations team has some basic data science competence. When there is an issue with model performance, for example, those in operational support roles need to be able to quickly judge if it's actually the model performance that is poor or if a data issue is causing the malfunctioning of the model.

Motivating AI Talent   Although it's not easy to understand until you have actually tried, recruiting the AI professionals that you need is difficult and expensive. Luckily, however, a high salary isn't the only thing that motivates a data scientist to switch jobs. There are other ways to "win over" a talented data scientist who can make the whole difference for your business. Some of these motivating factors are complex problems to solve, leading a team of junior data scientists who can do the less exciting work, a good location of the workplace, brand recognition, access to data, and the right AI/ML infrastructure. However, remember that even the junior data scientists usually want to work on the complex problems, so managing expectations will be critical.

So, if you find that you can't afford to pay a competitive salary for a data scientist, use long-term incentives and push for the motivating factors in the aforementioned list that fits your situation. Also, remember that not everyone thrives in environments at large tech companies. Expressing the differentiators between your business and leaders like Apple in what you provide could sway talent to accept your offer.

Sustainable Leadership   Yes, AI is reshaping business, but not with the speed most assume. It's true, however, that AI is now guiding decisions across many different areas, from crop harvests to bank loans. This is really the time to capitalize on AI. Indeed, McKinsey Global Institute estimates that AI will add $13 trillion to the global economy over the next decade (`www .mckinsey.com/featured-insights/artificial-intelligence/ notes-from-the-ai-frontier-modeling-the-impact-of-ai-on- the-world-economy`).

Despite the promise of AI, however, many organizations' efforts are still falling short. One of the most common mistakes leaders make is to view AI as a "plug-and-play" technology with immediate returns. Envision a scenario where the decision is made to invest in a few AI projects, get them up and running, and then start pumping in millions of dollars in data infrastructure, tools, and data science expertise. Then picture that some of the pilot projects manage to carve out small gains in pockets of the organization, but they are followed by months and possibly years passing without bringing the big wins that executives expected. It's a fact that companies struggle to move from pilots to companywide programs—and from a focus on discrete business problems, such as improved customer segmentation, to big business challenges, such as optimizing the entire customer journey.

Another challenge is that leaders tend to have a too-narrow focus on AI requirements. Although cutting-edge technology and talent are certainly needed, it's equally important to align a company culture, structure, and ways of working to support a broad AI adoption. Unfortunately, at most companies that aren't born digital, traditional mind-sets and ways of working run counter to those needed for AI.

These fundamental business transformations that need to happen don't come easy. They require leaders to dare to invest in full transformation and to prepare, motivate, and equip the workforce to make change happen. But leaders must also be prepared to change. Many failed AI initiatives come down to a lack of fundamental understanding of AI among senior executives. This needs to change. Remember that the way AI can be used expands continuously. New AI solutions might create fundamental and sometimes difficult changes in processes, roles, and culture, which leaders need to guide their organizations through carefully. There's no question that companies that excel at implementing AI throughout the organization, including mastering operational aspects, will find themselves at a great advantage.

The Technology Perspective

Deploying, scaling, and operating AI across your enterprise or as part of a commercial offering is a daunting task that requires complex, iterative end-to-end workflows from data to models to outcomes. And as the number of AI models multiplies in your organization or across your commercial portfolio, the road to successfully deploying and operating AI to gain the expected ROI can become slow and expensive to maintain.

It's also important to remember that the data science area is much more immature than the software engineering space when it comes to available tooling and standardized infrastructures. On top of that, it's even more immature in the production and operations part of the AI life cycle. It's actually so immature that even if it's clear that what's needed to succeed is an open, unified, collaborative, secure, and governed enterprise-grade environment to run and manage all AI models with transparency, consistency, reliability, and high performance, it's still not clear what that means in terms of platform selection. (This is explored in more detail in Chapter 3.)

While operating AI is one of the most difficult tasks in the AI life cycle, it's at the same time the most important part to unlock the business potential with AI. Therefore, it truly needs your attention! One example of the challenge is that the programming language that the ML model is written in could be different from the language the components in the production system are written in. Obviously, having to rewrite the code would significantly delay the model's deployment. Practitioners and platform architects must therefore be mindful about point solutions that appear to solve a particular deployment and operations problem short term but that introduce new security and governance problems. This could mean, for example, that data needs to be moved between multiple platforms or that a foundation for "shadow IT" must be created.

In many larger organizations, shadow IT tends to appear when users throughout the organization perceive that the central IT department doesn't respond to the user need fast enough or with sufficient technical capabilities. The purpose is to work around the shortcomings of the central IT systems. When shadow IT systems are well known and kept to a minimum it can be positive for a company and could even be seen as an important source of innovation, as these local systems may function as prototypes for future common IT solutions.

When implementing MLOps at scale, think holistically about the technology infrastructure and applications needed to deploy AI models and data pipelines. The scope includes everything from data science tools used to select and train models to the hardware that those models use to process data. It includes data storage solutions as well as message queues used to store, move, monitor, and track various technical metrics. Don't forget to spend some time thinking through those metrics. For each business setting, it's crucial to consider what is most important to measure for you. Is it model performance on a per-model level? Or is it more important to measure the business outcome when applying the model?

Furthermore, don't assume that the same production model will work optimally for all your use cases. What works best depends a lot on what type of use case you are trying to realize. Therefore, it's good to try to gather a list of different types of use cases you have, or are aiming to have, so that you can better understand what type of technical requirements different types of use cases drive in your business setting. And don't forget the operational requirements! The use case characteristics are more important than you think. For example, the level of business criticality of the model outcome will set different requirements on how you monitor and govern AI models in operation. Even the sensitivity of the data used or the use case sensitivity might impact your technology choices and could mean that you need to make different priorities than originally planned.

Something that you also need to consider is the packaging of models. This is important because it's necessary to enable automated deployment of models to production and to efficiently address multiple different deployment designs, such as batch, function-as-a-service (FaaS), and scoring at the edge. FaaS in this context refers to an event-driven computing execution model that runs in stateless containers, and those functions manage server-side logic and state through the use of services from an FaaS provider. Scoring at the edge means that instead of data being processed in algorithms located in the cloud, for example, data is processed locally in algorithms stored on a hardware device—for example, in a sensor. This flexible model packaging approach is important, because it allows developers to build, run, and manage those application packages as functions without having to maintain their own infrastructure.

Another vital aspect involves how your serving infrastructure will be approached. Model serving makes a trained model available to other components. Models can be built on different technology stacks, for different purposes. For example, assuming that you already have an AI development environment up and running, you might then have deep learning stuff on TensorFlow and some natural language processing (NLP) stuff on Keras. In that situation, it's important to consider what setup you're adding to, or moving from, to perform model serving. You also must consider whether your model serving needs to happen in real time or in batch. This includes deciding on your model training approach in operation. Should it be on request, and therefore manual, or on a recurring basis in batch, or should training perhaps happen online in live operations?

Finally, a fundamental technical element of the AI production environment is monitoring. Not only should monitoring occur during the production phase, but it should also be an integral part of the entire AI life cycle and include:

- Monitoring data flows and data quality
- Checking output distribution of model performance
- Identifying model skew, drift, and precision (potential accuracy change)
- Setting and managing model thresholds
- Measuring performance thresholds and triggering alarms

The technology stack you choose is not only important for managing your AI models in operation, but it's also vital for your end-to-end approach and setup. (See Chapter 3 for more details on the technology stack.) Getting an efficient and iterative AI life cycle up and running is critical from an ROI perspective but also to manage AI model quality, reliability, security, scalability, and innovation.

CHAPTER 2

Data Engineering
Focused on AI

It's well known that without data you can't develop and train an AI model and that you can't run an AI model in a live production setting if your data flow is interrupted or stopped. Still, companies tend to invest much less time and money on managing all aspects of the data needed than they do on developing new algorithms and models. Why is that?

Some say it's because working with the data is not that exciting, whereas developing cool algorithms is what everyone wants to do. However, in my opinion, it's the data that is cool. The data is the foundation of everything related to analytics and AI, and without it we would have nothing. It's the data that enables us to see what we previously didn't see, understand what we didn't know, and manage or achieve capabilities previously unattainable.

Treating data as one of the most valuable business assets should be the main priority in any company. It's truly the way to stay on top of what is going on in your company, and it will help you understand what is not working and why, as well as foresee what is coming in order to give you time to prevent it from happening or be prepared to respond to any challenge as quickly and efficiently as possible.

So, keeping your data in order is vital. But where do you start? A first good step is to understand what data is available to you already and how that is being used today. And before you embark on a journey to get more data, be sure to understand what data you really need in order to achieve your business objectives, for internal operations, as well as for enabling commercial business opportunities for your company.

Know Your Data

Data underpins machine learning (ML) research and development in order to structure what an ML algorithm learns and how models are evaluated and benchmarked. However, data collection and labeling can be influenced by unconscious biases, data access limitations, and privacy concerns, among other challenges. As a result, datasets can reflect unfair social or other biases along dimensions of race, gender, age, and more.

Investing in knowing your data—like where it comes from, what's in it, what it will be used for, and what it means in the context of a specific use case—will help product and compliance teams understand datasets with the goal of improving data quality and thus help to mitigate fairness and bias issues.

I know this book is all about *operating* AI, but if there is one piece of advice that you should take away from this book, whether you are a manager, business analyst, data scientist, or operational support engineer, this is it: without truly knowing your data, operating your AI solutions won't be a success. Although data practitioners don't tend to think that being familiar with a dataset and the surrounding systems is optional, it's definitely an approach that can held by people unfamiliar with the data science field.

So, what does "knowing your data" really refer to? There are many aspects to take into account when getting to know your data, as shown in Figure 2.1. Although I don't claim that these aspects are a complete set, it's a good way to get a pretty solid understanding of your data in order to move forward.

Know the Data Structure

The first aspect is in this model is described as *knowing the data structure*, meaning where it resides and how it is organized. This is essentially knowing what data is available. You simply must know this to even start working. But when scratching a bit deeper you'll find plenty of nuance involved. Are key constraints involved that you didn't know about?

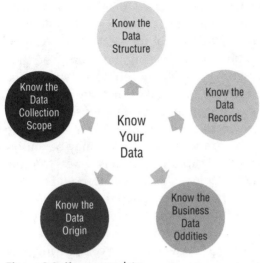

Figure 2.1: Know your data.

Has the data structure changed much over time; how'd those migrations and updates go? What's the default text encoding and time zone?

Other factors you need to consider are aspects such as which fields are automatically generated? What are the relevant indexes on the tables? What are the data types, and how is everything enforced? It's important to understand not just how the process works in theory but also how it's consistently (or not) applied in practice—which makes a huge difference to the reliability of the data quality.

Things get even more confusing when you have more complex production environments and the data you need is spread over many different instances. Database stuff like SQL data, tabular data, and columns is stored in one place, raw logs in other places, and processed logs in yet another place. Then you add third-party tools, which use other setups, and perhaps an on-premises data environment, which lives on another set of boxes. And, last but not least, perhaps there is data stored in the cloud, too.

Furthermore, you might realize that gaining access to all these different environments is a huge challenge in itself and even more so if the different environments have unmatched time stamps. Joining that data may turn out to be a real challenge. Just deciding on which system(s) you are going to use to join this stuff together is not as straightforward as it may seem. You also may not want to move data unnecessarily, since cost is associated with data shift. Instead, you might just want to fetch important parameters.

At the end of the day, the truth is that you need to be familiar with all the data and the data structures involved in order to get the job done. It's like knowing where all the ingredients in the kitchen are. Negotiating access can be an utter nightmare in some organizations, and then you have to marshal everything to a place where you can do your work.

On a deeper level, there are often multiple ways to measure something. For example, a sale might be recorded in the data warehouse but also in the base orders table, and it leaves traces in the raw server logs. There are layers of processing in between, and those specifics may be important someday and should therefore be captured, too. It is critical to know how data is manipulated, values calculated, and so on. It should be easy to look up where and how a data point is generated.

Another step deeper involves how the data is collected, as well as capturing where it came from. Which systems generated it, and what logic and technology was behind it? This step includes considering why certain pieces of data were collected and others weren't, as well as why certain metrics were chosen and others not.

But what do you do if the data you need is an entirely new data source? If that is the case, the data you need could still reside in the device or tool it was generated in and remains to be collected. In that case, don't forget to review your data collection options in relation to how you need to consume your data. Is a onetime batch sufficient, or do you need continuous collections over a period of time? Is every hour sufficient, or do you need every 30 or even 15 minutes? Perhaps you need to stream your data to secure a continuous data flow. Remember that by taking the time to understand your data properly already at the point of the first collection, you will stand a better chance of collecting all the related data and data attributes needed for your data science work.

Know the Data Records

A good way to get to know the data records is to play around with the data a bit, which is usually referred to as *data exploration*. When you explore the data long enough, you will come across weird things, even within the structured world of a relational database. Things are usually even worse in arbitrary logs.

Examples of data record problems could include:

- "0" nulls are inconsistently used to hard-code empty fields and to convey actual values.
- Time stamps are set in different ways, making it difficult to compare or structure data records in a consistent way.

- Code (e.g., JSON) is stored as plaintext because the system doesn't support it yet, and code is truncated because text fields have a maximum length.

- There are duplicated ID entries in a system where duplicates shouldn't exist.

- Field names get repurposed for a completely different use or are completely undocumented.

- Orphan IDs exist because no one really uses foreign key constraints in production.

Unfortunately, most data practitioners tend to spend the majority of their time cleaning and preparing data because of messy data records. This includes everything from bugs introducing erroneous data, to malicious or naive users giving you weird data, to bad system design, and so on. Sadly, there's no end to the list. Things tend to get even messier when you extract data from the web, a PDF file, or a randomly formatted Microsoft Excel sheet.

Fundamentally, most of these data issues will likely crash any code you write to do analysis. If you're lucky (or unlucky?) enough that your code runs despite weird data input, it will invalidate any conclusions you make and you need to be on point to realize what happened. When in doubt, ask other people when you see weird data. It's very often a bug that should be fixed in one or several underlying systems, processes, or data sources.

Know the Business Data Oddities

Businesses often collect special cases along the way, and those special cases can lead you the wrong way if you don't understand the business that the data reflects. Business data is dangerous because it manifests as valid data points but behaves differently.

Here are some examples:

- Same data is used differently by different groups, such as internal users, for various types of testing, for employees only, or for "friends of the business."

- Strategic partners get special deals. Maybe they have massively larger quotas and activities and get discounts, or they get features early.

- Reseller accounts effectively control multiple accounts' worth of activity under one account.

- Calendars in general—national holidays will mess with your data, and month lengths mess with your aggregations. An example of this is Easter because it's a different date every year and throws year-over-year (YOY) comparisons for a loop every year.

Domain experts and partners all across the business are key to dealing with this kind of data. All these things are part of the institutional knowledge you need to tap into in order to make sense of the data you see.

The only other guardrail you have is being vigilant about the distribution of activity and users. These special case entries tend to stand out from a more typical customer in some way so that you can hunt them down as if they were a big outlier and then be corrected partway through.

Know the Data Origin

In data science, it's important to meticulously document how data was collected and processed, because the details of the collection process matter. Tons of research has been invalidated based on the fact that there was a flaw in how data was gathered and used.

Let's look at a couple of examples:

- Do you depend on cookies? Don't forget that people can clear them or block them, or they can expire.

- Do you use front-end JavaScripts to send events like clicks and scrolls back to your systems? Do they work on all the browsers? Sometimes, remember, people block JavaScript, and *bots* rarely run JavaScript.

- If things are being tracked on the database, when does the update happen? Is it all wrapped in a transaction? Do state flags change monotonically or freely back and forth? What's the business logic dictating the state changes? Is it possible to get duplicate entries?

- How does your A/B testing framework assign subjects? Is it really assigning variants randomly without bias? Are events being counted correctly?

- What about Internet Protocol (IP) data? Don't forget the dynamics of IPs or network address translation (NAT) and how it all interacts with mobile devices. NAT is a way to map multiple local private addresses to a public one before transferring the data.

And then there are virtual private networks (VPNs), which extend a private network across a public network and enable users to send and receive data across shared or public networks as if their computing devices were directly connected to the private network. In this context, geolocations are just very complex lookup tables from a handful of vendors.

■ Are you relaying on physical sensors? Here you need to consider sensor calibration and wear effects, failures, and the real-world environment messing up your data.

As you might know, specific details matter a lot. At this point you are checking the integrity of the logic behind the data that exists. You need to be extremely aware of the wide range of biases and bugs that exist in the data. These details will often make or break a model. Remember all that talk about bias in various AI/ML solutions? This is where it starts.

Domain experts will be looking for these details, and you should leverage their precious knowledge. It's hard to beat collective institutional knowledge in this area. And you can help yourself uncover these issues by examining your data carefully, checking distributions, and questioning why they appear in a certain way.

Over time you should be able to develop a sense of what the engineers were trying to accomplish just by looking at the data table's structure and data. For example, this is a log of transactions, that's an audit trail of setting changes, orders go here and can have multiple shipments there. Status codes update this way, and one progression order is guaranteed but this other one isn't. With this sense of what a table's intent is, you can find all sorts of interesting bugs, many of which other engineers won't notice.

Know the Data Collection Scope

Someone made a choice, either consciously or unconsciously, to collect one piece of data and not another piece. Knowing those blind spots is important if you're concerned about biases in your data and models.

These collection decisions often stem from practical considerations. A certain data type might be impossible to collect, or it was decided not to collect a certain data type for privacy or ethical reasons, or because it wasn't seen as useful at the time. It's rarely with spite, but the effects of misuse of the data can be disastrous.

As an example, say you collect data about your own users because by definition non-users don't use your product. There is self-selection bias there, and this causes trouble when you are building a new product or entering a new market.

If you're aware of weaknesses, you can actively take measures to overcome them, but only if you know there's a problem to begin with. Maybe you go out and collect more data or rebalance the existing data. Sometimes you just need to conclude that something is a horrible idea and it should be scrapped.

So, what can you do to stay knowledgeable about your data? Well, you need to be prepared to keep learning. Remember that you're never going to have perfect data or a perfect understanding of all your data. And just when you think you've mastered something, you must be prepared for a new feature that has been added to the system you use as your main data source. Or perhaps the standards that you are dependent on change or entire systems are retired. So, keep learning and document what you can and just keep working with your data.

The Data Pipeline

A *data pipeline* starts by defining what, where, and how data is collected. It *automates* the processes involved in collecting or extracting, transforming, combining, validating, and loading data for further analysis and visualization. It delivers end-to-end velocity by eliminating errors and minimizing bottlenecks or latency. It can process multiple data streams at once. In short, it is an absolute necessity for a data-driven enterprise of today.

Another important aspect in an *AI in production* context is that a data pipeline views all data as streaming data, which allows for flexible schemas. Regardless of whether it comes from static sources (like a flat-file database) or from real-time sources (such as online retail transactions), the data pipeline divides each data stream into smaller chunks that it processes in parallel.

Furthermore, the data pipeline does not require the ultimate destination to be a data warehouse or a data lake. It can route data into any location—for example, another application, such as an analytics tool—or directly into an AI system. Think of it as the ultimate assembly line carrying your company's valuable data to wherever it's needed as part of improving internal operations or maybe enabling a commercial AI solution.

If architected in the right way, a data pipeline can provide data for internal usage, giving data science teams the needed datasets in an agreed frequency for developing and training AI models. At the same time it can also secure reliable data flows to AI models in live production environments, in so-called *production pipelines*. In a production pipeline, it's vital to secure sufficient speed, performance, and reliability of the data flow of both structured and unstructured data.

Many times, however, companies decide to separate the data pipelines for development and production. Sometimes the usage is constrained to different locations or environments, like on-premises versus in the cloud, or in a customer-controlled system environment versus your internal company system environment. Constraints on architectural choices for your data pipeline will also depend on what your commercial model and setup looks like, and if there are legal data aspects that you must take into account, such as the need to move data across country borders.

However, there are other reasons for separating your internal data pipeline from your production pipeline. As you might imagine, the production pipeline needs to be fully automated and easily scalable to be able to quickly adapt to potential changes in the production environment. You want to stay away from internal dependencies and processes that might be difficult or time-consuming to change. For example, a data pipeline can start off fine for one use case with a limited set of data sources, but as you start adding more data sources there is a risk of the data pipeline becoming less performant and reliable over time. This pipeline degradation can in turn result in longer data processing times, as well as increased compute cost—which in turn can create duplicated data records, partial failures in data processing, and data being late or completely out of order. You want to avoid ending up with a data swamp, especially for your production pipeline.

Figure 2.2 shows a simple view of the main components in a data pipeline. Data pipelines consist of three key elements: a source, a processing step or steps, and a destination. To the left you have the data sources, which could be coming from anywhere depending on your use cases and the objective of your data pipeline. The first step is to ingest the selected data into the system in its rawest form, before processing of the data can start. Part of the processing includes filtering, cleaning, and augmenting the data for the next step, where the business rules are applied in order to prepare the data for different types of user scenarios, which is the final destination of the data pipeline.

Data could then be pulled or pushed (depending on the setup) into an AI/ML development for getting to know your data through data exploration, then further into model development and training, and/ or to an AI/ML production environment directly for model execution

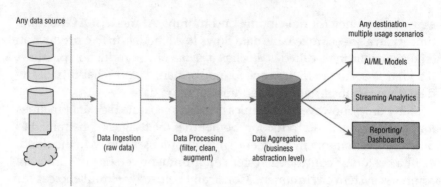

Figure 2.2: A data pipeline

of an internal AI solution or even a commercial solution. It all depends on the setup and purpose of the pipeline.

Another usage scenario could be real-time analytics using predefined models on streaming data, perhaps for automating different processes internally. And of course, the data pipeline can be used for updating your reports and dashboards with fresh data so that you can stay updated on the latest status of your operations, regardless if it involves financial performance, sales performance, or product quality.

One important thing to consider, though, is anonymization of your data. If you are collecting data that carries personal information of any kind, you need to anonymize the data as close to the data source as possible, usually at the point of collection, depending somewhat on how sensitive the data is and where you are collecting the data from and transferring the data to. This is especially important to take into account if you are collecting data that you do not own yourself but that you have acquired the right to use.

Let's say you are collecting the data with personal information from a customer´s site in one country, and according to the data pipeline setup you are transferring the data to the cloud (where the cloud server used is situated in another country, or even in another part of the world entirely). In this situation you might have to consider performing the anonymization of your data on a server located in the country of collection, rather than as the first step in your cloud environment. Again, it depends on the data sensitivity and the laws and regulations of the country in question, but also the business segment you're working in as well as customer requirements regarding certain data. Taking the time to learn how laws and regulations apply to the data you need (even if it involves your own company data) is vital to do early, because it might completely change how your company decides to build the data pipeline. For more details related to this, please see Chapter 6, "AI Is All About Trust."

So, how is a data pipeline related to an *ETL* (extract, transform, load) *process*? The terms *ETL* and *data pipeline* are sometimes used interchangeably, but there are significant differences to be aware of. The basic definition of an ETL system is that it extracts data from one system, transforms the data, and loads the data into a database or data warehouse. Legacy ETL pipelines typically run in batches, meaning that the data is moved in one large chunk at a specific time to the target system. Typically, this occurs in regularly scheduled intervals; for example, you might configure the batches to run at 12:30 a.m. every day when the system traffic is low.

A data pipeline, on the other hand, is a broader term that encompasses ETL as a subset. The data may or may not be transformed, and it's usually processed in real time (or streaming) instead of batches. When the data is streamed, it is processed in a continuous flow, which is useful for data that needs constant updating, such as data from a sensor monitoring traffic needed to run, for example, an AI solution in a production pipeline.

So, when do you need a data pipeline? A data pipeline is needed to secure a reliable infrastructure for consolidating and managing data and enables organizations to power their analytics tools and support daily AI operations in an efficient manner. And as organizations look to build applications with small code bases that serve a specific purpose (these types of applications are called *microservices*), they are moving data between more and more applications, making the efficiency of data pipelines a critical consideration in planning and development. Data generated in one source system or application may feed multiple data pipelines, and those pipelines may have multiple other pipelines or applications that are dependent on their outputs.

So, as the complexity of your data usage increases, and you become increasingly dependent on real-time data flows for decision making and operations, you need to move beyond traditional ETL thinking and embrace the data pipeline approach, if you haven't already.

Types of Data Pipeline Solutions

A number of different data pipeline solutions are available, each well suited to different purposes. Deciding on a data pipeline architecture requires many considerations. For example, does your pipeline need to handle streaming data? What rate of data do you expect? How much and what types of processing need to happen in the data pipeline? Is the data being generated in the cloud or on-premises, and where does it need to go? Do you plan to build the pipeline with microservices? Are there specific technologies in which your team is already well versed in programming and maintaining it properly?

Data pipelines may be architected in several different ways. The following list shows some popular types of data pipelines available. Note that these systems are not mutually exclusive. For example, it's common to have a data pipeline that is optimized for both cloud and real time in combination.

Batch   In the example of a batch-based data pipeline, you may have an application, such as a point-of-sale system that generates a large number of data points that you need to either push to a data warehouse and an analytics database, or for integrating the data points into a larger system for analysis. Batch processing is most useful for when you want to move large volumes of data at regular intervals and you do not need to move data in real time.

Real Time/Streaming   This type of data pipeline is optimized to process data in real time. Historically, data was typically processed in batches based on a schedule or some predefined threshold (e.g., every night at 1 a.m., every hundred rows, or every time the volume reaches 2 MB). But the pace of data has accelerated and volumes have exploded, and there are many use cases for which batch processing simply doesn't cut it. Stream processing has become a must-have for modern applications. Enterprises have turned to technologies that respond to data at the time at which it is created for a variety of use cases and applications. Stream processing allows applications to respond to new data events at the moment they occur. Rather than grouping data and collecting it at some predetermined interval, as in batch processing, stream processing applications collect and process data immediately as they are generated. Real time is useful when you are processing data from a streaming source, such as the data from financial markets or telemetry from connected devices.

Figure 2.3 shows an overview of how a streaming data pipeline could be architected. The data stream is managed by the fully automated stream processing framework where the data can be processed and delivered to various apps and/or solutions. The key is to build a flexible architecture that can grow and scale with your company's changing needs and priorities.

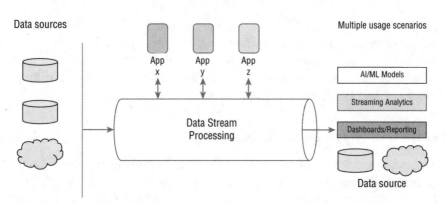

Figure 2.3: A streaming data pipeline

Cloud   This pipeline type is very good for working with cloud-based data, such as data from AWS buckets.

A *bucket* is a container for objects, where the data is stored in the form of objects, including any metadata that describes the data file. When the object (data) is in the bucket, you can open it, download it, and move it. These tools are hosted in the cloud, allowing you to save money on infrastructure and expert resources because you can rely on the infrastructure and expertise of the vendor hosting your pipeline.

Open Source   This pipeline type is most useful when you need an alternative to a commercial vendor and you have the expertise to develop or extend the tool for your purposes. Since open source tools are free of charge, they are often viewed as a cheaper alternative than their commercial counterparts; however, because open source tools lack support, the support cost is a trade-off with the cost of your own experts. So, low cost should not be the reason to choose open source, as it is seldom the case. It's more likely that you are forced to use a custom solution due to data restrictions. Open source solutions may also sometimes be more complicated to scale in a reliable manner.

So, what is the difference between a *data* pipeline and a *machine learning* pipeline? Well, when a data pipeline is built as part of feeding data to ML development and training, it usually becomes (by necessity) an integral part of the ML pipeline and its life-cycle management. A machine learning pipeline is a way to codify and automate the workflow it takes to produce a machine learning model. Machine learning pipelines consist of multiple sequential steps that do everything from data extraction and preprocessing to model training and deployment. Hence, they include all the steps of a pure data pipeline, but add the AI/ML parts to it and require the data pipeline to be configured with the objective of enabling an efficient ML pipeline. You will find more details on the key building blocks of an ML pipeline in Chapter 3, "Embracing MLOps."

Data Quality in Data Pipelines

Maintaining data quality is essential to any data pipeline initiative. Data-informed businesses rely on data in an ever-increasing manner today. It helps companies understand how their products are performing and how customers perceive their products, it provides valuable insights of the previously unknown and drives innovation, and it fuels any AI/ML solution that might be running on that same data. However, as a company expands its data collection, it also becomes more vulnerable to data quality issues. Insufficient quality data, such as inaccurate, missing, or inconsistent data, provides a poor foundation for decision making and can no longer be used to run AI solutions based on that data. And once trust in the information is lost, the data, the data team, the data infrastructure, and any internal or commercial AI solution, lose their value as well.

So, how can you prevent bad-quality data from finding its way into your organization and solutions? Well, let's start by sorting out what high-quality data means first. High data quality is usually defined by how you can rate the dataset in a number of aspects:

Accurate Data   When data is accurate, you can trust that what the data says happened, actually happened. Accurate data correctly captures the real-world event that took place. What's more, accuracy implies that data values are correct; you recorded what happened. Accuracy also means that the data is interpreted as intended in a consistent and unambiguous format. When this is done successfully, analysts can easily understand and work with the data, leading to more accurate insights or AI/ML models based on that data.

Complete Data   Complete data means there is no missing data. It also means that, to the extent possible, the data gives a complete picture of the real-world events that took place. Without comprehensive data, your visibility will be limited and you might end up building and training predictive AI models with unacceptable levels of accuracy.

Valid Data   This means how the data is collected rather than the data itself. Data is valid if it is suitable for the correct type and falls within the appropriate range. If data is not up to expected standards, you might have trouble organizing and analyzing it. Some software can help you change data to the correct format.

Relevant Data   The data you collect should also be helpful for the initiatives you plan to apply it for. Even if the information you get has all the other characteristics of quality data, it's not helpful to you if it's not relevant to your goals. It's essential to set goals for your data collection to know what kind of data to collect.

Timely Data   Timeliness refers to how recent the event the data represents took place. Generally, data should be recorded soon after or at the same time as the actual world event happens. Data typically becomes less valuable and less accurate as time goes on. Data that reflect events that happened recently are likely to show the reality. Using outdated data for data exploration and insights, or for AI model development and training, can lead to inaccurate AI models and results, which can have serious implications.

Consistent Data   When comparing a data item or its counterpart across multiple datasets or databases, it should be the same. This lack of difference between various versions of a single data record is referred to as consistency. A data item should be consistent both in its content and its format. Different groups may be operating under different assumptions about what is true if your data isn't consistent.

Securing an efficient and reliable data pipeline with high-quality data is a key element to successfully operating AI, regardless of whether it's internal AI operations or external, commercial AI operations. Next we'll explore in greater detail how to establish good routines in your data engineering function in order to secure high-quality data for your AI/ML development, training, and operations.

The Data Quality Approach in AI/ML

In a real-world AI/ML initiative, you must take several important data-related factors into account before you jump into AI/ML model development. Starting by defining precisely what the problem is that you are trying to solve, and then defining the success criteria for that, is usually a good idea. However, it's important to not take the detailing of this too far. It's all about finding the right balance of what you need to know before you start, and getting started so that you can understand and learn more from the experience you are gaining by actually doing it.

Success criteria that could be a target value for a metric might be data accuracy, or something more generic such as the satisfaction of a certain customer. However, don't forget to check that the data you need to satisfy the selected metric is available to you; you also need to find a way to collect the data needed.

After you've handled the data collection, you should explore the data before you can move into developing the ML pipeline. It's important not to jump into ML modeling before taking the time to "know your data," as described earlier in this chapter.

For example, you should know the value range for the features involved, their data type, whether there are outliers, and so on. You also need to identify and correct data problems, like missing data, or uninformative features that can be eliminated. Furthermore, you must test your assumptions about the problem at hand. For example, you might need to test that the distribution of the values of certain features are what you expect. By digging into the details of the data, you are able to discern what each variable means and check that your expectations of the quantity match reality. You can judge this by performing a *univariate analysis*, where you look at histograms and distributions for each feature.

Once that is done, you can move to a *bivariate analysis*, where you can look for correlations between features and other interesting relationships. You can also identify outliers and other types of anomalies that could challenge the assumptions about the data or conclude that further data cleaning is needed. As part of this step, you should also define appropriate strategies to fix certain types of missing values in your data.

Finally, don't forget to uncover biases in the data that could result in an unfair model. This aspect should not be discarded, especially for models where the model outcome has a direct impact on people's lives—for example, where an AI model is used to decide whether or not a person will be approved for a loan from their bank. Fair models are always important, but an unfair model can definitely have more serious implications in certain use cases.

Even though data exploration is an interactive step in data engineering, you probably still want to make it reproducible and you want to track it. This can be done by writing an MLflow component that installs the libraries that you need for your analysis, like pandas and matplotlib. The component also launches Jupyter itself, within the environment that MLflow created. You can then embed all the plots and computations that were performed during the data exploration step in the notebook. Remember that it's important to write comments and remarks in the notebook for traceability and documentation purposes. It's also vital to track the input of the notebooks so that you will know which version of the data you used for the data exploration.

The preprocessing step is quite limited in scope—and for a good reason. Only apply the preprocessing that is needed to make the training dataset look like the dataset that the model will see in production. All the preprocessing that needs to be applied on both the training data and the data at inference time *must* go in the inference pipeline to achieve data pipeline symmetry between development and production. In the context of AI/ML, an *inference pipeline* refers to when you apply your trained model on new live data in the production pipeline. For further details on the ML pipeline, see Chapter 3.

In data engineering for AI/ML, it's important to always think about the data that the model will see at inference time, meaning when it's applied in the live production pipeline. The dataset that you use for training and testing should look the same as the data in production. This means that it should not be modified by the preprocessing step in a way that makes it different from the data at inference time. Therefore, there are some examples of activities that should *not* be part of the preprocessing step:

- **Categorical encoding**—The categorical data encoding method transforms the categorical variable into a set of binary variables (also known as dummy variables). This type of encoding must be performed at both training and inference time and therefore should go in the inference pipeline.

- **Imputation of missing values when the feature could also be missing in production**—So, for example, if you are using the results of a web form as features, and one of the options is optional in the web form, you will get null values at inference time as well. In that case, you should *not* impute them during the preprocessing stage. Instead, you should impute them in the inference pipeline.

- **Dimensionality reduction**—This is the transformation of data from a high-dimensional space into a low-dimensional space so that the low-dimensional representation retains some meaningful properties of the original data. Since this operation modifies the features in the same way during training and during production, you should make it part of the inference pipeline.

Data validation is another important step to secure data quality in the data pipeline in preparation for your AI/ML activities. You need to validate your data in order to make sure that your assumptions about the data are correct and that they stay correct over time. Data validation is similar to unit testing for software, but it is applied to data instead. Data validation is fundamental to avoid the "garbage in/garbage out" problem, since problematic or incorrect data might give you a model that performs well in model training but fails completely on real data in production.

Data validation is important in order to catch bugs in the preprocessing step or in the data pipelines that produced the data. Another reason is to catch any significant changes in the data, because changes in the inputs of a training run will give you a significantly different model. Severe changes that violate the assumptions of the modeling—for example, around feature importance or the valid value range of a feature—might even completely break the model.

Data validation is especially important in the context of ML pipelines, which are supposed to be used to automatically retrain a model, up to the extreme of continuous training in live production environments.

Let's now look at three different types of data pipeline issues that can cause problems in your ML pipeline:

- **Example 1:** A person is rating the content on a website, like a movie, a song, or a book. The initial data had a 3-star rating system, whereas the new data you receive uses a 10-star rating system because of recent changes on the website that you were unaware of. This new situation might require a different modeling choice, such as different hyperparameters to account for the increased complexity of the rating.

- **Example 2:** Let's say you are preparing a regression model that predicts the price of big real-estate assets. Due to a bug in the new version of a data ingestion pipeline upstream, the target in the database went from having units of "millions of dollars" to just "dollars." Depending on the model you are using, this could cause significant problems, and it is a change you definitely want to be aware of.

- **Example 3:** Sometimes nothing has changed upstream in the pipeline, but the world has changed. For example, let's consider an example where you are predicting the price of houses for sale. Before COVID-19, the value was linked very strongly to the vicinity to the workplace. Now remote working is much more widespread, and therefore being very close to the workplace is now much less important, with a significant impact on your modeling strategy.

Another important step in data preparation for AI/ML is related to *data segregation*. In the simplest example of data segregation, you are just splitting the original dataset into three categories: *training*, *validation*, and *test*. You start by extracting the test dataset and later on, in the training and validation step, you will also take the remainder and split it further into training and validation.

You use the validation dataset for validating the model, optimizing hyperparameters, and so on. The training dataset is obviously used for training, and once the model development is finished, you measure the final performance of the model using the test dataset.

However, in some cases you want to perform k-fold cross-validation during training. This is also referred to as "out-of-sample testing," which is a model validation technique for assessing how the results of a statistical analysis will generalize to an independent dataset. It is mainly used in settings where the goal is prediction and you want to estimate how accurately a predictive model will perform in practice. In that case, you will not split the dataset into training and validation. You will instead only perform the first split and carry over the remainder dataset as a whole.

There are also more complicated forms of data segregation. For example, if you have enough data, you might want to split the test and the validation set into two different groups, say across protected categories. You then use these datasets to make sure that the model is performing equally well for the different groups. This is a fundamental practice for the ethical development of AI.

Scaling Data for AI

There are a lot of talks on how AI will advance society, but the debate remains as to how AI can and should be applied in practicality. Today, many enterprises continue to fail to effectively apply AI to solve their business problems and generate tangible value. The hype around AI has led to a trend where almost every vendor claims to leverage it in their technology, solutions, or products, causing extreme confusion, and in some cases, frustration among AI technology users.

Contrary to industry hype, AI cannot and should not be used to solve every problem. In fact, you can start to see companies using AI in situations where the capability isn't even needed to improve the product or software. Traditional analytics would be sufficient (and a faster and cheaper way) to meet the need.

To understand where AI should be used and will be most successful, it's important to revert back to what AI really is. AI, or machine learning, refers to a broad set of algorithms that can solve a specific set of problems, *if trained properly*. And this training requires high-quality data!

While integrating machine learning into a product is usually pretty straightforward, effectively training an algorithm to perform its task with the right intent and with expected performance level in production is not. Not to mention that it's now expected to have continuous learning capabilities and both run and learn securely and ethically in live environments, over time. Achieving such capable algorithms in every company across society assumes a lot from companies, not the least access to and utilization of high-quality data, not only for development and training but especially for continuous data flows in the production environments as well.

AI works best when large amounts of rich data are available. The more facets the data covers, the faster the algorithms can learn and fine-tune their predictive analyses. Successful machine learning depends on large and broad datasets. Remember, without data the algorithms cannot run!

From a technical standpoint, machine learning or AI features have never been more accessible than they are today. In the cybersecurity industry, when effectively leveraged, AI has the potential to help business leaders strengthen their resilience to all types of cyberattacks. AI's main promise in this space is the ability to consistently detect new and unknown threats in the absence of traditional indicators of compromise, such as a known piece of malware. With sufficient quality data available, AI techniques easily outperform traditional, signature-based approaches, which retroactively seek out the artifacts an attacker leaves during a breach.

Artificial intelligence can drive the creation of indicators of attack (IoAs), which can identify active attacks based on how an adversary behaves in the system, allowing organizations to prevent breaches. What's even more important, the algorithms will learn from those behaviors for future-proofed protection.

Scale is a critical component of getting AI applied effectively. In the cybersecurity example, it's vital in order to swiftly and accurately analyze billions of security events in real time, a capability that is needed for effective threat protection, and for that the algorithms require a sufficient level of computational power and scalability. In most cases, that degree of enablement cannot be accomplished using old-school, on-premises architecture and conventional database methods.

Analytics, AI, and machine learning are becoming fundamental for data-oriented industries and present significant opportunities for enterprises and research organizations. However, the potential for AI to improve business performance and competitiveness demands a different approach to managing the data life cycle.

Companies that are planning to fully embrace AI techniques should consider how *data*, which is at the heart of their competitive differentiation, will require *extensive scaling*. Current workloads may possibly still fit into in-node storage, but companies that are not considering what happens when deep learning is ready to be applied to larger datasets will be left behind by competition.

Key Capabilities for Scaling Data

The area of data science is advancing fast in the industry, and this is good news for data and technology leaders worldwide. There is no longer a need to start from scratch when building a scalable data architecture. The past few years have seen the emergence of data architectures that provide the agility to meet today's need for speed, flexibility, and innovation. Data architectures are available that have been road-tested in endless business and technology transformations across industries, with proven ability to reduce costs for traditional AI use cases and enable faster time to market and better reusability of new AI initiatives.

However, it's important to remember that building a scalable data architecture isn't a one-and-done exercise. Each quarter, technology leaders should review progress, impact, funding, and support for strategic business plans to ensure long-term alignment and a sustainable technology build-out in relation to the data architecture.

So, where do you start? What's needed to get this right? Let's look at a number of key capabilities for scaling data for AI success.

Maintain flexible and fast access to data.   Flexibility for AI means addressing data maneuverability. As AI-enabled data centers move from initial prototyping and testing toward production and scale, a flexible data pipeline should provide the means to independently scale in multiple areas: performance, capacity, ingest capability, and responsiveness for data scientists. Such flexibility also implies expansion of a namespace without disruption, eliminating data copies and complexity during growth phases. Flexibility for organizations entering AI also suggests good performance regardless of the choice of data formats.

Remove bottlenecks in your data pipeline.   Given the heavy investment from organizations into graphics processing units (GPUs)-based computer systems, the data pipeline must be capable of keeping ML systems saturated across throughput, input/output operations per second (IOPS), and latency, to eliminate the risk of being underutilized. A good saturation level for input/output (I/O) means cutting out application wait times.

Build a massive data ingest capability.   Ingest for storage systems means write performance and coping with large concurrent streams from distributed sources at a huge scale. Successful AI implementations extract more value from data, but they also can gather increasingly more data as a measure of success. Systems should deliver balanced I/O, performing writes just as fast as reads, along with advanced parallel data placement and protection. Data sources developed to augment and improve acquisition can be satisfied at any level, while concurrently serving machine learning compute platforms.

Apply a use case–based approach.   Organizations can realize results faster by taking a use case approach rather than initiating a major program with large (and inevitably slow) phases that impact the whole organization at once. In the use case approach, leaders start by building and deploying a minimum viable product that delivers the specific data pipeline components required for each desired use case. You can then make adjustments and scale up as needed based on feedback and experience from a real case.

Automate deployment using DataOps.   *DataOps* (data operations) is an Agile approach to designing, implementing, and maintaining a distributed data architecture that will support a wide range of open source tools and frameworks in production, software, and AI. The goal of DataOps is to create business value from data faster by creating predictable delivery and change management of data, data models, and related artifacts, whether the user needs the data for analytics or AI/ML.

DataOps applies a DevOps (development operations) approach to data, just as MLOps (machine learning operations) applies a DevOps approach to AI. (You can find out more about MLOps in Chapter 3.)

Like DevOps, DataOps is structured into continuous integration and deployment phases with a focus on eliminating "low value" and automating activities spanning the delivery life cycle across development, testing, deployment, and monitoring stages. A structured and automated pipeline, leveraging synthetic data and machine learning for data quality, can bring AI models and accompanying data-model changes into production much faster.

Let go of legacy technology.   Legacy solutions cannot match the business performance, cost savings, or reduced risks of modern technology, such as data lakes, and it won't enable businesses to achieve their full potential. Rather than engaging in detailed evaluations against legacy solutions, data and technology leaders will serve their companies better by educating business leaders on the need to let go of legacy technologies. Since delivering performance to the application is what matters, not just how fast the storage can push out data, integration and support services must span the whole environment, delivering faster results. This emphasizes the importance of partnering with a platform provider that really understands every aspect of the environment. Any AI data platform provider chosen to help accelerate analytics and machine learning must have deep domain expertise in dealing with datasets and I/O that well exceed the capabilities of applicable solutions, and they must have the tools readily at hand to create tightly integrated solutions at scale.

Not surprisingly, most companies are turning to public cloud vendors for fast, scalable, and cost-efficient data management solutions. However, as the industry dependency on the cloud vendors grows, businesses and buyers must continuously evaluate these public cloud vendors that are pushing their AI capabilities, keeping a keen eye to ensuring that the technology leverages the right data and capabilities to be truly effective over time. This will be of growing importance since in the next wave of AI evolution, the algorithms will be more commoditized, while whoever owns the data will be the leader.

Introducing a Data Mesh

A *data mesh* is a new approach to designing and developing data architectures. Much in the same way that software engineering teams transitioned from monolithic applications to microservice architectures, the data mesh is, in many ways, the data platform version of microservices.

Unlike traditional monolithic data infrastructures that handle the consumption, storage, transformation, and output of data in one central data lake, a data mesh supports distributed, domain-specific data consumers and views "data-as-a-product," with each domain handling their own data pipelines.

Figure 2.4 shows the distributed architectural approach in a data mesh with the foundation being the data-as-an-infrastructure. The data mesh then distributes the ownership by holding business owners accountable for providing their data as products. This also facilitates communication between data distributed across different locations.

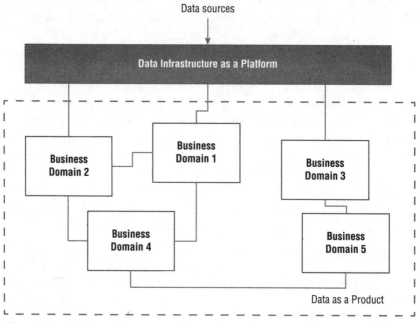

Figure 2.4: A data mesh

Whereas the data infrastructure is responsible for providing each domain with the solutions with which to process it, domains are tasked with managing data ingestion, cleaning, and aggregation of the data to generate assets that can be used by analytics and/or AI/ML applications. Each domain is responsible for owning its ETL pipelines but also a set of capabilities applied to all domains that stores, catalogs, and maintains access controls for the raw data. Once data has been served to and transformed by a given domain, the domain owners can then leverage the data for their analytics or AI operational needs.

Furthermore, data meshes leverage principles of domain-oriented design to deliver a self-serve data platform that allows users to stay above the technical complexity and focus on their individual data use cases. This means that the data mesh obtains and extracts domain-agnostic data infrastructure capabilities into a central platform that handles the data pipeline engine, storage, and streaming infrastructure. Meanwhile, each domain is responsible for leveraging these components to run custom ETL pipelines, giving them the support necessary to easily serve their data as well as the autonomy required to deliver a true self-service data platform.

So, why is a data mesh a well-suited data architectural approach going forward? Well, until recently, most companies have leveraged a single data warehouse connected to various business analytics and AI/ML platforms. Such solutions are usually maintained by a small group of specialists and frequently burdened by significant technical debt.

Additionally, implementing a data architecture with a data lake with real-time data availability and stream processing, with the goal of ingesting, enriching, transforming, and serving data from a centralized data platform, also tends to fall short in a few ways. For example, a central ETL pipeline gives teams less control over increasing volumes of data, and as every company becomes a data company, different data use cases require different types of transformations, putting a heavy load on the central platform. Therefore, such data lakes lead to disconnected data producers, impatient data consumers, and worst of all, a data team struggling to keep up with the demands of the business.

Instead, business domain-oriented data architectures, like data meshes, give teams the best of both worlds: a centralized database or a distributed data lake with different business domains responsible for handling their own pipelines.

When You Have No Data

Sometimes the data you need for developing and training your AI models is not accessible to you. The reasons for this may vary. Perhaps the data you need is owned by another party who refuses to give or sell you the data, or perhaps the data you need sits in another country and you cannot by any legal or practical means retrieve it.

One thing is clear. Understanding your data need early is key, and part of that is understanding the use case for the data. If there is something most data practitioners learn the hard way, it's that when it comes to data, nothing is ever as easy as it seems. Lead times are usually quite long when it comes to securing access to data you don't own but just want to use. And sometimes the dataset is too small for your specific use case. Or incomplete. Or perhaps you lack historical data records that are needed for building and training your prediction models.

So, what do you do then? Well, depending on the use cases, one option available to you is to use *computer-generated data*. Fake data that is created to mirror real data can be surprisingly effective for building and training a model in the lab. As long as the computer-generated data is as similar as possible to the real data, you can come quite far with this approach. However, it's important to synthesize data that is useful and prevent your ML model from becoming an inverted version of your data emulator.

However, be aware that you cannot expect an AI model trained only on synthesized data to perform in production at once. In fact, you cannot be sure it will work in production at all. Therefore, when you have built an AI solution using only computer-generated data, you need to take extra measures to ensure a confined environment for training your model in production. Also, be prepared for the model training in production taking longer than usual, since the real data in a production setting is more diverse.

The Role of a Data Fabric

The *data fabric* is the platform that supports all the data in the company—how it's managed, described, combined, and universally accessed. A data fabric is a design concept for attaining reusable and augmented data integration services, data pipelines, and semantics for flexible and integrated data delivery. It is an optimized combination of data management and integration technology, architecture design, and services delivered across multiple deployment and orchestration platforms. This results in faster, more informed, and in some cases, completely automated data access and sharing.

From a traditional perspective, a data fabric may consist of a combination of existing data delivery approaches in an orchestrated fashion. Modern data fabrics include new and upcoming data management technologies and data integration approaches delivered through collaborative data management practices (such as DataOps). These include (but are not limited to) stream data integration, data virtualization, semantic enrichment, AI/ML-assisted active metadata, and knowledge graphs.

Knowledge graphs are all about linking data. The goal of linking data is to publish structured data in such a way that it can be easily consumed and combined with other linked data. Linked data is the new de facto standard for data publication and interoperability on the web and is moving into enterprises as well. Big players such as Google, Facebook, Amazon, and Microsoft have already adopted some of the principles behind it.

As shown in Figure 2.5, it's easy to imagine how a knowledge graph is an advanced way to map all knowledge on a particular topic to fill the gaps on how the data is related. The data in the data fabric can represent concepts, objects, things, people—whatever you have in mind. The graph fills in the connections between the concepts.

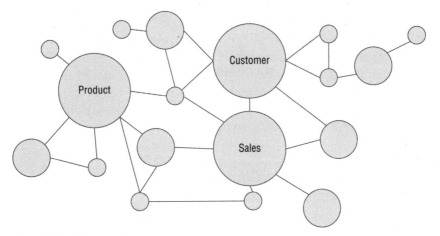

Figure 2.5: A knowledge graph

But what does the knowledge graph mean for your company? In the old-fashioned way, the data model in the data warehouse cannot absorb the huge amount of data that is coming at us. The process of creating relational data models just can't keep up with the speed at which new data is being generated and is needed for our various usage scenarios. In addition, the extracts of data that are used to power data discovery are also too small.

Unfortunately, data lakes based on Apache Hadoop Distributed File System (HDFS) or cloud storage have many times turned into data swamps, without the required management and governance capabilities. A concrete way to check the health of the data situation in your company is to ask your data engineers and data scientists if they understand the majority of the data your organization has. If they don't, it's probably a good idea to take control of your data situation before it turns into a data swamp.

Of course, it's extremely hard to analyze all the data you have and understand all the relationships behind it. That's where you can get help from a knowledge graph. They are more intuitive. An interesting thing is that people don't generally think in terms of tables, although that's how we organize data. But people do have a tendency to immediately understand the concepts of graphs—intuitively. When you draw the structure of a knowledge graph on a whiteboard, it is obvious what it means to most people.

Why a Data Fabric Matters in AI/ML

The current business demand for AI/ML-assisted and AI/ML-augmented data integration for new applications is driving practices away from custom-made design toward metadata-driven solutions. As a data leader you must introduce a data fabric design to rationalize cluttered integration environments that have become unmanageable over decades. Data integration must be made more dynamic and increasingly automated. Figure 2.6 gives a high-level view of the buildup of a data fabric.

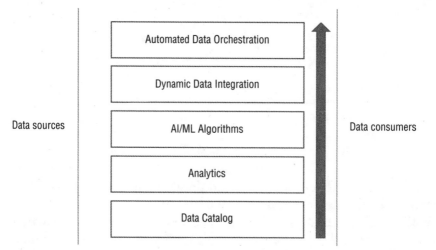

Figure 2.6: The concept of a data fabric

Figure 2.6 shows the different layers that should be included in a data fabric. The purpose of the data catalog is to help companies (on a continuous basis) find, integrate, catalog, and share all forms of *metadata*. Metadata refers to a set of data that describes and gives information about other data. The data fabric should be able to share this metadata across all environments, including hybrid and multicloud platforms, and at the edge. The metadata should then be represented, along with its intricate relationships, in a connected knowledge graph model that can be understood by the business teams.

With the data fabric you also gain the ability to perform *analytics* over connected metadata in a knowledge graph. The resulting output can be used as input (in the form of training data) to inform and enrich the AI/ML algorithms that are delivered as part of the fabric. These AI/ML algorithms assist with delivering a dynamic integration design that can adjust to changing data integration requirements.

Furthermore, with a data fabric approach, you gain the ability to use *AI/ML algorithms* in your own data management infrastructure and processing maps for data integration use cases. It means that these maps will adjust dynamically and provide guidance and recommendations on key data management and integration considerations with the assistance of AI/ML capabilities. By using AI/ML in your data management infrastructure, it will also enable you to answer important questions, such as:

- What is the optimal processing environment for this workload?
    1. For example, Spark versus an existing data warehouse
- What is the best way to deliver the integrated data?
    2. For example, extract, transform, and load (ETL) processes, data virtualization, or a combination of the two approaches

A strong data integration is essential to good data fabric design. A data fabric must be flexible enough to deliver *integrated data* through a combination of required data delivery styles (including, but not limited to, ETL, streaming, replication, messaging, and data virtualization). A comprehensive data fabric must also support data delivery in all necessary latencies (batch or streaming) and all types of data consumers, including IT users (for complex integration requirements) and business users (for self-service data preparation).

In addition, a good data fabric implementation should be able to perform data integration across a multicloud and hybrid cloud environment and treat integration as a discipline regardless of environment, vendor, platform, or cloud.

Finally, the data fabric should possess the ability to *automate data orchestration*, since it's a key component of any successful data fabric design. The separation of storage and compute is becoming critical in managing data across a hybrid/multicloud environment. This means that data fabrics now require automation to manage and orchestrate their data pipelines that often traverse organizational boundaries and ecosystems.

The various facets of orchestration in today's data environments include coordination, maintenance and operationalization of data flows, performance optimization, scheduling of integration workloads, and more. Managing these requires your data fabric to automate most parts of orchestration to make data management teams more productive.

Key Competences and Skillsets in Data Engineering

A great data engineer is a problem-solver focused on building and preparing things that are useful for others. It´s also important for a data engineer to have detailed knowledge of tools and programming languages relevant in the data management space. Data engineering represents a combination of software engineering and data science, so it helps to have skills from each discipline. In fact, most data engineers start off as software engineers, which is almost mandatory competence, given that data engineering relies heavily on programming.

Data engineers usually work in a variety of settings to build and manage systems focused on collecting and managing raw data and turning it into usable information for data scientists and business analysts to analyze and draw insight from. Their ultimate goal is to prepare and process data and make data accessible so that teams and organizations can use it for various purposes ranging from data exploration and analytics to training ML models or securing reliable data quality and a stable data flow for ML models in an operational production setting.

But before we dive into the detailed skillsets needed by data engineers, let's briefly look at the difference between a data engineer and a data scientist.

- **Data engineer**—Data engineers are mainly tasked with transforming data into a format that can be easily analyzed. This is achieved by developing, maintaining, and testing infrastructures for data generation. Data engineers work closely with data scientists and are largely in charge of architecting solutions for data scientists that enable them to do their jobs. Data engineers are therefore tasked with developing a robust and scalable set of data processing tools/platforms and must be comfortable with SQL/NoSQL database wrangling and building/maintaining data pipelines. So, a data engineer is an engineering role within a data science team or any data-related project that requires creating and managing technological infrastructure of a data platform.

■ **Data scientist**—Data scientists uses various techniques in statistics and machine learning to process and analyze large sets of both structured and unstructured data. A data scientist is responsible for building and training models to explore what can be learned from data, and the role combines different disciplines such as computer science, statistics, and mathematics. Data scientists could be viewed as analytical experts who use their skills in both technology and social science to build models to identify trends and predict outcomes. They use industry knowledge, and contextual understanding and question existing assumptions to uncover hidden insights and to find new solutions to business challenges. However, some of the best data scientists are those who are prepared to also do a lot of data engineering work. Understanding the data is as important as understanding the business problem. Ultimately, the success of a data scientist will depend on identifying which data is needed to train the model to solve the business problem at hand.

In general, you could say that there is not a clear division between key roles in a data science team when it comes to skills and responsibilities. However, the difference mainly involves which focus they have. In short, you could say that while data engineers are focused on building infrastructure and architecture for data generation, data scientists are focused on using advanced mathematics and statistical analysis to build models built on that generated data. The ML engineer role is then to take these models and industrialize them in a production setting, although ML engineers have started to get more involved with designing the solutions, too. This is positive, as it facilitates practically applying the operational perspective into the design phase.

Data scientists are engaged in a constant interaction with the data infrastructure that is built and maintained by the data engineers, but they are not responsible for building and maintaining that infrastructure. Instead, they are internal clients, tasked with conducting high-level market and business operation research to identify trends and relations—things that require them to use a variety of sophisticated machines and methods to interact with and act upon data. In contrast, data engineers work to support data scientists and analysts, providing infrastructure and tools that can be used to deliver end-to-end solutions to business problems. Simply put, data scientists depend on data engineers.

Succeeding in AI requires a team effort, it´s as simple as that. However, the role of the data engineers in the data science team should not be underestimated. Unfortunately many companies get fixated on how many data scientists they have employed and forget about the data engineers. Remember that it´s the responsibility of the data engineers to know how to build and maintain database systems, be fluent in programming languages such as SQL, Python, and R, be excellent at identifying suitable warehousing solutions, and of course excel at using ETL (Extract, Transfer, Load) tools, as well as understanding basic machine learning techniques and algorithms. This is a very broad and versatile skillset, crucial in enabling an efficient data science team.

A great data engineer should also master communication and collaboration. The importance of *clear and concise writing* should not be underestimated but is often a forgotten skillset. This is important because it helps to solidify the data science results and hence the expertise of the data engineer and ultimately the whole team's combined effort. Writing blogs is another way to consolidate and validate the understanding of complex professional concepts and explain complex data and results to business stakeholders or even just within the data science team.

Another important skill to master is *time management*. When exploring and managing data, there are many ways you can get stuck in the details of a particular problem, or have difficulties with accepting that the data quality never will be perfect. However, to become a great data engineer you need to be able to manage your time efficiently. An experienced data engineer is usually great at balancing the efforts and planning the workday in a good way. Apps like Forest and HabitMinder as well as many books are available to help you improve time management skills.

Data science is a highly collaborative field, and data engineers work with a range of stakeholders, from data analysts to chief technology officers (CTOs). In fact, the role of the data engineer is probably the role that requires the broadest technical skillset. Examples of *technical skills* for data engineers are:

Data Warehousing   Data engineers must be familiar with the basic concept of data warehousing and the tools related to this field, such as Amazon Web Services and Microsoft Azure. Data warehousing is among the fundamental skills required for data engineering professionals. The data can come from multiple sources such as enterprise resource planning (ERP) software, accounting software, or a customer relationship management (CRM) solution.

Machine Learning   As a data engineer, you only need to be familiar with the basics of machine learning and its algorithms. Being familiar with machine learning will help you in understanding your organization's requirements and collaborate with the data scientists more efficiently. Apart from these benefits, learning about machine learning will help you in building the right data architecture and provide data pipelines that meet the needs of the data scientists.

Data Structures   Although a data engineer usually performs data optimization and filtering, knowing about the basics of data structures is important. A data structure is a collection of data values, the relationships among them, and the functions or operations that can be applied to the data. Getting familiar with an organization's data structures will assist a data engineer in understanding the various aspects of the organization's goals, as well as act as a common base for cooperation with other teams and business stakeholders.

ETL Tools   As explained earlier in this chapter, ETL represents how you extract data from a source, transform it into a format, and store it into a data warehouse. ETL uses batch processing to ensure that users can analyze relevant data according to their specific business problems. It gets data from multiple sources, applies particular rules to the sources, and then loads the data into a database where anyone in the organization can use or view it. Although ETL tools represent a more traditional and manual approach to data management, mastering the ETL toolsets is necessary as a data engineering professional, as many organizations usually have different data management maturity across the organization as well as different data management setups. This requires data engineering flexibility and ability to handle both legacy toolsets, as well as the latest and most advanced toolsets in the industry for the more demanding data management activities.

Programming Languages   Python, Java, Golang, and Scala are some of the most popular programming languages. Python is a must-have for a data engineer as it helps you perform statistical analysis and modeling. Python is the core programming language that remains in high demand. Data engineers are expected to be fluent in Python to be able to write maintainable, reusable, and complex functions. This language is efficient, versatile, and perfect for text analytics. Java helps you work with data architecture frameworks, and while Scala also is a Java Virtual Machine (JVM) based language and produces the same byte code as Java, the higher optimization in Scala makes it faster to compile code.

Golang is very useful for writing lightweight microservices and for generating APIs that interact with front-end applications. If you want to build a small functional microservice quickly, then Golang is an easy language for developers to learn quickly. However, you should note that nearly 70 percent of job descriptions for this field require Python as a skill. As a data engineer, you must have strong coding skills since you'll need to work with multiple programming languages. Apart from Python, other popular programming skills are .NET, R, Shell Scripting, and Perl. Java and Scala are vital as they let you work with MapReduce, a vital Apache Spark component. Similarly, Python helps you in performing data analysis. You must master at least one of these programming languages. Another language to watch out for is C++. It can compute vast amounts of data in the absence of a predefined algorithm. Apart from these advantages, C++ lets you apply predictive analytics in real time and retrain the algorithm. It's among the most important skills required for data engineers.

Distributed Systems   A distributed system is a computing environment in which various components are spread across multiple computers (or other computing devices) on a network (see Figure 2.7). These devices split up the work, coordinating their efforts to complete the job more efficiently than if a single device had been responsible for the task. Distributed systems are an important development in data science as an increasing number of related jobs are so massive and complex that it would be impossible for a single computer to handle them alone. But distributed computing also offers additional advantages over traditional computing environments. Distributed systems reduce the risks involved with having a single point of failure, bolstering reliability and fault tolerance. Modern distributed systems are generally designed to be scalable in near real time; also, you can spin up additional computing resources on the fly, increasing performance and further reducing time to completion.

Historically, distributed computing has been expensive, complex to configure, and many times quite difficult to manage. But with the emergence of software-as-a-service (SaaS) platforms these things started to change. SaaS platforms offer more functionality, making distributed computing more streamlined and affordable

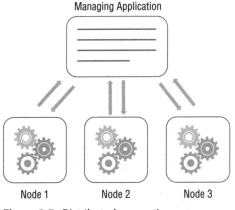

Managing Application

Node 1   Node 2   Node 3

Figure 2.7: Distributed computing

for companies of any size. As a result, all types of computing jobs now more or less use distributed computing. In fact, distributed computing has become so critical in the SW industry that many types of software, such as cryptocurrency systems, scientific simulations, blockchain technologies, and AI solutions, wouldn't be possible at all without using distributed computing. Previously, the cost associated with data storage, data preparation, and data analysis were quite high because organizations had to keep investing in larger and larger storage solutions to manage their growing data volumes. With distributed computing systems such as Apache Spark, this has changed and as a data engineer it´s important to be familiar with them.

Data engineering is very much a framework-driven discipline, and the data engineering tools that a data engineer needs to master include:

Apache Spark   Apache Spark is a must-have framework to be familiar with as a data engineer. Spark is an open source distributed general-purpose framework for cluster computing. It has an interface where you can program clusters with fault tolerance and data parallelism. Spark uses in-memory caching and optimized query implementation to process queries quickly against any data size. It's an essential tool for large-scale data processing. Apart from its capabilities of processing large amounts of data quickly, it is compatible with Apache Hadoop, making it quite a useful tool. Apache Spark lets you perform stream processing on a data flow, which has constant data input and output. Spark is more efficient than Hadoop, which is why it has become such a popular tool for data engineers.

Apache Hadoop Apache Hadoop is the legacy version of Apache Spark. Although it's not the preferred solution for the future, many enterprises are still using Hadoop for parts of their data architecture, so being familiar with it as a data engineer will be helpful. It's an open source framework that lets you store and manage data applications that run within cluster systems. Hadoop is a framework to manage these clusters. It has a wide collection of tools that make data implementations easier and more effective. Hadoop lets you perform distributed processing of large datasets by using simple programming implementations. You can use R, Python, Java, and Scala. This framework makes it affordable for companies to store and process large amounts of data as it performs the tasks through a distributed network.

Amazon Web Services Amazon Web Services (AWS) is a popular cloud platform that programmers use to become more agile, innovative, and scalable. Data engineering teams rely on AWS to design automated data flows, so you'll need to know how to design and deploy a cloud-based data infrastructure with this tool. Nearly every data engineering job description requires familiarity with AWS.

Microsoft Azure Microsoft Azure is a cloud-based technology that can help you with building large-scale analytics solutions. Like AWS, it's a must-have for any data engineer. Azure automates the support of applications and servers with a packaged analytics system. Primarily, Azure is popular for building, deploying, testing, and managing services and applications through data centers. It has various solutions available, such as as IaaS (infrastructure as a service), SaaS (software as a service), and PaaS (platform as a service). Azure helps you set up Windows-based server applications quickly and efficiently. Because Windows is widely popular, the demand for this tool is quite high.

Amazon S3 and HDFS Amazon S3 (Amazon Simple Storage Service) is a part of AWS that offers you a scalable storage infrastructure; HDFS is a distributed storage system for Apache Hadoop. Both of these tools let you store and scale easily. With the help of these two solutions, an organization can store virtually an unlimited quantity of data. Moreover, both solutions offer cloud-based storage so you can access the data from anywhere and work on it. These solutions are popular for offering storage to mobile applications, Internet of Things (IoT) applications, enterprise applications, websites, and many others.

SQL and NoSQL   SQL (Structured Query Language) and NoSQL are must-haves for any data engineer since moving a lot of data around is one of their main tasks. SQL is the primary programming language for managing and creating relational database systems. It's a domain-specific language designed for managing data held in a relational database management system (RDBMS), or for *stream processing* in a relational data stream management system (RDSMS). It is particularly useful in handling structured data—that is, data incorporating relations among entities and variables. Relational database systems are tables that contain rows and columns and are quite popular. NoSQL databases are nontabular and are of various kinds according to the data model. Common examples of NoSQL databases are documents and graphs. You should know how to work with database management systems (DBMSs) and for that, you need to be familiar with SQL and NoSQL. Some additional SQL skills include MongoDB, Cassandra, Big Query, and Hive. Some examples of NoSQL include Apache River, BaseX, Ignite, Hazelcast, and Coherence. By learning about SQL and NoSQL, you can work with all kinds of database systems.

Apache Kafka   Apache Kafka is an open source processing software platform for handling real-time data feeds. You can use it to build real-time streaming apps, which is something that businesses require. Kafka-powered apps can help discover and apply trends and react to customer needs almost in real time.

Then there are other data engineering tools of interest for various usage, such as the following:

- **Amazon Redshift** is a fully managed and easy-to-use cloud warehouse. The tool allows you to set up your data warehouse and scales easily.

- **Big Query** is also a fully managed cloud data warehouse and is commonly used in companies that are familiar with the Google Cloud Platform (GCP). Analysts and engineers can start using it when they are small and scale with the tool as their data grows. It also has built-in ML capabilities.

- **Tableau** is one of the oldest data visualization solutions, but it's still widely used. The main function is to gather and extract data that is stored in various places using a drag-and-drop interface to make use of data across different departments. The data engineer works with this data to create dashboards.

- **Looker** is a business intelligence (BI) software that helps employees visualize data. Unlike traditional BI tools, Looker has created a useful LookML layer. This layer is a language for describing dimensions, aggregates, calculations, and data relationships in a SQL database. By updating and maintaining this layer, data engineers can make it easier for nontechnical employees to use company data.

- **Apache Airflow** is an open source workflow management platform. It started at Airbnb in October 2014 as a solution to manage the company's increasingly complex workflows. Creating Airflow allowed Airbnb to programmatically author and schedule their workflows and monitor them via the built-in Airflow user interface.

- **Apache Hive** is a data warehouse software built on top of Apache Hadoop. Its purpose is to provide capabilities for data query and analysis. Hive gives a SQL-like interface to query data stored in various databases and filesystems that integrate with Hadoop. The three important functionalities for which Hive is deployed are data summarization, data analysis, and data query. The query language, exclusively supported by Hive, is HiveQL. This language translates SQL-like queries into MapReduce jobs for deploying them on Hadoop.

- **Snowflake** is built on a shared data architecture that delivers performance, scale, elasticity, and concurrency. In Snowflake, the data workloads scale independently from one another, making it a platform well suited for data warehousing, data lakes, data engineering, data science, and developing data applications.

- **Fivetran** is a comprehensive ETL tool that allows efficient collection of customer data from related applications, websites, and servers. The data collected is moved from its original state to the data warehouse and then transferred to other tools for analytics, marketing, and warehousing purposes.

- **great_expectations** is a Python-based, open source library for monitoring, validating, and understanding your data. It focuses on helping data engineers maintain data quality and improve communication between teams. Software teams have used automated testing software for some time to test and monitor their code, and great_expectations brings the same processes to data engineering teams.

- **Stitch** is a cloud-based, open source platform for rapidly moving data. Stitch has a simple and powerful ETL service that connects most data sources to SaaS applications like Salesforce and Zendesk, and it can replicate the data to any destination.

- **Prefect** is an open source tool used to ensure that data pipelines operate as expected. The company's dual products are Prefect Core, which is a data workflow engineer tool, and the Prefect Cloud, a workflow orchestration platform.

CHAPTER 3

Embracing MLOps

As the key factor behind succeeding with operating AI is embracing an operational mindset from start, the key to do that is to embrace the concept of *MLOps* (machine learning operations). In ML development the problem has never been to technically develop, train, or implement ML models; instead, the main problem is mostly related to poor communication and lack of efficient cross-functional team collaboration. It might sound like an easy task to correct, but the fact remains that most AI projects do not make it to production due to this communication gap between the data scientists and the business. And that's where MLOps can help.

MLOps refers to best practices of operationalizing ML models. This approach is all about bringing data scientists and engineers closer together through improved collaboration to achieve speed and robustness throughout the ML life cycle. A key success factor for MLOps practices is also the emphasis on continuous feedback from business stakeholders.

The main challenge that MLOps is trying to solve is building an integrated AI system for continuous operations in the production environment, without any major disconnects.

By adopting sustainable MLOps best practices, you will gain:

- **Improved visibility** providing end-to-end visibility of data extraction, model creation, deployment, and monitoring for faster processing

- **Faster auditing**, including improved ability to replicate production models by storing all related artifacts such as versioning data and metadata

- **Simplified model retraining** for various environments and requirements

- **Reliable ML system testing**, enabling faster, more secure, and accurate testing of the ML systems

MLOps as a Concept

MLOps is also sometimes referred to as *DevOps* (development operations) *for ML*, where the term DevOps comes from the software engineering world and is concerned with developing and operating large-scale software systems. There are similarities between the two, but also fundamental differences, which will be sorted out later in this chapter.

So, what does MLOps mean? According to Technopedia, MLOps seeks to improve communication and collaboration between the data scientists who develop machine learning models and the operations teams who oversee an ML model's use in production. MLOps is a multidisciplinary approach to managing machine learning algorithms as ongoing products, each with its own continuous life cycle. It's a discipline that aims to build, scale, and deploy algorithms to production consistently. It achieves this by reusing ML pipelines and automating as many repetitive tasks as possible, as well as improving the feedback loops used by data scientists, ML engineers, developers, and operations teams.

As shown in Figure 3.1, MLOps operates in the intersection of data engineering, ML development, and DevOps, bridging the gap between the different disciplines.

Although MLOps started as a set of best practices, it is now starting to transform into an independent approach to ML life cycle management. This is true since MLOps actually applies to the entire life cycle, from integrating with model generation, orchestration, and deployment, including its retraining, tuning, everyday use in a production environment, and model retirement. It also includes performance, diagnostics, governance, and business metrics.

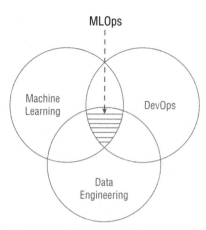

Figure 3.1: The scope of MLOps

An interesting aspect is that MLOps was originally developed with the knowledge that not all data scientists and ML engineers have experience with programming languages and IT operations. Therefore, MLOps is built on a concept based on continuous feedback loops that allow employees outside the data science domain to focus solely on what they know best, instead of having to stop and learn new skills. However, it's also an opportunity for all parties to learn from one another and continue to develop their skills; as noncomputer scientists learn more, the whole process becomes easier.

MLOps has obvious benefits for data science and data engineering teams. Since members of both teams sometimes work in silos, using a shared infrastructure boosts transparency. But MLOps can benefit other colleagues, too. This discipline offers the operations side more autonomy over regulation, and as an increasing number of businesses start using machine learning, they'll come under more scrutiny from the government, media, and the public. This is especially true of machine learning in highly regulated industries like healthcare, finance, and autonomous vehicles.

Here are some of the main benefits of MLOps:

- Rapid innovation through robust machine learning life cycle management
- A reproducible workflow and models
- Simplified deployment of high-precision models in any location
- Effective management of the entire machine learning life cycle
- Machine learning resource management system and control

When it comes to difficulties with MLOps, the real challenge isn't building an ML model; the challenge is building an integrated ML system and to continuously operate it in production. An ML system is a type of software system, so similar practices apply to help guarantee that you can reliably build and operate ML systems at scale.

ML models can have reduced performance not only due to suboptimal coding but also due to constantly evolving data profiles. In other words, models can decay in more ways than conventional software systems, and you need to consider this degradation as part of your life cycle management setup and track summary statistics of your data and monitor the online performance of your model to send notifications or roll back when values deviate from your expectations.

Other challenges to implementing MLOps are as follows:

- A high failure rate when it is not implemented properly, with the most common reason being poor staff communication and lack of compatibility between departments
- Difficulty to scale the MLOps setup
- Complex monitoring and management procedures
- Automation and diagnostics issues
- Low reproducibility of models and results

As shown Figure 3.2, a successful MLOps rollout requires five important components, also referred to as MLOps best practices.

Figure 3.2: The essential components of MLOps

- **Cross-functional teams in operations**—Interconnected teams are needed to bridge the gaps in knowledge and skill between data engineers, data scientists, and DevOps teams. The exact composition, organization, and titles of the team could vary, but the essential part is realizing that a data scientist alone cannot achieve the goals of MLOps. Even if an organization includes all the necessary skills, it won't be successful if they don't work closely together.

- **ML pipelines**—ML pipelines where data gets extracted, transformed, and loaded are essential for successful machine learning operations because data often needs to be transformed into different formats. Normally formatted in graphs that display each node to represent dependencies and executions, these pipelines are a vital part of data management. With ML, data transformation will always be required. Therefore, pipelines are an essential component.

- **Monitoring**—Within MLOps, managing and monitoring, both controllable and uncontrollable factors like latency, traffic, and errors, is a top priority. But since ML uses nonintuitive mathematical functions, it becomes a black box that requires continuous monitoring to ensure that outcomes remain within predefined limits. You may have to retrain models periodically, and determining how and when to do so requires critical collaboration between the teams involved.

- **Versioning**—In a traditional software world, you only need to version your code because it determines all the behavior of your system. In ML, things are a little different. In addition to versioning code, other elements, such as training data, metadata, and model versions, need to be tracked and altered. It is also important to understand the raw data and how it affects features, models, and so forth. In order to secure reproducibility, you need to store data long enough to be able to achieve that.

- **Validation**—Both models and data require validation for MLOps to be successful. Tests need to be performed both on the end product and on its separate elements during development.

Today, ML plays an essential role in developing reliable and trustworthy AI applications. As the proper use of ML helps AI applications grow and evolve semi-automatically, MLOps has become an essential part of automating the entire AI life cycle from start to finish, allowing companies to make the most of their investments and resources. Realistically, without the ability to automate the growth and the deployment process, the expected value of AI cannot be achieved. Despite that fact, only some 15 percent of businesses reported using MLOps and AI in their regular operations in 2020, according to Forbes (www.forbes.com/sites/forbestechcouncil/2021/09/17/will-ai-ever-be-able-to-offer-an-roi-for-enterprises/?sh=16087d202025).

From ML Models to ML Pipelines

Pipelines have been growing in popularity, and now they are everywhere you turn in data science, ranging from simple data pipelines to complex machine learning pipelines. An ML pipeline is used to help automate machine learning workflows, so that the ML model is trained and deployed in a continuous flow aimed at achieving the model objective. ML pipelines automate that flow, enable better model management, and facilitate refinement of the model over time, including model retraining in production. The main objective of having a proper pipeline for any ML model is to exercise control over it. A well-organized pipeline makes the implementation more flexible on one hand, but remember that automation can also lead to "overfitting" and thereby decrease flexibility. There is always a balance.

However, this automated approach to the ML pipeline is what makes it different from how ML development was previously approached. Not so long ago, the mainstream approach was a manual ML workflow, and to be honest, in many enterprises new to AI, this seems to still be the fact. Furthermore, once that manual approach is realized in the organization, the technical debt can make it costly to move to automated pipelines, which then becomes an additional hurdle.

So, what is the main difference between a manual versus an automated approach to ML? Well, a main aspect to understand is that in a *manual* ML workflow *the model is the main objective*, whereas in an *automated* ML workflow *the actual ML pipeline is the main objective*.

The manual ML workflow is also often ad hoc and turns out to be unstable when a team begins to speed up its iteration cycle since manual processes tend to be difficult to repeat and document. The main characteristics of a manual ML pipeline usually include the following:

- The ML model as the target
- A manual or script-driven process
- A disconnect between the data scientist and the engineer

- Slow iteration cycle
- No automated testing or performance monitoring
- No version control

The fact is, as your company's investment in AI scales up and becomes more important, your data science teams will move from a stage where they are occasionally updating a single model to having multiple frequently updating models in production. As you might guess, in that situation a pipeline approach becomes paramount.

The ability of an ML pipeline to split the problem solving into reproducible, predefined, and executable components forces the team to adhere to a joined process.

Characteristics of an automated ML pipeline include these:

- The ML pipeline as the target
- Fully automated process
- Cooperation between the data scientist and the engineer
- Fast iteration cycle
- Automated testing and performance monitoring
- Version-controlled

Figure 3.3 shows a conceptual view of the difference in approach for a sentiment analysis when using a manual ML workflow versus an automated ML pipeline. The steps used in the sentiment analysis are the same in both approaches and include (1) ingest data, (2) clean data, (3) preprocess data, and (4) model data. The difference lies in how the components of the workflow are executed. However, there's an additional problem with the manual approach. If we assume that engineers are inherently lazy, they will copy the steps that are the "same" and then start making minor changes, which could lead to an even bigger mess with regard to reproducibility and version control.

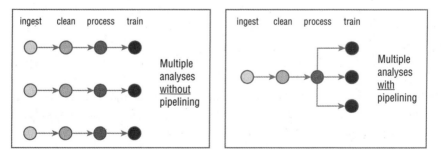

Figure 3.3: A manual vs. a pipelined approach

With the pipelined architecture as visualized in the box to the right in Figure 3.3, it's easy to swap out the algorithms with other algorithms, update the cleaning or preprocessing steps, or ingest additional data without breaking the other elements of your workflow. There is no copying and pasting changes into all iterations, and this simplified structure with fewer overall pieces will run smoother. However, in order to atone for multiple models, the pipeline may need to include more steps than in the separate flows.

Transitioning from a manual cycle to an automated pipeline may have many iterations in between, depending on the scale of the company's ML efforts and the team composition. Ultimately, the purpose of an ML pipeline is to allow you to increase the iteration cycle with the added confidence that codifying the process gives and to scale how many models you can realistically maintain in production. Eventually you may need to split the pipeline to be able to maintain control as the number of models increases.

The ML Pipeline

Machine learning pipelines consist of several steps to train a model. In this context, the term *ML model* refers to the model that is created by the training process. Machine learning pipelines are iterative as every step is repeated to continuously improve the accuracy of the model and to achieve a successful algorithm.

The learning algorithm finds patterns in the training data that map the input data attributes to the target (the answer to be predicted), and it outputs an ML model that captures these patterns.

A pipeline consists of a sequence of components, which are a compilation of computations. Data is sent through these components and is manipulated with the help of computation. As shown in Figure 3.4, ML pipelines are not one-way flows. They are cyclic in nature, and each step in the pipeline assumes iteration to improve the scores of the ML algorithms and make the model scalable. At any step in the pipeline, you might also want to iterate to the previous step—for example, for further data processing if there are data quality issues or if other refinements are needed in previous steps in order to move forward in the pipeline.

As there is no fully standardized way in the industry to define and specify the exact steps in an ML pipeline, Figure 3.4 should be seen as a reference example rather than the absolute truth. As shown in the figure,

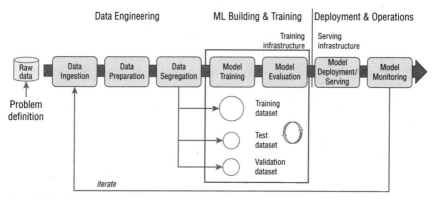

Figure 3.4: An ML pipeline

an ML pipeline has many steps, but it all starts with a problem definition and access to data. The different steps are as follows:

Problem Definition   The first step in any project is defining your problem. You can use the most powerful and shiniest algorithms available, but the results will be meaningless if you are solving the wrong problem. So, start by properly describing what the problem is and why the problem needs to be solved, and offer some ideas on how you would solve the problem. This definition in turn identifies what *raw data* you need in your ML pipeline.

Data Ingestion   Directing incoming raw data into a data store is the first step of any ML workflow once the data scope has been set by the problem definition. The key point is that data is persisted without undertaking any transformation at all, to allow us to have an indisputable record of the original dataset. Data can be fed from various data sources, either obtained by request or streamed from other services. However, it's worth mentioning that depending on whether the data being collected is privacy-related data, you may have to anonymize the dataset at the point of collection. (For more details on this topic, see Chapter 6, "AI Is All About Trust.")

In the *offline data ingestion layer*, data flows into a data storage solution for raw data via an ingestion service, which encapsulates the data sourcing and persistence. When the data is saved in the data storage solution of choice, a unique batch ID is assigned to the dataset to allow for efficient querying and end-to-end data lineage and traceability in the next step. The offline ingestion service runs regularly on a time schedule (once or multiple times per day) or on a predefined trigger related to the specific dataset.

In the *online data ingestion layer*, the entry point is the streaming architecture as it decouples and manages the flow of information from data sources to the processing and storage components by providing reliable, high throughput and low latency capabilities. In other words, it functions as an enterprise-scale *data bus*. Data is saved in long-term data storage for raw data but is also a pass-through layer to the next online streaming service for further real-time processing. Examples of online technologies used are Apache Kafka (pub/sub messaging system) and Apache Flume (data collection to long-term database), but you will come across others, depending on your enterprise's tech stack. The newest one is Apache Pulsar, which is a cloud-native, distributed messaging and streaming platform originally created at Yahoo!.

Data Preparation   This step generally starts with activities such as *data exploration* and *data transformation*. So, once the data is ingested, a distributed pipeline is generated that assesses the condition of the data—looking for format differences; outliers; trends; incorrect, missing, or skewed data; and rectifying any anomalies along the way.

Feature Engineering   This step includes the important *feature engineering process* and the preprocessing steps that transform raw data into features that can be used in machine learning algorithms, such as predictive models. Predictive models consist of an outcome variable and predictor variables, and it is during the feature engineering process that the most useful predictor variables are created and selected for the predictive model. Automated feature engineering has been available in some machine learning software since 2016.

Data Segregation   As shown in Figure 3.4, data segregation splits subsets of data to train the model and further validate how it performs against new data. Remember that the fundamental goal of the ML system is to apply an accurate model on new data that has not yet been trained and, based on the quality of the pattern prediction of the model, be able to get the same result. Therefore, existing labeled data is used as a proxy for future/unseen data by splitting it into training and evaluation subsets before model training happens.

Model Training   The approach is to use the training subset of data to let the ML algorithm recognize the patterns in it. The model training pipeline is offline only, and its schedule varies depending on the criticality of the application at hand, from every couple of hours to once a day. Apart from predefined scheduled training, model training can also be time and event triggered. Model training must be implemented with *error tolerance* in mind. Also, data checkpoints and failover on training partitions should be enabled, meaning that each partition can be retrained if the previous attempt fails due to some transient issue, such as timeout.

Model Evaluation   The purpose of this step is to assess the performance of the model using the *test subset* of data to understand the accuracy of the prediction. Like the model training step, model evaluation is also performed offline. The predictive performance of a model is evaluated by comparing predictions on the evaluation dataset with true values using a variety of metrics. The model that performs best (with the most accurate predictions) on the evaluation subset is selected to make predictions on future and new instances. A library of several evaluators is designed to provide a model's accuracy metrics using, for example, a receiver operating characteristics (ROC) curve, which is a graph showing the performance of a classification model at many classification thresholds, or a precision-recall (PR) curve. Much like the ROC curve, the PR curve is used for evaluating the performance of binary classification algorithms. Like ROC curves, precision-recall curves provide a graphical representation of a classifier's performance across many thresholds, rather than a single value like accuracy.

Drift in data and model concept are also important aspects to evaluate. So, what does *data drift* mean? A helpful way to think about this is to consider feature segments. A segment here refers to a specific categorical value or a continuous value range in our input features. Example segments include an age group, a geographical origin, or customers from particular marketing channels. Let's say your model works well on the entire dataset but does not produce good results on a specific segment (e.g., because of too little exposure). Low segment-level performance is not a problem if the segment's proportion is small and you aim only for aggregate results. However, your overall performance drops when the model receives new data with a high proportion of the poorly predicted segment. The input distribution shift makes the model less capable of predicting labels.

Model concept drift, on the other hand, refers to the situation when the functional relationship between the model inputs and outputs changes. The model context has changed, but the model doesn't know about the change and the patterns that the model has learned are not relevant anymore. It's vital to establish good practices for monitoring and handling data and model concept drift in production. (For more details and practical examples on data drift and model concept drift, see Chapters 4 and 5.)

Model Deployment/Serving   Once the chosen model is produced, it is typically deployed and embedded in decision-making frameworks. Remember that model deployment is not the end; it is just the beginning! This step of "operationalizing an ML model" or "putting an ML model into production" is also referred to as *ML inference*. An ML life cycle can be broken up into two main, distinct parts. The first is the *training phase*, in which an ML model is created or "trained" by running a specified subset of data into the model. ML inference is the second phase, in which the model is put into action on live data to produce actionable output. So, once the best model is selected, it's deployed for offline (asynchronous) and online (synchronous) predictions. More than one model can be deployed at any time to enable safe transition between old and new models—for example, when deploying a new model, the services need to keep serving prediction requests. This is also called *canary deployment*, meaning that you start with a subset of the whole population on a new model and then transfer the rest to that model. Traditionally, a challenge in model deployment has been that the programming languages needed to operationalize models have been different from those that have been used to develop them. Porting a Python or R model into a production language like C++, C#, or Java is challenging and often results in reduced performance, such as reduced speed and less accuracy, of the original model.

Model serving is an activity within model deployment focused on applying an ML model to a new dataset in order to uncover practical insights that will help solve a business problem. The insights could include a list of recommended items, numeric values for time series models and regression models, a probability value indicating the likelihood that a new input belongs to some existing category, the name of a category or cluster to which a new item is most similar, and a predicted class or outcome for classification models. (For more details on model deployment/serving, see Chapter 4, "Deployment with AI Operations in Mind.")

Model Monitoring   The model is continuously monitored to observe how it behaves in the real world and is continuously calibrated accordingly. Any ML solution requires a well-defined performance monitoring solution. An example of information that we might want to see for model serving applications includes a model identifier, deployment date/time, number of times the model has been served, average/minimum/maximum model serving times, distribution of features used and predicted versus actual/observed results, and so on. This metadata is calculated during the model scoring and then used for monitoring. This is another offline pipeline.

The performance monitoring gets notified when a new prediction is served, executes the performance evaluation, and persists the results and the relevant notifications are raised. The evaluation itself takes place by comparing the scores to the observed outcomes generated by the training dataset. The basic implementation for monitoring can follow different approaches. with the most popular being logging analytics like Kibana, Grafana, Splunk, and so on. Model monitoring is a continuous process, where a shift in prediction might result in a need to restructure the model design. Normally there is also a fallback baseline model for worst-case scenarios. Remember that to continuously provide accurate predictions and recommendations to drive the business forward is what defines the benefits of an ML pipeline! (See Chapter 5, "Operating AI Is Different from Operating Software," for more details on model monitoring.)

The main objectives that a production-ready ML pipeline should try to address are:

- Reduced latency
- Pipeline components are integrated but loosely coupled with the other parts of the ML end-to-end workflow
- Scalability both horizontally and vertically
- Efficient computation with regard to workload management
- Fault-tolerance and self-healing (i.e., breakdown management)
- Supporting batch and real-time processing

Another consideration when building your ML pipeline is that every step should be seen as a reusable component. It's important to consider all the steps that go into producing your ML model. It's good to start with how the data is collected and preprocessed and work your way from there. It's generally encouraged to limit each component's scope to make it easier to understand and iterate.

Furthermore, you need to codify tests into the components. Remember that testing should be considered an inherent part of the pipeline. If in a manual process you do some sanity checks on how the input data and the model predictions should look, you should codify this into a pipeline. A pipeline gives you opportunities to be much more thorough with testing since you will not have to perform tests manually each time.

It's also vital to set up ML orchestration. There are many ways to handle the orchestration of a ML pipeline, but the principles remain the same. You define the order in which the components are executed and how inputs and outputs run through the pipeline.

Finally, you should automate the pipeline steps as much as possible. However, while building a pipeline already introduces automation since it handles the running of subsequent steps without human intervention, the ultimate goal is to automatically run the ML pipeline when specific criteria are met. For example, through automated model monitoring, you may want model drift in production to trigger a model retraining run or to schedule automated retraining sessions to happen on a daily basis.

Adopt a Continuous Learning Approach

In software engineering, CI/CD (or CICD) is the combined practices of *continuous integration* (CI) and either *continuous delivery* or *continuous deployment (CD)*. In the context of this book, I will use the definition *continuous deployment* (CD) since it's closer to what CD refers to in the context of AI/ML practices.

CI/CD bridges the gap between development and operation activities and teams by enforcing automation in building, testing, and deploying applications. The process contrasts with previous traditional software engineering methods where all updates were integrated into one large batch before rolling out the newer version. Modern DevOps practices involve continuous development, continuous testing, continuous integration, continuous deployment, and continuous monitoring of software applications throughout the development life cycle. The CI/CD practice, or CI/CD pipeline, forms the backbone of modern DevOps operations.

An ML system is a software system, so similar practices apply to help guarantee that you can reliably build and operate ML systems at scale. However, ML systems differ from other software systems in a couple of ways:

Other skillsets in the teams are needed.   In an ML project, the team usually includes data scientists or ML researchers, who focus on exploratory data analysis, model development, and experimentation. These members might not be experienced software engineers who can build production-class services.

An experimental approach to model development is required. ML is experimental in nature and requires you to try different features, algorithms, modeling techniques, and parameter configurations to find what works best for the problem as quickly as possible. The challenge is tracking what worked and what didn't, and maintaining reproducibility while maximizing code reusability. This is very much dependent on the data scientists being skilled enough to understand *which* changes had an impact and *how* the changes affected the results.

More aspects must be covered during testing. Testing an ML system is more complete than testing other software systems. In addition to typical unit and integration tests, you need data validation, trained model quality evaluation, and model validation.

Deployment requires more automation to be added. In ML systems, deployment isn't as simple as deploying an offline-trained ML model as a prediction service. ML systems require you to deploy a multistep pipeline to automatically retrain and deploy a model for efficient model management in production.

Model performance must be carefully monitored in production. ML models can have reduced performance not only due to less optimal coding but also due to constantly changing datasets. In other words, models can deteriorate in more ways than traditional software systems, and you need to consider this proactively. Therefore, to manage this successfully you need to track summary statistics of your data and monitor the online performance of your model by sending notifications or roll back when performance metrics deviate from your expectations. An efficient rollback requires that you have a baseline model in place, which could be less capable but that guarantees a certain performance.

ML and other software systems are similar in continuous integration of source control, unit testing, integration testing, and continuous delivery of the software module or the package. However, in ML, there are a few important differences:

- ■ CI is no longer only about testing and validating code and components but also about testing and validating data, data schemas, and training models.

- CD is no longer about a single software package or a service but a system (an ML pipeline) that should automatically deploy another service (model prediction service). The loosely coupled components also allow for more gradual changes in a properly designed cloud native pipeline.

- Continuous training (CT) is a new component that is added, unique to ML systems, that's concerned with automatically retraining and serving the models in production.

The Maturity of Your AI/ML Capability

When it comes to assessing maturity in a company's AI/ML capabilities, it's worth noting that although AI technology is already in fact transforming our society in terms of how we live and work and how we do business, some companies have still not realized that AI will matter in their line of business too. For quite a lot of companies, it's still not on the company agenda, although they might already be losing competitiveness because of this lack of understanding.

First of all, a prerequisite for companies to start applying AI is that they have gone through a digital transformation. Why? Well, without digitizing the data assets, there can be no automation or AI. AI requires machine-readable data. Whether it's for using AI internally or for commercial purposes, data must be digitized. It's as simple as that.

However, even for companies that have started to apply AI in practice or even matured into a situation where MLOps is starting to be seen as a key to streamlining AI development as well as scaling up and improving delivery efficiency, it's still not just a check in the box. The fact is that there are many "AI maturity models" floating around in the industry, and unfortunately standardization is missing with reference to this. Therefore, in this book you will not find a precise model for AI maturity assessment, but rather just three different categories of AI/ML capabilities to reference against. Each category comes with its limitation and/or benefits so that it becomes clear why enhancing your company's AI/ML capabilities actually matters.

Furthermore, the ML pipeline architecture design for your company will also depend very much on the enterprise ambition and strategic approach in AI/ML. For example, a global company with a broad product and service portfolio across several business segments will most probably set up and implement several ML pipelines independently of each other.

A large company will most probably also clearly separate between its internal ML pipeline and any commercial ML pipeline in a live production environment. For a small to medium-sized company, this might be approached differently.

On a high level, you could say that most companies' maturity in AI/ML is based on their capabilities, which can be grouped into one of three main categories, as shown in Table 3.1.

Table 3.1: Levels of maturity in AI/ML capabilities

MATURITY LEVEL	LEVEL FOCUS	LEVEL CAPABILITIES
Level 0	Model focus and no MLOps	■ The models are the development target. ■ Monolithic code. ■ Limited reusability. ■ Experimentation over production. ■ No monitoring in production.
Level 1	Pipelines rather than models	■ The ML pipeline is the development target. ■ Reusable components through ML pipelines. ■ Code, artifact, and experiment tracking. ■ Retraining models is easy. ■ Balance between development and production. ■ Models are monitored in production.
Level 2	Leveraging continuous learning	■ The pipeline components are the development target. ■ Continuous integration where every change in components is merged automatically. ■ Continuous deployment where every change that passes the tests is deployed in production. ■ Continuous training where every time the pipeline changes or new data arrives, the pipeline is automatically triggered and a new model is released. ■ High levels of automation is in place, including support for AutoML.

As you can see from Table 3.1, the levels range from a manual and ad hoc approach to a fully integrated, automated, and continuous ML pipeline.

Level 0—Model Focus and No MLOps

The first level is level 0, which is characterized by an ad hoc approach to AI/ML activities and that there is no MLOps capability present at all. At this capability level, AI might still be seen as something to "try out first" rather than being approached as an important investment that requires management's full attention, or even as a necessity for company survival. At this maturity level, activities are usually spread out over different parts of the company, where investments in infrastructure and competence are not synchronized or based on an agreed strategy. AI-related activities are more of a happening than something strategically intentional.

Practically, a result of this is that data scientists usually produce monolithic code where, for example, one or more Jupyter notebooks or scripts do all the necessary steps to produce a trained model. Since the code is inside the notebooks or scripts, it is easy to iterate, but there is very limited reusability with this approach.

It's also common that the produced outcome is a model rather than an inference pipeline for deployments in production, since the focus is on the experimentation and on the test metrics, rather than on the model in production. In fact, in many cases, there is no intention to use the model in production at all at this capability level.

If you use this approach in a company, you will have to hand over the model to a production team that will have to engineer a solution to deploy your model, possibly reimplementing parts of your preprocessing and data cleaning system. Retraining is usually manual and difficult. In a production environment, this process is relevant for very small teams and for companies at their early stages. In fact, if the AI solutions are deployed in production at all, it's very cumbersome and difficult, and there is very little reusability from one project to the next. Also, typically at this stage there is no awareness about the fact that a model deployed must be monitored. Eventually this will become yet another monolith and might lose all the flexibility, which was the whole point of the experimental setup. If it's handed over to a traditional computer scientist, they will most likely turn it into a programmatic model, which removes the retraining possibility. On the positive side, however, the process is very easy to set up and the infrastructure needed is minimal. Remember that all organizations start at this point before a more mature setup can be achieved. The important thing is to not get stuck with this approach.

Level 1—Pipelines Rather than Models

If your company has moved past the proof-of-concept approach to AI/ML, a more mature process is in place. This is referred to in Table 3.1 as Level 1, which is the first level where MLOps practices are introduced. Another major difference on this level is the development target. Whereas the development target on Level 0 is a trained model, the target is now instead an entire training pipeline. This makes retraining easy, and the process can be automated. This process is relevant for small and medium teams, and typically for small and medium-sized companies. This is a relatively easy and production-ready process, with some infrastructure needs that are manageable in a small or medium-sized company. The entire process can reasonably be managed by data scientists with some help from software engineering and DevOps.

This pipeline is made of reusable components and can regenerate the model at any time, using the original dataset or a new dataset. All the code, the experiments and their parameters, and the produced artifacts are tracked and versioned. This makes it easy to reproduce and also to train with new data. Since the product of a training pipeline is an inference pipeline, there is symmetry between development and production, meaning that the preprocessing code that was used during training is the same that will be used in production. At this stage, monitoring of the model in production is also introduced.

The Level 1 process produces some important results:

- The process of training a model is standardized, which makes it easier to collaborate with a team of people.
- It's easier to reuse large parts or even entire pipelines for rapid prototyping of new products.
- Time to market for new products or new solutions is reduced drastically.
- Having an ML pipeline that can be retriggered at any time minimizes the risk of lower model performance due to the data drift typical of ML models in production. For example, when models can be retrained every day, every week, or every month it's much easier to catch up with the model drift that you know will eventually happen.

Level 2—Leveraging Continuous Learning

The next step in your AI/ML capability, Level 2, includes adding even more automation capabilities to your MLOps setup, with continuous learning in focus. At this maturity level, the company is fully aware of the transformational potential of AI and is fully investing in it; AI may even be seen as necessary for the company's survival. Capabilities at this level enable parts of or the entire company business model to be relying on AI capabilities—either for internal operations only or a combination of internal AI capabilities and for commercial and externally facing solutions.

In the data science environment, the starting point is existing pipelines in production, and the focus is shifted toward improving the single components of the pipelines. At this level the entire system of testing and deployment is automated so that a change in any part of a component will trigger tests, and if the tests pass, the change will make it all the way to production automatically, without manual releases.

This means that this change will be included the next time a given pipeline will be triggered, which can be on a schedule such as daily or weekly, or any time new data arrives.

At Level 2 there are typically large teams with complex operations, which also require significant infrastructure support. However, the rewards for these investments come in terms of significantly improved development speed and time-to-market. There is also the possibility of iterating very quickly on production pipelines, drastically reducing the time for a new solution to be deployed. *Continuous integration* (CI) is enabled since every change in components is merged automatically, and *continuous deployment* (CD) is applied since every change that passes the tests is deployed in production. Furthermore, *continuous training* (CT) is in use since every time the pipeline changes or new data arrives, the pipeline is automatically triggered and a new model is released. (For more details on CI/CD/CT, see the section "Adopt a Continuous Learning Approach" earlier in this chapter.)

It also helps to facilitate tasks like A/B testing. A/B testing refers to when a certain change is deployed to only a part of the customers. The customers who receive the change are sample B, and those who don't are sample A. Then, the difference between the two groups is studied statistically to understand the impact of the change.

Other interesting results that are achieved once you reach Level 2 in AI/ML include:

- It's easier for large teams to work concurrently on the same pipelines.
- The level of automation is much higher. This includes automated machine learning, also referred to as automated ML or AutoML, which is the process of automating the time-consuming, iterative tasks of machine learning model development. It allows data scientists, analysts, and developers to build ML models with high scale, efficiency, and productivity all while sustaining model quality. Although traditional machine learning model development is resource-intensive—requiring significant domain knowledge and time to produce and compare dozens of models—with automated machine learning, you'll accelerate the time it takes to get production-ready ML models with great ease and efficiency.
- The iteration speed is very fast, and the time-to-market is very short.
- Achieving full Level 2 maturity is difficult. Be aware that it requires a high level of automatic testing of code, data, and models. It also requires a tight coupling with the inference system, as well as computing and DevOps resources to orchestrate it. Consequently, it requires a collaboration between data scientists, software engineers, and DevOps dedicated to this process. It also requires investing in a fully capable infrastructure, including cloud readiness or a significant investment in an appropriate and ready-to-use, end-to-end ML platform.

The Model Training Environment

Although machine learning projects may at first seem a lot like software development projects, the structure of an ML project more closely resembles scientific investigation. Successful projects consist of a series of experiments that may be prosperous, result in a dead end, or inspire completely different courses of investigation, which may lead to useful insights.

As you probably know, a software development project starts with the question "How can we build X?" and finishes when it's built. You might also know that during development, the team typically has to refine the definition of X, because it was vague and incomplete. In successful projects, however, the requirements, design, and development ultimately turn into something that hopefully resembles what was asked for.

ML model development, on the other hand, as well as data science in general, is more likely to start with the question "What can we build to solve this problem?" and stop when one of three outcomes has been reached:

- Results have been found that are good enough to release or use.
- Constraints like legal issues, time, and/or compute power limit further progress.
- Efforts are redirected or abandoned altogether.

And since an ML model won't run without data, even concrete objectives must be forsaken if the data won't support them.

So, with these fundamentally different approaches, how does that impact the model training environment you need to establish in order to succeed with your objectives in AI? This section explores some aspects regarding your training environment, such as enabling ML experimentation, using a simulator for model training, and environmental considerations related to model training.

Enabling ML Experimentation

An experiment usually involves systematically varying one or more independent variables and examining their effect on some dependent variables and to find dependencies. In AI/ML, however, an experiment requires more than a single learning run; it requires a number of runs carried out under different conditions through an iterative cycle. Each step of the entire ML cycle is visited again and again. The question is, what makes the ML cycle iterative?

AI is an evolving field of technology and the answer lies in the nature of the problems that AI/ML is trying to solve. As new algorithms are being developed, there are new opportunities found in the real world to solve, or vice versa, and AI as a solution is primarily used in the areas where traditional programming ceases to have a viable solution. Examples of this could be:

- Too complex problems to code, such as face recognition, extractions, and understanding text from a variety of documents in different languages

- Analysis of enormous amounts of data—for example, stock market predictions

- Real-time recommender systems like movie recommendations on Netflix, Amazon, and so forth, which are highly dependent on your last transaction or the current transaction you are executing

Remember that even when an infant tries to learn to walk, it has to go through the same process of walking, falling, standing, walking, balancing, and so on, again and again until it achieves a certain degree of confidence to walk independently. The same fundamental concept applies to AI as it goes through the model training iterations until the desired confidence level is achieved.

According to the nature of AI/ML, it's applicable to all those applications/systems that are trying to learn and that don't require you to code exactly how to solve the problem. However, it is not right to assume that there is no coding required at all. The machine learning field allows you to code in a way so that the application or system can learn to solve the problem on its own.

So, it is evident that AI/ML requires a highly iterative process, much closer to scientific experimentation with a lot of trial and error rather than a strict software process with a clear implementation. So, how do you enable an efficient approach to ML experimentation?

Let's start by reflecting on how the ML development process works in reality. There are several steps in the ML pipeline where you might encounter problems and issues that will require changes upstream. For example, during the preprocessing step you might encounter issues in the data that will need solving by modifying the data itself. Or, during the data checks, you might realize that your dataset is not large enough or is more unbalanced than you thought. You could also find bugs in the preprocessing step, for example. Indeed, you probably want to optimize the hyperparameters of your model, or iterate over architectures and algorithms, to find the best-performing one. During validation you might realize that you actually need more or different data, and you have to go back to square one and collect more data. You should also be aware that this actually invalidates any experiments done so far.

This iterative process might easily lead to chaos, which makes it more difficult to learn lessons and to clearly articulate why a certain decision was taken. Therefore, more control is needed. A good starting point for that is, from the beginning, assume that there's going to be a lot of iterations and plan accordingly. Consequently, you need to allocate enough time for the iterative approach in the process but of course without missing the project deadlines.

As part of improving the control, it's very important to be systematic; for example, you should normally only change one thing at a time. By doing so, you can with certainty know what, for example, the model performance change was caused by.

It's also vital to realize that every experiment contributes to improved understanding in how to approach the problem at hand. With that mindset, you realize that every experiment matters and it should not be lost. On the other hand, when experimenting, you also need to know when to stop. For that, it's crucial to have a clearly formulated objective and stop once you reach it. Typically experimentation has diminishing returns, so knowing when to stop also prevents you from wasting a lot of time for limited gains. Finally, sometimes it is hard to think about going back to collect more data at a point where investments are already made and models are already trained. However, remember that many times it's much more efficient to just go back and collect the data you need rather than trying to invest in some complicated, bleeding-edge solution that takes a long time to implement and that might not work at all.

So, how do you achieve this required order? Consider the following advice:

- Start off by versioning your data so that you can reproduce a given experiment using the data that was originally used.

- For the same reason, you absolutely need to version all the code that you use.

- Start tracking every experiment from the very beginning of the project. This is fundamental to gain insights on what works and what doesn't, and it allows you to back out from dead ends. For example, let's say you've invested a few hours in a different algorithm or architecture that required significant changes in the code. However, the results turn out to be worse than the previous iteration. With experiment tracking, you can easily go back to the best result so far, restore the code at that stage, and try something different instead.

Using a Simulator for Model Training

While AI is impacting the world in different ways, the capability of ML algorithms very much depends on access to data. This is specifically true in *reinforcement learning* (RL), where the model learns from feedback from the environment. And it takes a lot of time and data to train a model, deploy it in production, and use it to generate reliable predictions in the real world.

So, in many instances, researchers who are working to train advanced AI/ML models are restricted by both the quality and the amount of data. The real live data your algorithms need to train on is often not available from the start, and even if it is, it may not contain all the features you want to train your algorithm on.

So, on the off chance that you need to show a vehicle how to drive itself, you will require a great many miles of human driving data. And to be honest, you really don't want a car to learn how to drive by crashing. On the other hand, with the help of simulation, just as humans do in their brains, researchers can create a great many training datasets and come up with innovative models.

Researchers have created models on autonomous vehicle fleet control in which vehicles self-learn where they position themselves in a simulated environment. In such a model, each car is an agent and learns in an optimal way where different cars are moving in different positions. Amazon's Aurora self-driving vehicle unit runs many simulations in parallel to train its models to explore urban conditions. The organization is preparing Alexa's conversational resources, drones, and robotic systems for logistics purposes across its fulfillment facilities.

An algorithm in order to develop an intelligent policy needs to experience a multitude of experience, running in millions of parameters. In a situation where there is a lack of data, simulation is what allows it to do that. Over the past few years, superhuman accuracy is starting to be the result of using machine learning algorithms in a wide variety of complex problems. It's up to the point where the entire AI training process is done as a simulation, without needing to go through the tedious process of data collection that is both difficult and expensive.

Apart from using simulation to train models for autonomous driving, the research in this area has also been focused on the gaming industry, where algorithms are finding newer and more clever ways to win over humans in, for example, DeepMind's AlphaGo. But researchers have proposed use cases for using simulated models for solving business problems as well. For example, for textiles that are heavily automation-based, researchers created a model to enhance the efficiency of the processes. Production processes were simulated to make regression from the time-series data with machine learning. The errors that occur in the production process were created using random parameters in the simulation, and the variables showing the number of faulty products could be forecast successfully.

The idea of using a simulated training environment is the idea that you can potentially learn how to optimally generate scenes so that a deep learning network can either learn a very good representation or that the model can perform well in a downstream task. Learning to simulate can be seen as a meta-learning algorithm that adjusts parameters of a simulator to generate synthetic data so that a machine learning model trained on this data achieves high accuracy on validation and test sets, respectively.

One pitfall here is that the complexity of the simulation is often under-estimated, and in some cases, you may end up with a model that is the inverse of your simulator and will perform poorly in the real world.

Environmental Impact of Training AI Models

The AI industry is sometimes compared to the oil industry, or rather it's the value of data that is referred to, meaning that once the data is mined and refined, like oil, it can be a highly valuable asset. Now it seems the metaphor may extend even further. Like its fossil-fuel counterpart, the process of training deep learning models has turned out to have an unexpectedly high environmental impact.

In the paper "Energy and Policy Considerations for Deep Learning in NLP" (*MIT Technology Review*, June 2019, `https://arxiv.org/pdf/1906.02243.pdf`), the authors performed a life cycle assessment for training several common large AI models. They found that the process itself can emit more than 626,000 pounds of carbon dioxide, equivalent to nearly five times the lifetime emissions of the average American car, including the car manufacturing process.

The paper specifically examines the model training process for *natural language processing* (NLP), the subfield of AI that focuses on teaching machines to handle human language. The recent advances in this area have required training ever larger models on datasets scraped from the Internet. The approach is both computationally expensive and highly energy intensive.

The researchers found that the computational and environmental costs of training grew proportionally to model size and then exploded when additional tuning steps were used to increase the model's final accuracy. In particular, they found that a tuning process known as *neural architecture search* (which tries to optimize a model by incrementally tweaking a neural network's design through exhaustive trial and error) had extraordinarily high associated costs for little performance benefit. Without it, the most costly model, BERT, had a carbon footprint of roughly

1,400 pounds of carbon dioxide equivalent, close to a round-trip trans-America flight for one person.

What's more, the researchers note that the figures should only be considered as baselines, since training a single model is the minimum amount of work you can do. In practice, it's much more likely that AI researchers would develop a new model from scratch or adapt an existing model to a new dataset, either of which can require many more rounds of training and tuning.

To get a better handle on what the full development pipeline might look like in terms of carbon footprint, the researchers at the University of Massachusetts applied their findings to a case study and found that the process of building and testing a final paper-worthy model required training 4,789 models over a six-month period. Converted to CO_2 equivalent, it emitted more than 78,000 pounds and is likely representative of typical work in the field of AI.

In my view, that also raises serious concerns regarding how ROI from AI is calculated. Considering and limiting the environmental impact from AI development may actually bring some sense into what AI development will be allowed to cost. In many cases, this is probably not even addressed, resulting in companies spending x dollars, to save two times x dollars.

So, what can be done about this? Well, one conclusion was that since human brains can do amazing things with little power consumption, AI research should spend time figuring out how machines can be built in that way too.

Considering the AI/ML Functional Technology Stack

The focus so far has been on explaining concepts and approaches to embracing an operational mindset to ML development. In this section you will learn more about the AI technology stack and its components from an operational perspective.

AI technology is built on top of a stack of underlying technologies, and in order for your ML pipeline to deliver an optimized AI/ML model serving in production, you need to understand what makes up a fit-for-purpose functional tech stack (see Figure 3.5).

According to the defined layers in Figure 3.5, the layer at the bottom includes the *silicon chips*. As you can see in the following list, these different hardware chips are designed for specific functionalities in the AI/ML perspective:

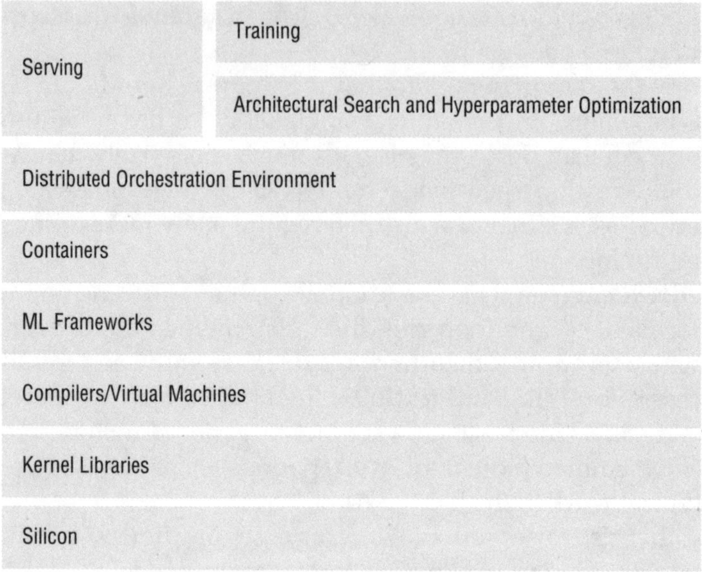

| Serving | Training |
| | Architectural Search and Hyperparameter Optimization |

| Distributed Orchestration Environment |

| Containers |

| ML Frameworks |

| Compilers/Virtual Machines |

| Kernel Libraries |

| Silicon |

Figure 3.5: An AI/ML functional technology stack

- **Central processing units (CPUs)** are the electronic circuitry that executes instructions in a computer program. The CPU performs basic arithmetic, logic, controlling, and input/output (I/O) operations specified by the instructions in the program. This contrasts with external components, such as main memory and I/O circuitry, and specialized processors, such as graphics processing units (GPUs). In general, you could say that CPUs are more versatile and better for sequential instructions.

- **Graphics processing units (GPUs)** are specialized electronic circuits designed to rapidly manipulate and alter memory to accelerate the creation of images in a frame buffer intended for output to a display device. GPUs are used in embedded systems, smartphones, personal computers, workstations, and game consoles. Modern GPUs are very efficient at manipulating computer graphics and image processing. Their highly parallel structure makes them more efficient than general-purpose CPUs for algorithms that process large blocks of data in parallel.

- **Tensor processing unit (TPU)** is an "AI accelerator" application-specific integrated circuit (ASIC) developed by Google specifically for neural network machine learning, particularly using Google's own TensorFlow software. Google began using TPUs internally in 2015 and in 2018 made them available for third-party use, both as part of its cloud infrastructure and by offering a smaller version of the chip for sale.

- **Field-programmable gate arrays (FPGAs)** are semiconductor devices that are based around a matrix of configurable logic blocks (CLBs). FPGAs can be reprogrammed to desired application or functionality requirements after manufacturing.

- **Application-specific integrated circuit (ASIC)** is an integrated circuit (IC) chip customized for a particular use rather than intended for general-purpose use. For example, a chip designed to run in a digital voice recorder or a high-efficiency bitcoin miner is an ASIC.

On top of the hardware chip layer, the *kernel libraries* help handle the basic computation optimizations based on the hardware specifications of the chips. These kernel libraries could include the following:

- **AMD Optimizing CPU Libraries (AOCL)** are a set of mostly open source libraries compiled for AMD64 processors, in the 64-bit processor architecture.

- **Basic Linear Algebra Subprograms (BLAS)** is a specification that prescribes a set of low-level routines for performing common linear algebra operations such as vector addition, scalar multiplication, dot products, linear combinations, and matrix multiplication. They are the de facto standard low-level routines for linear algebra libraries. Although the BLAS specification is general, BLAS implementations are often optimized for speed on a particular machine, so using them can bring substantial performance benefits.

- **Compute Unified Device Architecture (CUDA) Deep Neural Network library (cuDNN)** is a GPU-accelerated library of primitives for deep neural networks. CuDNN provides highly tuned implementations for standard routines such as forward and backward convolution, pooling, normalization, and activation layers. Deep learning researchers and framework developers worldwide rely on cuDNN for high-performance GPU acceleration. CuDNN is developed by NVIDIA.

- **LLVM** (not an acronym) **Core libraries** provide a modern source- and target-independent optimizer, along with code generation support for many popular CPUs. These libraries are built around a well-specified code representation known as the LLVM intermediate representation. The LLVM Core libraries are well documented, and it is particularly easy to invent your own language (or port an existing compiler) to use LLVM as an optimizer and code generator.

On top of the kernel libraries, you need *compilers* or *virtual machines* to generalize the computations so that data scientists can develop AI algorithms with the *ML frameworks* with increased productivity. Here are examples of these compilers:

- **ONNX** (not an acronym) **compilers** are built in an open format to represent both deep learning and traditional models. With ONNX, AI developers can more easily move models between state-of-the-art tools and choose the combination that is best for them. ONNX is developed and supported by a community of partners such as Microsoft, Facebook, and AWS.

- The **NNVM** (not an acronym) **compiler** is a new, enhanced compiler for deep learning. NNVM differs from other existing deep learning frameworks such as TensorFlow since NNVM compiles given graph definitions into execution code through a runtime-agnostic compiler, while in TensorFlow you need to write a specific graph definition.

- The **NGraph compiler** is a graph compiler that supports both training and inference acceleration for all three of the most popular deep learning frameworks: TensorFlow, PyTorch, and MXNet. This open source graph compiler is able to look for patterns (subgraphs, sequences of specific operations, etc.). NGraph is developed by Intel.

- **Tensor Virtual Machine (TVM)** is an open deep learning compiler stack intended to compile various deep learning models from different frameworks to the CPU, GPU, or specialized accelerators. TVM supports model compilation from a wide range of front-ends like TensorFlow, ONNX, Keras, MXNet, DarkNet, CoreML, and Caffe2.

So, what is the purpose of a *machine learning framework*? An ML framework is an interface, library, or tool that allows developers to more easily and quickly build machine learning models without getting into the nitty-gritty of the underlying algorithms. It provides a clear, concise way to define ML models using a collection of prebuilt, optimized components. A good ML framework should

- Be optimized for performance
- Be developer friendly and utilize traditional ways of building models
- Be easy to understand and code on
- Not be completely a black box
- Provide parallelization to distribute the computation process

Overall, an efficient ML framework reduces the complexity of machine learning, making it accessible to more developers. For examples of ML frameworks, see the section "MLOps Toolsets" later in this chapter.

Once the models are built in the ML frameworks, the models can be *containerized* in the next layer. A container is a standard unit of software that packages code and all its dependencies so that the application runs quickly and reliably from one computing environment to another. Containerization can be done using Docker containers. Docker is a set of platform-as-a-service (PaaS) products that use OS-level virtualization to deliver software in containers. Because all the containers share the services of a single operating system kernel, they use fewer resources than virtual machines (VMs). For more details on containers, see the section "MLOps Toolsets" as well as Chapter 4.

These containers are then *orchestrated in a distributed environment* (for example, Kubernetes). Using container orchestration, engineers can manage when and how containers start and stop, schedule and coordinate components' activities, monitor health, distribute updates, and institute failover and recovery processes. Engineers who work in DevOps cultures use container orchestration platforms and tools to automate that process throughout the life cycle of containers.

Modern orchestration tools use *declarative programming*, which is focused on the outcome to ease container deployments and management. This is different from using *imperative language*, which is focused on how to achieve the objective. The declarative approach lets engineers define the desired outcome without feeding the tool with the step-by-step details of how to do it and can be done serverless in a cloud environment. In contrast, an imperative approach requires engineers to give detailed instructions on how to orchestrate containers to accomplish a specific goal. This increases complexity, depriving containers deployed in this way of their advantage over VMs after all.

Let's use an example to explain the difference. Think about how you order an Uber. You do not need to instruct the driver how to drive their car, which shortcuts to take, and how to get to a particular destination.

You just tell them you are in a hurry and, well, that you need to arrive at your destination in one piece. They know what to do next.

Using the Uber analogy, an imperative approach would be similar to taking a ride to a destination the driver is unfamiliar with. It is crucial that you know precisely how to get there and clearly explain all the turns and shortcuts to the driver, or you may get lost in an unfamiliar neighborhood.

So, what is container orchestration used for? Orchestrating containers has various uses:

- Configuring and scheduling
- Load balancing among containers
- Allocating resources among containers
- Monitoring the health of containers and hosts

Orchestration simplifies container management. In addition, orchestration tools help determine which hosts are the best matches for specific pods. A *pod* represents a single instance of a running process in your cluster. Pods contain one or more containers. When a pod runs multiple containers, the containers are managed as a single entity and share the pod's resources. That further eases your engineers' job while reducing human error and time used. Orchestrating also promotes optimal resource usage. So, if a failure occurs somewhere in that complexity, popular orchestration tools restart containers or replace them to increase your system's resilience.

So, when the models are containerized and orchestrated in a distributed environment, they're ready for *serving* (or being deployed in production) in the next layer—through, for example, model serving frameworks such as TensorFlow Extended (TFX) (also called TensorFlow Serving) or BentoML. (For additional details about model serving, see the section "MLOps Toolsets" later in this chapter and Chapter 4.)

The serving layer needs to be closely connected to the model training/retraining environment, architecture search, and hyperparameter optimization, ensuring that best performance of the models is achieved for specific applications, at any time, anywhere. Hyperparameter optimization (or tuning) in this context refers to the problem of choosing a set of optimal hyperparameters for a learning algorithm. A hyperparameter is a parameter whose value is used to control the learning process. By contrast, the values of other parameters (typically node weights) are learned.

Key Competences and Toolsets in MLOps

While having the competence to train AI/ML models is essential, developing a practical production model demands highly skilled professionals. However, the industry still has varying metrics on what being a good MLOps engineer actually means and how it differs from the role of a data scientist. So, let's start by sorting out some key differences as a basis in this book.

A *data scientist* can best be described as a business-focused scientist who studies, finds, and solves problems within the company with ML algorithms. The main objective is usually to make a process both more accurate and efficient compared to how it was previously done. This definition sounds quite similar to a software engineering role; however, this position focuses, of course, more on the algorithms and how they work as a solution, rather than more handmade and object-oriented programming code solutions.

The workflow of a data scientist usually includes the following tasks:

1. Explore the company data and products.
2. Understand internal and external business pain points.
3. Capture and define a business problem statement that highlights the issue at hand.
4. Obtain the data in some way, or work with a data engineer to digest newer data from other, new sources.
5. Perform exploratory data analysis on the chosen dataset.
6. Compare several models to a baseline model.
7. Choose the main algorithm.
8. Identify key features (feature engineering).
9. Remove redundant and unnecessary features.
10. Create an ensemble or stepwise algorithm process (if needed).
11. Account for outliers.
12. Save the model and test in a development environment.
13. Provide details on accuracy or error metrics.
14. Present the results to business stakeholders and propose improvements to the product.

So, as you can conclude, the data scientist role is not intended to go beyond model development. That's where the MLOps engineer role comes into play. Also keep in mind that not every company can afford or deems it necessary to have an MLOps engineer alongside a data scientist. Instead, many times key competences in data science work in both roles. However, sometimes it can be more beneficial if a data scientist focuses on the machine learning algorithms and the MLOps engineer focuses on the deployment, pipelines, and productionalization of the model. It can help to improve on the model's accuracy or reduce its error metrics when the data scientist doesn't have to worry about the software engineering–heavy aspects of implementing the actual model into the business, application, and other parts of your company's software.

A solid *MLOps engineer*, on the other hand, should have strong programming and ML expertise, as well as hands-on experience with ML frameworks, libraries, agile environments, and deployment of machine learning solutions using DevOps principles. The role should be engaged with creating pipelines, scaling ML, and taking models to production. Furthermore, MLOps engineers should focus on putting the architecture, systems, best practices, and governance in place to ensure smooth deployment of models in production.

MLOps calls for a combined set of ML, data engineering, and DevOps practices, and since ML relies heavily on data, a skilled MLOps engineer should know data structures, data modeling, and database management systems inside and out.

The MLOps engineer should understand the tools serving different purposes in the pipeline, including CI servers, configuration management, deployment automation, containers, infrastructure orchestration, monitoring and analytics, testing and cloud quality tools, as well as network protocols. Since MLOps is modeled on the existing discipline of DevOps, it's a necessity to know how to automate the entire DevOps pipeline, including application performance monitoring, infrastructure settings, and configurations.

Moreover, since successful deployment of ML models in production remains heavily dependent on two critical factors, code and data, understanding the relationship between the two is vital. While data originates from the real world, code is carefully developed in a controlled development environment, so it's important to remember that real-world data sees constant change without an engineer controlling it.

Because MLOps includes several different phases, each phase demands slightly different skillsets. For example, when identifying an ML problem and selecting appropriate input data, as well as preparing and processing data, the skillset must include data cleaning (imputations, checking for outliers, formatting, etc.), feature engineering, and selecting features. The ability to design and code a complete pipeline is a must.

Understanding the system's requirements, such as triggers, computing needs, and parameters, is helpful. Additionally, a good MLOps engineer should be able to construct training and testing pipelines and perform data validation activities. This includes being able to deploy an ML model to the production system, using either static or dynamic deployment.

Again, there's no MLOps skillset formally agreed on in the industry, but for successful MLOps practices, key competences and related toolsets include the following:

- Monitoring of build and production systems using automated monitoring and alarm tools

- Experience with MLOps tools such as ModelDB, Kubeflow, Pachyderm, and Data Version Control (DVC)

- Experience in supporting model builds and model deployment for integrated development environment (IDE)-based models and AutoML tools, experiment tracking, model management, version tracking, and model training (Dataiku, DataRobot, Kubeflow, TensorFlow Extended [TFX], MLflow), model hyperparameter optimization, model evaluation, and explainability (SHAP [SHapley Additive exPlanations], TensorBoard)

- Knowledge of machine learning frameworks: TensorFlow, PyTorch, Keras, Scikit-Learn

- Experience with container technologies (Docker, Kubernetes, EKS, ECS)

- Experience with multiple cloud providers (AWS, GCP, Azure, etc.)

- Experience in distributed computing

Furthermore, the scope and responsibilities of an MLOps engineer role mainly include the following operations-related activities, which happen after model development. However, it's important that the data scientist is kept in the loop, as decisions made by the MLOps engineer may contradict the purpose of the model—for example, taking shortcuts that can alter the model's outcome. (For more details, see Chapters 4 and 5.)

- Deploying and operationalizing MLOps, specifically implementing
  - Model hyperparameter optimization
  - Model evaluation and explainability

- Model training and automated retraining
- Model workflows from onboarding operations to decommis- sioning
- Model version tracking and governance
- Data archiving and version management
- Model and drift monitoring
- Creating and using benchmarks, metrics, and monitoring to mea- sure and improve services
- Providing best practices, executing proof-of-concepts for automated and efficient model operations at scale
- Designing and developing scalable MLOps frameworks to support models based on client requirements
- Being the MLOps expert for the sales team, providing technical design solutions to support RFPs

Remember that no single person or role will achieve all of this by themselves. To succeed, you need to think about MLOps as a team effort, where competences are distributed across the MLOps team, and that MLOps engineers work closely with data scientists and data engineers throughout the life cycle of your AI initiative.

Clarifying Similarities and Differences

It's obvious that the way the data scientist role and the MLOps engineer role are implemented will vary from company to company, but in gen- eral, key similarities and differences exist between these two positions that can mostly be applied anywhere. Some of the similarities between the two roles are usually that both

- Need to understand the business, problem, and solution (at least a high-level overview)
- Need to know the data of the company well and where to look for more if needed
- Are proficient in database technologies like SQL and programming languages such as Python
- Are used to working with versioning control and code repositories such as Git and GitHub
- Need to know the concept of training and testing

Some of the key differences between the data scientist role and the MLOps engineer role are as follows:

- Data scientists usually work or develop in their notebooks or something similar.

- Data scientists tend to be more research-oriented, whereas MLOps engineers focus on production-ready code and programming.

- MLOps engineers work with DevOps tools like Docker and CircleCI as well as with AWS/EC2, Google Cloud, or Kubeflow.

- MLOps tend to focus more on object-oriented programming (OOP).

- Data scientists must understand the math behind how the actual machine learning algorithm works (e.g., gradient descent, regularizations, parameter tuning, etc.).

- Data scientists focus on choosing and creating the algorithm (e.g., is it supervised, is it unsupervised, is it regression, is it classification?).

- Schooling/education is different between the roles. Usually, a degree in data science is needed for data scientists, whereas a degree in software engineering is required for MLOps engineers.

MLOps Toolsets

MLOps toolsets enable data science teams to easily build models and provide developers with easy access to these models. Overall, these tools simplify the complex machine learning process, saving developers time. MLOps tools offer a broad variety of features depending on the tool, but here are some of the most common features offered by MLOps tools:

- IDE integration
- Automated ML model development (AutoML)
- Model serving
- Model explainability
- Machine learning model performance monitoring
- Data governance/security
- Machine learning notebooks

Here are a few key aspects that are important to consider when you're choosing MLOps tools for your business:

- Many MLOps tools offer some features to support machine learning, such as automated model training and analysis. If you don't already have a tool for model analysis, be sure to choose an MLOps tool that offers robust analysis features.

- MLOps tools integrate with other development tools, including IDEs, storage solutions, and more. When choosing an MLOps tool, be sure to select one that integrates with all the tools you already use, as well as tools you plan to use in the future.

- MLOps tools include features for data governance and security. How robust these features are depends on each specific solution. If you don't already have a strong data security tool, you should select a tool that offers those features.

Regarding pricing, many MLOps tools are open source or offer some limited free version, whether that includes partial feature access or access to a number of compute hours for free. Beyond that, most MLOps tools are offered as a service (aaS) and charge on an hourly basis, with rates increasing as memory needs increase. A company should expect to pay at least $0.05 an hour, but understand that if the highest performance is needed, the price could increase to up to $6.00 an hour or more.

Most MLOps tools also include charge-as-you-go pricing, so if your organization needs high performance for a single workload, most tools enable them to just pay more for that workload, without having to commit to a more expensive plan long term.

When it comes to MLOps, no one tool can do it all. It takes an array of best-of-breed tools to truly automate the entire ML life cycle. To start with, there are a number of ML frameworks you should be aware of. An ML framework is any tool, interface, or library that lets you develop ML models easily without understanding the underlying algorithms. There are a variety of machine learning frameworks geared toward slightly different purposes. The following are some of the most popular frameworks:

- **TensorFlow** is a free and open source software library for machine learning and artificial intelligence built by Google. It can be used across a range of tasks but has a particular focus on training and inference of deep neural networks. TensorFlow can be used in a wide variety of programming languages, most notably Python, as well as JavaScript, C++, and Java. This flexibility lends itself to a range of applications in many different sectors.

- **PyTorch** is an open source machine learning framework that accelerates the path from research prototyping to production deployment. PyTorch is an optimized tensor library primarily used for deep learning applications using GPUs and CPUs. It is a machine learning library for the Python programming language, mainly developed by the Facebook (Meta) AI Research team.

- **Keras** is an open source software library that provides a Python interface for artificial neural networks. Keras acts as an interface for the TensorFlow library. From the beginning, Keras supported multiple backends, including TensorFlow, Microsoft Cognitive Toolkit, Theano, and PlaidML, but the newer versions only support TensorFlow. Keras is designed to enable fast experimentation with deep neural networks and focuses on being user-friendly, modular, and extensible.

- **Scikit-learn** is a free software machine learning library for the Python programming language. It features various classification, regression, and clustering algorithms, including support vector machines, random forests, gradient boosting, k-means, and density-based spatial clustering of applications with noise (DBSCAN). Scikit-learn is designed to interoperate with the Python numerical and scientific libraries NumPy and SciPy. *NumPy* is the fundamental package for scientific computing in Python. It is a Python library that provides a multidimensional array object, various derived objects (such as masked arrays and matrices), and an assortment of routines for fast operations on arrays, including mathematical, logical, shape manipulation, sorting, selecting, input/output (I/O), discrete Fourier transforms, basic linear algebra, basic statistical operations, random simulation, and much more. *SciPy* is an open source library used for solving mathematical, scientific, engineering, and technical problems. It allows users to manipulate the data and visualize the data using a wide range of high-level Python commands. SciPy is built on the Python NumPy extension.

- **Apache MXNet** is a modern open source deep learning framework used to train and deploy deep neural networks. It is scalable, allowing for fast model training, and supports a flexible programming model and multiple programming languages, including C++, Python, Java, Julia, MATLAB, JavaScript, Go, R, Scala, Perl, and Wolfram Language. The MXNet library is portable and can scale to multiple GPUs and multiple machines. MXNet is supported by public cloud providers such as AWS and Microsoft Azure.

The public cloud providers have also developed their own ML frameworks, and their usage is increasing due to the ease of access (it already runs where your data is) and ease of use:

- **Amazon Machine Learning (Amazon ML)** is a robust, cloud-based service that makes it easy for developers of all skill levels to use machine learning technology. Amazon ML provides visualization tools and wizards that guide you through the process of creating ML models without having to learn complex ML algorithms and technology. Once your models are ready, Amazon ML makes it easy to obtain predictions for your application using simple APIs, without having to implement custom prediction generation code or manage any infrastructure.

- The **Microsoft Cognitive Toolkit**, which was previously known as CNTK, empowers developers to harness the intelligence within massive datasets through deep learning by providing uncompromised scaling, speed, and accuracy with commercial-grade quality and compatibility with various programming languages and algorithms.

Usually, data scientists prefer to use specialized tools for different parts of the life cycle, but there are some tools that aim to manage the full MLOps life cycle:

- **Kubeflow** is a free, open source machine learning platform that offers an end-to-end ML stack orchestration toolkit that makes it possible for machine learning pipelines to orchestrate complicated workflows running on Kubernetes as a way to deploy, scale, and manage complex systems.

- **Pachyderm** provides the data layer that allows machine learning teams to productionize and scale their machine learning life cycle. Pachyderm's data versioning, pipelines, and lineage enables data-driven automation, petabyte scalability, and end-to-end reproducibility. Pachyderm is good for building machine learning pipelines and ETL workflows and for tracking every model/output directly to the raw input datasets that created it.

- **Data Version Control (DVC)** tracks ML models and datasets. It's built to make ML models shareable and reproducible and is designed to handle large files, datasets, machine learning models, and metrics as well as code. DVC is a new type of data versioning, workflow, and experiment management software that builds upon Git (although it can work stand-alone).

- **Dataiku Data Science Studio (DSS)** is a platform with the ambition to span the needs of all main data science roles, like data scientists, data engineers, business analysts, and AI consumers. DSS also spans the machine learning process end to end, from data preparation through MLOps and application support.

- **MLflow** is an open source platform for managing the end-to-end machine learning life cycle. Its Tracking feature allows you to track experiments to record and compare parameters and results.

Then there are tools that are more focused specifically on ML model serving (deploying models in production) or serving of ML pipelines:

- **TensorFlow Extended (TFX) or TensorFlow Serving** is an end-to-end, open source platform for deploying production ML pipelines. When you're ready to move your models from model training to production, you can use TFX to create and manage a production pipeline. TensorFlow Serving is a flexible system for machine learning models, designed for production environments. It deals with the inference aspect of machine learning. TFX can serve multiple models, or multiple versions of the same model, at the same time and exposes both gRPC and HTTP inference endpoints. It also allows deployment of new model versions without changing your code and lets you flexibly test experimental models. TFX offers efficient, low-overhead implementation and adds minimal latency to the inference time.

- **BentoML** is a framework for serving, managing, and deploying machine learning models. Its aim is to bridge the gap between data science and DevOps and enable teams to deliver prediction services in a fast, repeatable, and scalable way. BentoML packages models trained with any ML frameworks and reproduces them for model serving in production, and they can then be deployed anywhere for online API serving or offline batch serving. BentoML has a high-performance API model server with adaptive micro-batching support. It works as a central hub for managing models and the deployment process via a web UI and APIs, and the modular and flexible design allows you to adapt the tool to your infrastructure.

- **Cortex** is an open source platform for deploying, managing, and scaling machine learning models. It's a multiframework tool that lets you deploy all types of models. Cortex is built on top of Kubernetes to support large-scale ML workloads and can automatically scale APIs to handle production workloads. Cortex allows running inference on any AWS type and deployment of multiple models in a single API. Deployed APIs can also be updated without downtime. Cortex also supports monitoring of API performance and prediction results in production.

■ **KFServing** provides a Kubernetes custom resource definition (CRD) for serving machine learning models on arbitrary frameworks. It aims to solve production model serving use cases by providing performant, high-abstraction interfaces for common ML frameworks like TensorFlow, XGBoost, Scikit-learn, PyTorch, and ONNX. The tool provides a serverless machine learning inference solution that allows a consistent and simple interface to deploy ML models. KFServing offers a simple, pluggable, and complete support for your production ML inference server by providing prediction, preprocessing, postprocessing, and explainability. It has a customizable inference service to add your resource requests for CPU, GPU, TPU, and memory requests and limits, and it can batch individual model inference requests. KFServing supports traffic management, revision management, and request and response logging, and it offers scalable multiple-model serving.

■ **Multi Model Server (MMS)** is a flexible and easy-to-use tool for serving deep learning models trained using any ML or deep learning framework. It can be used for many types of inference in production settings. It provides an easy-to-use command-line interface (CLI) and utilizes REST-based APIs to handle state prediction requests. You can use the MMS Server CLI or the preconfigured Docker images to start a service that sets up HTTP endpoints to handle model inference requests. MMS allows advanced configurations and lets you develop customized inference services. It supports unit tests and allows Apache JMeter to run MMS through the paces and collect benchmark data for MMS benchmarking. MMS also supports model serving with Amazon Elastic Inference, and the ONNX model export feature supports different models of deep learning frameworks.

Then there are a few ML tools for model explainability from an MLOps perspective. This capability is becoming increasingly important as the trustworthiness in AI models is directly associated with our ability to understand why a certain recommendation or decision was made by the model. However, the area of model explainability is still pretty weak when it comes to capable software. The ability to explain the model outcome is also related to which ML technique has been used. However, the following two approaches are applicable for any model:

- **SHAP (SHapley Additive exPlanations)** is a game theoretic approach to explain the output of any ML model. It connects optimal credit allocation with local explanations using the classic Shapley values from game theory and their related extensions. SHAP values interpret the impact of having a certain value for a given feature in comparison to the prediction you would make if that feature took some baseline value.

- **TensorBoard** is a visualization toolkit from TensorFlow used to display various metrics, parameters, and other visualizations that help you debug, track, fine-tune, optimize, and share your deep learning experiment results. TensorBoard allows you to track metrics like loss and accuracy change with every epoch and tracking loss, and accuracy over the ML training cycle will help you determine whether the model is overfitting. It will also help you model graphs and visualize deep learning models to determine whether they are built correctly. Furthermore, it supports distribution histograms, where you can visualize the histograms of weights and biases over epochs. TensorBoard supports images so that you can visualize arbitrary images for your dataset.

Container technology has changed the way data science gets done. The original container use case for data science focused more on managing the ML environment, since configuring software environments is a constant task, especially in the open source software space, the space in which most data scientists work. It often requires trial and error. This tampering may, however, break dependencies such as those between software packages or between drivers and applications. Containers therefore provide a way for data science professionals to isolate environments from each other, allowing data scientists to experiment and freeze golden-state environments. Container orchestration has the following benefits in data science work:

- Removal of central IT bottlenecks in the MLOps life cycle
- Improved collaboration for data scientists when sharing code and research
- Capability to instantly reproduce and rerun old projects

Getting models into production is a critical stage in the MLOps life cycle. You can read more about the role that container technology plays in getting ML/AI models into production in Chapter 4. Container technologies available include the following:

- **Docker** is an open source, Linux-based containerization platform. It enables developers to package applications into containers— standardized executable components combining application source code with the OS libraries and dependencies required to run that code in any environment.

- **Kubernetes** is an open source container-orchestration system used for automating computer application deployment, scaling, and management. It was originally designed by Google and is now maintained by the Cloud Native Computing Foundation. It works with a range of container tools and runs containers in a cluster, often with images built using Docker. Kubernetes originally interfaced with the Docker runtime; however, that changed in 2016 and Kubernetes is now directly interfacing with the container through `containerd`, a runtime that is compliant with the Container Runtime Interface (CRI). Many cloud services offer a Kubernetes-based platform as a service (PaaS) or infrastructure as a service (IaaS) on which Kubernetes can be deployed.

- **Amazon Elastic Kubernetes Service (Amazon EKS)** is a managed Kubernetes service that makes it easy for you to run Kubernetes on AWS and on-premises.

- **Amazon Elastic Container Service (ECS)** is a cloud computing service in AWS that manages containers and allows developers to run applications in the cloud without having to configure an environment for the code to run in.

Deployment with AI Operations in Mind

Although AI models are developed and trained in the lab, it's important to remember that's not where they will generate any business value. It's not until you deploy your models in a production setting that the potential value of AI can fully be realized. This is true whether your models are more informally deployed as part of an internal process, or a vital part of an internal decision-making framework or even deployed for commercial purposes. However, moving your models from the lab to production is far from an easy task. Successful model deployment is about a lot more than just running your model in another execution environment.

When deploying AI models in production, you need to consider various areas, from legal rights and data access to managing retraining and redeployment of models in a live production setting. Remember that even when the model is deployed in an internal process, people and decisions will depend on it differently from when you run it in the lab. Depending on what type of solutions or operational settings will depend on your model, you also need to consider how to seamlessly deploy a fallback solution if, for example, the model performance degrades to unacceptable levels, or if the model stops working entirely.

This chapter will explain how to be more successful in operating AI by adopting an operational approach in the deployment phase.

Companies in the software industry currently deploying AI are reporting that the top five most important ways their organizations use AI are as follows:

- Data security (36 percent)

- Automation of processes (31 percent)

- Virtual assistants/chatbots (26 percent)

- Business process optimization (24 percent)

- Sensor data analysis/Internet of Things (24 percent)

These statistics result from an IBM survey of 4,514 businesses in the United States, European Union, and China (`https://filecache` `.mediaroom.com/mr5mr_ibmnews/183710/Roadblock-to-Scale-exec-` `summary.pdf`). You can also see from the figures that AI utilization in production environments are still mainly focused on improving processes (55 percent) and not on empowering existing or enabling new commercial solutions in their portfolio offerings.

One reason for this is that AI is still seen as new technology whose uses must still be explored. Another reason could be that most companies want to start by using AI internally to build competence and learn to master it before using the technology in commercial solutions. However, as AI has matured and spread across most industry segments over the past years, it has also become obvious to many companies that infusing AI in a commercial portfolio is significantly different from just releasing new software features.

One of the major reasons behind why many companies hesitate when it's time to deploy AI in a production setting relates to the lack of standardization in the data science space. AI is, as we know, very much open source driven and constantly evolving. This means it's also constantly changing. In a lab environment this doesn't matter that much, but in a production setting the situation is different. Data flows must be stable and reliable, and the AI model must perform over time and also be able to scale with increased data volumes, as well as adapt to changing behaviors and preferences reflected in the data. Therefore, one key to succeeding with deploying AI in production relates to how well your company can industrialize AI. But before going into the details of what AI industrialization means and how to achieve it, let's sort out two important aspects of AI deployment: model serving and the inference pipeline.

Model Serving in Practice

A common fact among data science or machine learning researchers and practitioners is that putting a model in production is difficult and time consuming. As a result, some claim that between 85 and 90 percent of models never see the light of the day in production due, it seems, to the lack of insights into how to deploy a model in production, a basic understanding of how the ML tech stack needs to be set up in production for a specific purpose, and last, but not least, which MLOps tools are recommended for use.

Although questions like these have no simple answer, there are some acceptable and common technical considerations and pitfalls to keep in mind when considering your ML stack and tools.

The ML model development cycle paradigm differs from the traditional software development cycle. A number of factors influence an ML model's success in production, including being able to perform training at scale and tracking model experiments.

First, the outcome of a model is measured by its metrics, such as an acceptable accuracy.

Second, achieving an accuracy that satisfies the business objective means experimentation with not only one model or ML library, but with many models and many ML libraries while tracking each experiment runs: metrics, parameters, artifacts, and so on. As vital as accuracy is, so is a developer's choice of ML libraries to experiment with.

Third, accuracy is directly linked to the quality of the acquired data: bad data results in a bad model. Steps taken in data preparation—including feature extractions, feature selection, standardized or normalized features, data imputations, and encoding—are all imperative before the cleansed data lands in a feature store, accessible in the model training and testing phase or for inference in deployment. A *feature* in data science represents a measurable piece of data (usually a column) that can be used for analysis like, for example, name, age, and sex. Features are also sometimes referred to as *variables* or *attributes*. Depending on what you're trying to analyze, the features you include in your dataset can vary widely.

Fourth, another key success factor for ML in production is using a programming language that is not only familiar to your data science team but also supported by many ML libraries used during model experimentation and training phases. For the data science community, Python is usually the de facto choice. Alongside a choice of a programming language is the choice of an ML framework for handling compute-intensive ML workloads related to, for example, deep learning, distributed training, hyperparameter optimization (HPO), and inference. This is all done at a horizontal scale from your laptop, single-node multiple cores to multiple nodes with multiple cores.

Finally, to succeed in production, the ability to easily deploy models in diverse environments at scale is of vital importance. This includes deploying ML models as part of web applications, inside mobile devices, and as a web service in the cloud.

Feature Stores

Feature stores are a way to manage data, particularly for MLOps. With feature stores, the expertise of ML teams can increase because the data they need is more easily seen.

Data used to sit comfortably in a server somewhere and data scientists would access the data when it was needed for analysis. Or, users would query the server to display data. In ML and the construction of AI systems, however, different data needs to be pulled from its sources, and then transformed and combined to create a standard feature set to serve a model. Those features can then be retrieved and served to model training jobs or scoring applications at any point in time. For this workflow to function optimally, data scientists need to be able to easily

- Verify the validity of the data
- Check its quality
- Know it's fresh
- Version the data and share it with others

To address these needs, feature stores are starting to emerge as essential components in the modern machine learning development cycle. As more data scientists and ML engineers work together to successfully put models in production, having a singular storage point to preserve cleaned and featurized data is becoming an increasing necessity. Feature stores are used to reuse features across models when building and operating operational ML applications. However, remember that not all features for a model may end up in a feature store.

With a feature store, the data science and machine learning teams can search for features that are already available. They can reuse existing features and thus avoid doing the heavy data engineering required to generate the features. This approach comes with noticeable benefits: it can reduce the infrastructure costs and improve the access control and governance of features, to just mention a few. The flip side is that it creates dependencies across models for features, which means if a feature is changed, multiple models can be affected.

As shown in Figure 4.1, feature stores are positioned between the ML models and the data sources to accommodate the kind of accessibility that data science teams require. The metadata layer coordinates data access between the applications that need the features and the data sources. With this feature management layer comes a set of benefits:

- Discoverability and ability to search for features
- Reuse of existing features
- Computed statistics on the features for distribution validation and anomaly detection
- Documentation of feature sources, generators, and consumers
- Versioning of features
- Cost reduction due to data reuse
- Data format flexibility to serve multiple types of consumers and ML libraries
- Point-in-time data accuracy through the metadata store
- Consistent set of data between training and inference
- No data skew or unintended data leakage

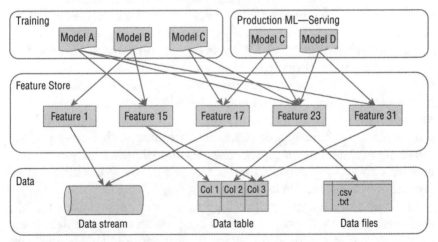

Figure 4.1: The role of a feature store

Not surprisingly, model accuracy depends on good data, and feature stores help manage precomputed and cleansed features for your model training and production inference during model serving. As a basic rule, you should consider feature stores as a vital part of your model development process. Feature store solutions are provided by Feast, Tecton, Amazon SageMaker, and Databricks, among others.

However, building and managing a feature store is no small undertaking. Your current understaffed ML infrastructure team has more urgent things to do than to include yet another dependency in their stack. This sort of investment starts making sense when a combination of elements begin creating chaos in your ML pipelines:

- Your organization starts having to maintain and evolve at least a dozen models that run in production.

- These applications start demanding online serving as well.

- If the apps do not have an online serving component to them, then at least they need to demand frequent model retraining and scoring from recent interaction data.

- The apps that benefit the most from a feature store are the ones with a high number of structured data sources.

For companies with ML applications with few data sources, the data is available all at one time, like for a whole image or document to train on. Features, in this case, are extracted using the pixel values of an image or words from a document. Though very unstructured, these sorts of applications can be deployed while depending only on one or two data sources.

The situation is different for ML applications with a large number of data sources, such as a personalized ranking of products for an e-commerce application. In this case, the feature search is composed of multiple tables, files, streams, and other enterprise APIs. The data is collected on the fly as consumers interact with the predictive service or the products they are interested in. This can include, for example, changing product attributes/availability, past purchases, user attributes, user social interactions, current cart items, current search words, current session paths, past impressions, and clicks by a user.

In the case of a use case with a high number of data sources, the ML engineering team will be spending a lot of time choosing and iteratively curating the datasets used for their ML applications. This is precisely the type of use cases that will benefit from a feature store to automate, record, and expose feature engineering pipelines.

Deploying, Serving, and Inferencing Models at Scale

Once the model is trained and tested, with confidence that it met the business requirements for model accuracy, you must consider a set of important requirements for scalable model serving frameworks:

- **ML framework agnostic**—A model serving framework should be as ML framework agnostic as possible. That is, it can deploy any common model built with most commonly used ML frameworks, such as PyTorch, TensorFlow, XGBoost, or Scikit-learn, each with its own algorithms and model architectures. However, remember that the complexity of your deployment increases with the number of frameworks, so you might need to make a few choices here to reduce overall complexity.

- **Business logic**—Model prediction often requires preprocessing, postprocessing, or the ability to request data by connecting to a feature store or any other data store for validation. Model serving should allow this as part of its inference.

- **Replication of models**—Some models are compute-intensive or network-bound. As such, the serving framework should be able to fan out requests over to model replicas, load balancing among replicas to support parallel request handling during peak traffic.

- **Batch serving**—Not all models in production are deployed for real-time serving. Often, models are scored in large batches of requests. For example, for deep learning models, parallelizing these image requests to multiple cores, taking advantage of hardware accelerators to expedite batch scoring and utilize hardware resources, is worthy of consideration.

- **High concurrency and low latency**—Models in production require real-time inference with low latency while handling bursts of heavy traffic of requests. This is crucial for best user experience to receive millisecond responses on prediction requests.

- **Model deployment in a CI/CD pipeline**—A ML engineer who is responsible for deploying a model should be able to use a model server's deployment APIs or command-line interfaces (CLIs) simply to deploy model artifacts into production. This allows model deployment from within an existing CI/CD pipeline or workflow.

Consider a real production scenario at an e-commerce website, where the data science team has trained and deployed a simple logistic regression model that predicts whether a customer is likely to buy a product based on their behavior on the website. The model was trained on historical data. A logistic regression model requires imputing missing values and normalizing the features (in order to be interpretable), so the team performed these operations before training. That means that the model expects new data to have gone through the same preprocessing. Therefore, when deploying the model in the production environment, you need to perform the same transformations or the model won't work as expected.

Now consider another example with a website selling food for pets. The user is asked to upload the image of their pet, and a computer vision model is used to classify the pet into dogs or cats and suggest the appropriate food. The neural network expects images to be of a fixed size and normalized in a specific way. When the team has trained it, these operations are performed, so the same operations must be performed in production as well—otherwise, again the model will not perform as promised.

One of the foundational principles of MLOps is the idea of development/ production symmetry. You should not reimplement the same operations in multiple systems. So if you're doing some preprocessing that is needed at training time as well as at inference time, you should reuse the same code. Many companies instead still duplicate the functionality in the production environment. It is an error-prone process, especially when the teams responsible for model development and production are different. Instead, you should embed all the preprocessing in the inference artifact itself so that the code that runs during development is exactly the same that runs in production.

So the inference artifact is a minimal pipeline in itself, consisting of two steps: a preprocessing step where all the needed data transformations are applied, and then using the trained model to perform inference on the preprocessed data. By structuring the process in this way, you're guaranteed that the same operations that happened during model development will also take place in production. It is therefore much easier to deploy the model, since the artifact itself is pretty much self-contained.

Most machine learning frameworks allow you to save the preprocessing steps as well as the model into one artifact that can be deployed. For example, in Scikit-learn you can use the `Pipeline` class to chain together transformers and models. In PyTorch, you can make most transformations part of the model graph and then export them with `torch.script`.

Sometimes your preprocessing step includes some feature engineering, which refers to creating a new feature combining existing features, which should ideally be stored separately in the feature store. In some cases, including some simple feature engineering step within the inference pipeline is a sensible solution. However, depending on your use case, you might not have enough time or resources at inference time to compute the features that you need. Or, you might have several models needing the same feature engineered at inference time and you might have to share the computation. In these cases, you should invest in a feature store solution, as explained earlier in this chapter.

The ML Inference Pipeline

Machine learning (ML) *inference* is the second phase of the ML pipeline, in which the model is put into action on live data to produce actionable output.

According to a technical report (`https://dancrankshaw.com/publication/inferline-pub`) by Dan Crankshaw in InferLine in 2018, the dominant cost in production machine learning workloads is not training individual models but serving predictions from increasingly complex prediction pipelines spanning multiple models, machine learning frameworks, and parallel hardware accelerators. Due to the complex interaction between model configurations and parallel hardware, prediction pipelines are challenging to provision and costly to execute when serving interactive latency-sensitive applications. This challenge is exacerbated by the unpredictable dynamics of bursty workloads. From a single model perspective, however, model serving or inference is normally much less computationally intense than model training.

The setup of your inference pipeline therefore depends a lot on how you want to serve your ML system. There are multiple ways to serve your ML model, and often you are required to decide the serving architecture even before training your model. This means that this step should be part of the ML development phase. Why? Well, if you don't know how your ML system needs to operate in the live production environment, how will you know what to expose your model to during training?

So, what is a serving architecture for your ML system? It's simply the conceptual model that defines the structure, behavior, and more views of the ML system. A serving architecture description is a formal description and representation of the system, organized in a way that supports reasoning about the structures and behaviors of the system.

A serving architecture can consist of system components, and the subsystems developed, that will work together to implement the overall

ML system. So, to select the best approach for your serving architecture, you need to know and consider the requirements for your ML system. For example:

- What will ensure a good user experience? To answer this, you need to be clear on who the user of your solution is. Remember, the user could be an actual person, or a consumer (downstream service) such as a backend service.

- What parts of the solution are the most critical to implement for a good user experience?

- What is the minimum viable product you can implement as soon as possible to get the first version to your users and collect feedback?

The two most common architectures for model serving are precomputed model prediction and microservice-based model serving. These architectures are useful for different types of ML systems.

Precomputed model prediction is one of the earliest used and simplest architectures for serving ML models. It is an indirect method for serving the model, where you precompute predictions for all possible combinations of input variables and store them in a database. This architecture is generally used in *recommendation systems* where recommendations are precomputed and stored, and shown to the user at login.

This type of serving architecture has both advantages and disadvantages:

Pros:

- It enables low latency during model inferencing.

- Productionization is easy since retraining the model and bringing it back to production is very simple and less time-consuming.

- Cost efficiency is high since a database is all you need—no special infrastructure is required.

Cons:

- Since you need to precompute predictions for all possible combinations, you need to keep independent variable space discrete and bounded. Therefore, you can't use continuous variables directly.

- Adding a new variable is painful, since every new variable exponentially increases inference latency, storage, and so on.

In *microservice-based model serving*, the model is served independently of the application, and predictions are provided in real time as per request.

This type of architecture provides flexibility in terms of model training and deployment.

Before selecting a microservices-based architecture for model serving, you need to consider the following benefits and drawbacks:

Pros:

- It serves real-time (RT) predictions online, which meets the need of many applications.

- Deployment is flexible since it's an independent service. The model can be deployed with ease and can be in-house, in a cloud environment, or at the edge (device).

- It is highly scalable since the model is an independent service and can be scaled independently.

Cons:

- Infrastructure costs can be high since cloud, GPU, database, and so forth might be required, depending on the model requirements.

- It is more difficult to secure low latency optimization depending on the model's complexity. Extra effort in inference optimization is required to minimize latency.

Model Serving Architecture Components

Let's use an example in order to better understand how to approach the specifications for each component of the ML system based on its deployment and operational need. Consider an AI use case where a service should recommend the top 10 articles a user is likely to read based on their interest for a given log-in session through the mobile application or the website homepage. The following descriptions exemplify how the ML system components should be approached differently depending on the purpose and scope of each specific case in the areas described.

Data Acquisition and Feature Management Specifications   Since the articles are acquired from a variety of sources, it makes sense to centralize the data access into a data warehouse so that it can easily ingest the production data into a data pipeline.

You'll need a feature store to store the transformed feature values extracted from the production data for retraining the machine learning model offline.

Data versioning should also be enabled in order to allow for tracing the data lineage for auditing, debugging, or other purposes.

Furthermore, you should monitor the quality of the data needed for the automated workflow—completeness of the data, data validity, data consistency, and so forth.

Experiment Management and Model Development Specifications: Training should happen offline with existing data on users and their interaction with previous articles during the last 24 hours. Selecting this data refresh cycle makes sense based on expected interaction patterns with the articles and since new items are added each day.

A dynamic training architecture will be needed to compensate for the freshness in the articles released to avoid a stale model and ultimately stale recommendations.

You'll need a model registry to store details of the experiments and metadata from our training runs. This will also enable lineage traceability of the model being deployed and that of the data as well.

A training pipeline will be needed because you'll have to automate the retraining process as fresh articles come in every day.

To stay on budget, ensure that the model is trained every day for a reasonable amount of time. You may have to cap the amount of data it trains on for each training run because it is expensive, with extensive training periods on very high volumes of data, based on new article releases.

In the training architecture, you might also want to take advantage of model checkpoints so that training and retraining don't take too long (preferably under a few hours from the time they come in since that is often the peak login time for users).

Deployment and Serving Specifications   A batch inference system is probably a good idea since you don't need to serve predictions to users in real time while they browse the platform. The recommendations can be computed offline, stored in a database, and served to the user when they log in. To interface with the existing system, you could serve the model as a service with a RESTful interface.

Try to avoid dealing with serving dependency changes so that your automated pipeline runs don't fail due to these changes.

You want to ensure that it's easy to continuously deploy new model versions after successful evaluation and track them, since training will occur every day.

Model Monitoring Specifications   Model drift should be monitored in real time so that users aren't getting stale recommendations. The news events are quite dynamic, and users' reading behavior can become uncertain too.

It's important to monitor data quality issues because there will be times when there might be fewer fresh articles than is typically expected in a single day. Also take into account corrupted data.

Since you'll frequently be retraining the model, it's vital to keep track of the training metadata for each run so that when a model fails to perform, it's possible to audit its training details and troubleshoot.

Since you are dealing with pipelines, you'll need monitoring components to gauge the health of the pipelines.

It's important to collect ground truth labels on how long a person spends on an article to measure the model performance and the model drift.

Data drift should also be monitored alongside model drift to capture changes in user preferences and article features.

Another important part of model monitoring involves being able to get reports in the form of dashboard views and alerts when a pipeline performance degrades or fails, as you want to make sure your model is constantly updated.

Model Management Specifications   Since a large number of articles come in at random times based on events, it's possible to set up a pull-based architecture that executes a workflow on schedule to retrain the model on new data.

Model versioning will also need to be in place for each retrained and redeployed model version so that you can easily roll back if the retrained model underperforms. A/B testing, as discussed in Chapter 3, "Embracing MLOps," can also be used for this.

Retraining will happen based on data that has been transformed and loaded to a feature store.

Model Governance Specifications   Remember that it's important that model decisions are explainable. This is usually something that your customers care about, and since it could also be audited, it needs to be regulated.

System Operations (Ops) Specifications   A vital step in your ML system architecture is defining how the models will be able to run in production environments. What are the criteria for services to interact with each other, and how will that define the operations of the entire system? Basically, you'll need to understand and account for the performance requirements for an optimal system operation. For example, this could be

- 95 percent service level agreement (SLA) between the recommendation service and the backend server

- Low latency and high throughput when serving batch predictions through the data storage to thousands of users

Therefore, you need to track the number of successful, failed, and timed-out API calls, and the training pipelines and the overall system should be monitored in terms of how much resources they consume, such as I/O, CPU usage, and memory. To enforce low serving latency and high throughput serving, you could specify the targeted number of requests per second or, for example, maximum latency accepted per request in relation to x number of users or requests per second.

Furthermore, it's important to ensure that the infrastructure is model- and runtime-agnostic.

The production environment should not require frequent dependency changes that might cause the data and model pipelines to fail while executing. The production environment should mostly be deterministic.

The environment also needs to be reproducible because it will enable a rollback strategy when the system fails.

It's essential to ensure that you properly version every infrastructure package so that conflicts due to dependency changes can be easily debugged.

It's worth noticing that to get to this point, it's more about designing a system with the business ambition and end user in mind, without getting caught up and influenced by tooling or implementation preferences. While designing your architecture, you should be as technology-agnostic as possible and only focus on the requirements and specs. The structure should be completely agnostic to the ML problem you're solving. This means that it could work whether you're working on a computer vision project or a natural language processing task—I´m stating the obvious here, but, of course, some data management specifications will most probably change.

Considerations Regarding Toolsets for Model Serving

Because MLOps is still a nascent field, building an efficient ML system requires a combination of best practices and use of robust tools. This essentially means that while deciding on which tools you want to use in implementing the various components of your structure in line with your requirements and specifications, you have to be deliberate. In other words, look out for tools that are robust enough for the component you want to implement them for—preferably, one platform that has you covered across the horizontal stack (of managing your data, experiments, and model) and is dynamic enough for you to integrate with your existing ecosystem.

When deciding, you may want to consider the following:

- How soon do you need a minimum viable product (MVP) out and what will it take to release one?

- What are the results from the risk assessment you carried out? How crucial are the security needs of the platform in terms of data, model, and the entire system?

- Will this tool be hard to learn and integrate with your existing ecosystem of tools?

- Do you have the right experience on the team to use a particular tool or set of tools?

- Is the cost of these tools in the budget you have set aside for this project in terms of subscription or licensing fees (if you're buying), hosting fees (if you're building), and maintenance fees?

You want to choose what's optimal for your project based on the scope, requirements, risks, and constraints (such as costs and stakeholder skepticism).

The Industrialization of AI

So, what does it mean to industrialize AI and why is that important? *Industrialization* is the process of expanding the application of a technology so that a business can benefit from it at scale. The fact is that it's not enough to just deploy AI in a production setting; enterprises must also take the leap of industrializing AI to truly realize the benefits of the AI capabilities they have developed.

Just consider if a company built each component of its product from scratch with every order without any standardized or consistent parts, processes, and quality-assurance protocols? Chances are that any CEO would view such an approach as a major red flag preventing economies of scale and introducing unacceptable levels of risk and would seek to address it immediately.

Yet every day this is how many organizations approach the development and management of AI and analytics in general, putting themselves at a tremendous competitive disadvantage. Significant risk and inefficiencies are introduced as teams are scattered across an enterprise and regularly start efforts from the ground up, working manually without enterprise mechanisms for effectively and consistently deploying and monitoring the performance of live AI models.

To use another analogy, creating an AI application today is like building a house. Imagine that you want to build a row of 10 rental houses, and you use a different contractor for each one. Each contractor brings their own customized materials to the build site, so every house is built with different-sized nails, nuts, and bolts. The contractors might all be master craftspeople, and each house may be beautiful, but what happens after a tenant moves in and the natural wear-and-tear occurs? Because each house was built with customized parts and there are no blueprints or documentation available, the only person who can make repairs is the same contractor who built it.

In AI, this is analogous to how each application today is built with unique tools and processes, meaning that if the application's creator leaves a company, there is nobody left to maintain and update the system. For businesses, the AI investment could simply go to waste.

There's a need to industrialize AI in order to ensure uniform quality for an unlimited number of products and to produce them in a timely fashion. One way to achieve this in a company is to strive for a common toolset for AI and common processes that can be used by all practitioners. This is especially important as part of the deployment phase.

However, AI has some unique characteristics that make the AI industrialization challenge especially daunting. First and foremost, the term *AI* encompasses several distinct families of mathematical, statistical, and algorithmic methods. It's difficult for any one individual to truly be an expert in all areas of AI. For this reason, standardization requires a concerted effort from an organization with a wide representation of AI talent. To make things even more complicated, AI standardization also includes the computing equipment that businesses use to deploy AI in different target environments, such as edge devices, mobile devices, laptops, data centers, and cloud environments.

Ultimately, for AI to make a sizable contribution to a company's bottom line, organizations must scale the technology across the organization, infusing it in core business processes, workflows, and customer journeys to optimize decision making and operations daily. Achieving such scale requires a highly efficient AI production line all the way to live operations, where every AI team quickly delivers, deploys, and runs dozens of ready-to-go, risk-compliant, and reliable models.

Figure 4.2 shows an overview of the layers involved in getting an AI solution to an operational stage, and it also shows a matrix of steps involved in industrializing your AI solution, where each layer has its own challenges. The journey toward industrialization of AI usually starts with manual processes, leveraging local or disintegrated training environments, where the AI model life cycle management is manual and model serving is customized for each model deployment.

However, with improved streamlining and more efficient system design, manual processes should be replaced by reusable processes and other reusable and common assets over time, including ML frameworks and toolsets.

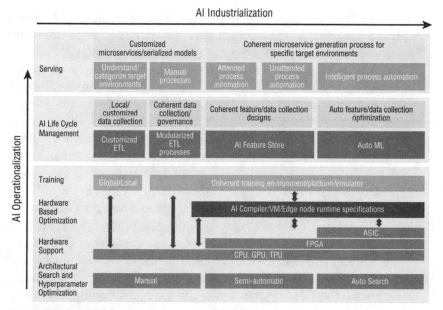

Figure 4.2: AI industrialization with operations in mind

In the training environment described in Figure 4.2, there are three separate layers, each with its own steps toward AI industrialization:

Architectural Search and Hyperparameter Optimization   In this part of the AI industrialization, the steps include manual, semi-automatic, and auto search. Neural architecture search (NAS) and hyperparameter optimization (HPO) are used to make deep learning accessible to nonexperts by automatically tuning the employed neural network architecture and the hyperparameters of a deep learning algorithm. However, it's worth noting that while both fields have been studied extensively in recent years, NAS methods typically assume fixed hyperparameter configurations, and vice versa. Little work exists on jointly optimizing hyperparameter configurations and neural network architectures.

Hardware Support   A critical aspect to speed up data science project cycles is to ensure that the training environment emulates the deployment environment early on so that the hardware environment dependencies are addressed early in the development cycle and the ML performance and footprint is fully optimized according to these constraints. (For more details on target environment, see Chapter 5, "Operating AI is Different from Operating Software.")

AI Compiler/VM/Edge Node Runtime Specifications   As part of industrializing AI, the AI compiler/VM/edge node runtime specifications become very important and *hardware-software codesign* should be practiced. Hardware–software codesign techniques target system-on-chip (SoC) design or embedded core design that involves integration of general-purpose microprocessors, digital signal processors (DSPs) structures, programmable logic (field-programmable gate arrays [FPGAs]), ASIC cores, memory block peripherals, and interconnection buses on one chip. The purpose is to manage AI power consumption by considering the whole system design process and attempt to partition the various tasks of the system between hardware and software from the early stages of the design process. These techniques attempt to find an optimal partitioning and assignment of tasks between software running on microprocessors or DSPs and hardware implemented on ASIC or FPGA for a given application. A system-level power optimization approach that deploys hardware–software partitioning based on a fine-grained (instruction/operation-level) power estimation analysis will achieve up to 94 percent savings in energy consumption.

The next layer in AI industrialization, as shown in Figure 4.2, regards *AI life cycle management*, where each of the steps is divided into two sublayers: data/model aspects and supporting technology. Furthermore, each of the AI life cycle management steps also corresponds with steps in the serving layer (where models are deployed and made available) describing the industrialization from a production environment perspective. The *serving* layer is also divided into two sublayers: the delivery aspects (commercial or internal) and the supporting methodology.

From an AI life cycle management perspective, the first step in the manual approach is having *local and customized data collection* setups. That is, every time a dataset is needed, it becomes a happening and is therefore time consuming and resource demanding. There is also a high risk of human error involved in this type of setup. Furthermore, if the data needed to run the model is owned by a third party, this could be even more cumbersome and time consuming because of data collection permissions and usage. The technology supporting this type of setup is usually handled through *customized ETL*, since the data collection method and data sources, and therefore the APIs, might change regularly—again, with poor cost efficiency and longer lead times as a result.

When the organization is ready to take a step toward AI industrialization in its life cycle management, this usually includes coherent data collection, as well as adding data governance. *Coherent data collection* in data science is an indication of the quality of the data, either within a single dataset or between similar but not identical datasets. Fully coherent data is logically consistent and can be reliably combined for analysis. Moving toward coherent data collection needs technical support through a *modularized ETL* approach. When data teams are forced to piece together products to get the job done, they risk creating overlapping dependencies between them. Doing so is problematic in that it limits an organization's ability to scale technically and in team structure, thus slowing down AI industrialization. The way to avoid this is to encourage openness and continuous communication between teams.

A modular approach to ELT is a cleaner design that improves the current and future prospects of a data team. In a nutshell, ETL modularization involves abstracting common tasks into reusable units of work. For a more concrete example, let's consider the scenario of downloading a file from an FTP server, a common task in an ETL infrastructure. Since most ETL software suites have built-in tasks to handle FTP downloads, a common design pattern is to include that task (with hard-coded paths to the source file and local destination folder) in each ETL process requiring an FTP download.

A modularized design involves breaking out common operations into separate and distinct processes that can be invoked generically. These modularized processes are parameterized to allow the passing in of operational values at runtime, and they are centrally stored so that they are available and visible for common use. A modularized ETL process means flexibility in choosing and changing products and vendors, as well as cleanly splitting the responsibility of moving data (extract, load) and modeling data (transform) between data engineers and analysts. Figure 4.3 illustrates the difference between a traditional ETL workflow, which works splendidly for a single process, and a modularized ETL process. However, you'll never have just a single ETL process that downloads a file from FTP. These things always travel in herds, so the odds are good you'll have a lot of related tasks.

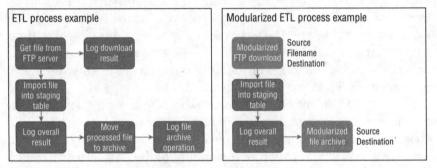

Figure 4.3: ETL modularization

In the ETL process example to the left in Figure 4.3, there are two easily identifiable opportunities for modularization: the download of files from FTP and the movement of files to an archive. Because these types of operations are common, and because each includes logging steps to capture some information about the operation, these will both be good candidates for modularization. By encapsulating the common behaviors and parameterizing the values needed at runtime, the design in the modularized ETL process to the right in Figure 4.3 is reusable and much easier to maintain.

In the manual step in the model serving layer, deliveries are being made through customized microservices, as well as serialized models. Customized microservices in model serving are needed since a standard product application cannot fit all the requirements of any customer and therefore often needs to be customized. A drawback of a customized microservice is that it becomes less secure as the customization code developed by the third parties or customers cannot be trusted to be dynamically compiled and executed within the execution context of the main service. There are ways to get around that, though—for example, by testing after compiling.

Another technology limitation hindering AI industrialization is that the customization code has to be written in the same language as interpreted by the product code.

Model serialization refers to the process of converting an object into a stream of bytes to store the object or transmit it to memory, a database, or a file. Its main purpose is to save the state of an object in order to be able to re-create it when needed. Serialization of models is appealing since it's easy to use and can be customized and the serialized stream can also be encrypted, authenticated, and compressed. A drawback hampering AI industrialization is that it should ideally not be used with large-sized objects since it offers significant overhead. Large objects also significantly increase the memory requirements of your application since the object I/O streams cache live references to all objects written to or read from the stream until the stream is closed or reset. Figure 4.4 shows the steps included in model or data serialization.

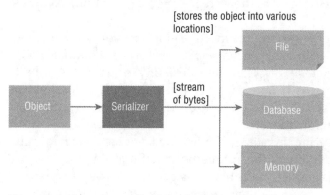

Figure 4.4: The concept of serialization

Another important aspect in the first manual setup in the serving layer is that there are no deployment processes in place and the activity to *understand and categorize target environments* therefore becomes entirely event triggered. Since this means that each model deployment also becomes a "happening," it includes manually triggered investigations as to where the AI model will be deployed and run. Hopefully this doesn't come as too much of a surprise for the team when it's time to deploy but that it has been taken into account during model development and training. If not, teams run the risk of having to redo or at least retrain your model. To mitigate this event-triggered approach, the next step toward industrializing AI means adding basic manual processes, which will create a repetitive and more reliable procedure, where important aspects are taken into consideration by the deployment team in time. It's still manual, but it creates a foundation for reuse and automating tasks in the next step.

The next step toward AI industrialization in AI life cycle management includes *coherent designs for data collection and feature management*. By focusing on a coherent design, you will build a solid and reliable foundation for managing your data and models efficiently over time, enabling industrialization and scale-up. The pieces must fit together, the process must be clear and predictable, and the design must allow reusability and flexibility. Technology-wise, this should ideally be supported by an *AI feature store*. A feature store is a data warehouse of features for machine learning. Different from a data warehouse, it is dual-database: one serving features at low latency to online applications and another storing large volumes of features. From an AI life cycle management (LCM) perspective, securing coherent designs and enabling easy, fast, and structured access to AI models are key pieces to enabling AI industrialization.

Even from a model serving perspective, the next step sets coherence as a priority, primarily securing a *coherent microservice generation process for specific target environments*. This offers flexibility in terms of reusability and consistency across various target environments (e.g., cloud versus edge deployments) and allows for controlled configurations rather than uncontrolled customizations.

Process-wise, during this step in the serving layer there are two maturity steps, and with any of the automation methods you use, the process automation is going to be either *attended* or *unattended*. In attended (human-initiated) scenarios, the process automation is suitable when you want to automate tasks and processes at an individual level. The automation is often triggered manually whenever the user wants to run it. The process might require human interaction or decisions between steps.

In unattended process automation scenarios, a designated computer or a server is set up to run the automation on behalf of a user. No interaction or decision is made by a human (with the exception of approval flows, in which the person doing the approving is considered to be technically a "third party" to the automation). The automated process can be triggered automatically from another system or service, or based on a schedule.

In the final step of AI industrialization as part of the AI life cycle management, *auto feature/data collection optimization* is introduced. Based on the coherent design established in the previous step, it can now be automated and continuously optimized based on automation results. Technology-wise, it is supported by *AutoML*. AutoML refers to the process of automating the tasks of applying machine learning. AutoML covers the complete pipeline, from the raw dataset to the deployable machine learning model. One major benefit of AutoML that is contributing to its growing popularity is its high degree of automation, which allows non-experts to make use of machine learning models and techniques without requiring them to become experts in machine learning. However, there are several concerns with AutoML related to lack of understanding what's actually going on. In other words, AutoML tends to become a "black box" solution.

On the positive side, automating the process of applying machine learning end to end offers the advantages of producing simpler solutions, faster creation of those solutions, and models that often outperform hand-designed models, making AutoML a major cornerstone in industrializing AI from an AI life cycle management perspective. Figure 4.5 illustrates the simplicity and speed enabled by AutoML.

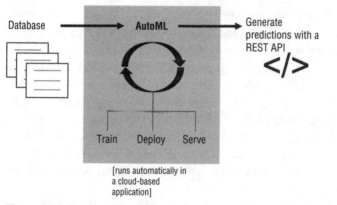

Figure 4.5: How AutoML works

Over the past few years, automatic machine learning algorithms have been used in areas such as image recognition, natural language processing, speech recognition, interactive AutoML optimization, semi-supervised learning, and reinforcement learning. But it comes with its own set of challenges.

AutoML faces problems such as data and model application. For example, high-quality labeled data is far from enough, and data inconsistencies during offline data analysis will impact model training. In addition, teams need to do automatic machine learning processing of unstructured and semi-structured data, which is technically difficult.

Furthermore, the current AutoML system optimization objectives are fixed, while real-life problems are often a combination of multiple objectives, such as the need to make subtle differences between decision making and cost. With this kind of multi-objective exploration, people have limited ways to effectively judge the model outcome on a real scenario before the results are obtained.

The actual business need may include customized requirements for the machine learning process, such as in a situation where only a certain type of data processing tool can be used. Such requirements cannot be met in a current black box AutoML solution.

Another drawback with AutoML is that it is more difficult to perform in a dynamic environment than in a static environment, since the environments keep dynamically changing. For dynamic feature learning, companies will need to adapt to changes in data in real time, detect distribution changes, and automatically adapt models. For AutoML to be efficient in a dynamic environment, it needs to be able to automatically perform model adaptation based on changes in the data distribution.

However, while automated machine learning models can find solutions, it may not necessarily be what the user wants. The user may want an explainable model instead. In fact, experts say explainability itself has great uncertainty, because everyone's understanding is different, and it has a relationship with personal judgment. It is even more challenging to make the model explainable when using AutoML, especially for people who don't understand ML. To manage this challenge, organizations have to work on advancing the development of standards related to explainable machine learning. AutoML can give the results, but then it's up to the experts to judge whether they meet the company standards for interpretable, explainable, and consistent models. For more on explainability in AI, see Chapter 6, "AI Is All About Trust."

In the serving layer, the final step toward AI industrialization introduces *intelligent process automation (IPA)*. IPA is an emerging set of new technologies that combines fundamental process redesign with robotic process automation and machine learning. It is a suite of business-process improvements and next-generation tools that assists the knowledge worker by removing repetitive, replicable, and routine tasks, simplifying interactions and speeding up processes.

IPA can also mimic activities carried out by humans and, over time, learn to optimize them. Traditional levers of rule-based automation are augmented with decision-making capabilities thanks to advances in deep learning and cognitive technology. The promise of IPA is radically enhanced efficiency, increased worker performance, reduction of operational risks, and improved response times and customer journey experiences—a true enabler of AI industrialization.

The Importance of a Cultural Shift

Getting to that ultimate state where the AI models are easily and automatically operationalized and the AI production line is fully industrialized is not an easy task, and an absolute must is a clear and fully management supported AI strategy. It's also important to understand that it will take time to get there. Teams, processes, and the organization all need to mature into this over time. Even your customers might not be ready to move too fast to the final stage, depending on the customer situation and product. In a business-to-business scenario, it's necessary to be prepared for the possibility that some customers will be requesting a fully industrialized and self-optimized AI solution early, whereas others might want to stay manual or semi-manual longer, until their own operations or product and services portfolio is ready to incorporate, deploy, and launch to their customers.

Company CEOs often recognize their role in providing strategic pushes for the cultural changes, mindset shifts, and domain-based approach necessary to scale AI, but few recognize their role in setting a strategic vision for the organization to build, deploy, and manage AI applications with required speed and efficiency. The first step toward taking this active role is understanding the value at stake and what's possible with the right technologies and practices. The highly customized and risk-laden approach to AI applications that is common today is partly a function of decade-old data science practices, necessary in a time when there was no easy way for practitioners to share work and there were few (if any) readily available AI platforms, automated tools, or building blocks that could be assembled to create models and analytics applications. In recent years, massive improvements in AI tooling and technologies have dramatically transformed AI workflows, expediting the AI application life cycle and enabling improved consistency and more reliable scaling of AI across business domains, although it should still be seen as somewhat volatile.

Gone are the days when organizations could afford to take a strictly experimental approach to AI and analytics broadly, pursuing scattered pilots and a handful of disparate AI systems built in silos. In the early days of AI, the business benefits of the technology were not apparent, so organizations hired data scientists to explore the art of the possible with little focus on creating stable models that could run reliably 24 hours a day. Without a focus on achieving AI at scale, the data scientists started creating entire system environments using their preferred tools to fashion custom models from scratch and preparing data differently for each model—so-called shadow IT. They left on the sidelines many scale-supporting engineering tasks, such as building crucial infrastructure on which all models could be reliably developed and easily run.

Today, market forces and consumer demands leave no room for such inefficiencies. Organizations recognizing the value of AI have rapidly shifted gears from exploring what the technology can do to exploiting it at scale to achieve maximum value. Tech giants leveraging the technology continue to disrupt and gain market share in traditional industries. Moreover, consumer expectations for personalized, seamless experiences continue to ramp up as they are delighted by more and more AI-driven interactions.

Thankfully, as AI has matured, so too have roles, processes, and technologies designed to drive its success at scale. Specialized roles such as data engineer and machine learning engineer have emerged to offer skills vital for achieving scale, although the really good ones are still hard to find and usually very expensive.

A rapidly expanding stack of technologies and services has enabled teams to move from a manual and development-focused approach to one that's more automated, modular, and fit to address the entire AI life cycle, from managing incoming data to monitoring and fixing live applications. Start-up technology companies and open source solutions now offer everything from products that translate natural language into code to automated model-monitoring capabilities. Cloud providers now incorporate MLOps tooling as native services within their platform, and tech natives such as Netflix and Airbnb that have invested heavily in optimizing AI workflows have shared their work through developer communities, enabling enterprises to stitch together proven workflows.

Alongside this steady stream of innovation, and as described in Chapter 3, MLOps has arisen as a blueprint for combining these platforms, tools, services, and roles with the right team operating model and standards for delivering AI reliably and at scale. MLOps is poised to do the same in the AI space by extending DevOps to address AI's unique characteristics, such as the probabilistic nature of AI outputs and the technology's dependence on the underlying data. MLOps standardizes, optimizes, and automates processes; eliminates rework; and ensures that each AI team member focuses on what they do best.

In many companies, the availability of technical talent is one of the biggest bottlenecks for scaling AI and analytics in general. When deployed well, MLOps can serve as part of the proposition to attract and retain critical talent. Most technical talent get excited about doing cutting-edge work with the best tools that allows them to focus on challenging analytics problems and seeing the impact of their work in production. Without a robust MLOps practice, top tech talent will quickly become frustrated by working on transactional tasks (for instance, data cleansing and data integrity) and not seeing their work have a tangible business impact.

Implementing MLOps requires significant cultural shifts to loosen firmly rooted, siloed ways of working and focus teams on creating a factory-like environment for AI development and management. Building an MLOps capability will materially shift how data scientists, engineers, and technologists work as they move from custom builds to a more industrialized production approach. As a result, the company leadership team plays a critical role in three key areas: setting aspirations, facilitating shared goals and accountability, and investing in talent.

CHAPTER 5

Operating AI Is Different from Operating Software

AI model monitoring is an operational stage in the machine learning (ML) life cycle that comes after model deployment. It refers to monitoring your ML models for things like errors, crashes, and latency, but most importantly, to ensure that your model is maintaining a predetermined desired level of performance in production. Monitoring ML models is an essential feedback loop of any MLOps system to keep deployed models current and predictions accurate, and ultimately to ensure that the ML models deliver value long term. Therefore, it's vital that the setup of your model monitoring has a good balance between these different aspects.

Observing and monitoring AI models in production, however, is often an overlooked part of the ML life cycle, almost like an afterthought, whereas it should be seen as critical to a model's viability in the post-deployment phase. Models have an afterlife of viability, and that viable life in production needs a constant watchful eye. Because AI is built on continuous learning principles, it requires another operational support model than traditional software. The feedback loop becomes fundamental, along with highly automated monitoring of model performance and data quality.

Model Monitoring

Model monitoring is vital to detect and address up front, since your models will degrade over time as you use them, a process known as *model drift*. Model drift, also known as *model decay*, refers to the degradation of a model's prediction accuracy due to various reasons.

Generally, a machine learning model is trained only on a sample size of the total data population and is typically due to a scarcity of labeled data, also called ground truth, or computational constraints of training on a significant amount of data. And although an ML model is built to minimize the impact of bias and to be able to generalize based on the data, there will always be data samples that your model interprets incorrectly, inaccurately, or simply below standards. Regardless how well trained your model is, continuous model monitoring will be required to ensure that deviations in model performance are detected without delay.

Furthermore, all AI models are optimized based on the contextual variables and parameters which are identified as relevant during model development. As a comparison, imagine how a spam detection model that was created 20 years ago would perform today. The Internet was barely a thing 30 years ago. Spam emails have become much more sophisticated and have changed significantly, so the spam detection model would probably not perform at all today.

Another factor that affects the contextual environment of a model, and its relationships between its variables, is our interpretation of data and how that varies over time. For example, a sentiment model created 10 years ago may falsely classify the sentiment of various words and phrases as the way we speak and words that we use as a constant, while in reality, the slang that we develop changes with time.

Another reason why model monitoring is important is related to upstream data changes, which refers to operational data changes in the data pipeline. In practice, this is a fairly common problem, as the data science team usually doesn't have control over every system where data is acquired from. For example, if a completely siloed software engineering team would change the measurements of a variable from Celsius to Fahrenheit even though the rest of the data is stored in Celsius, it could make it difficult to find the average temperature over time. Another example of an upstream data change is when a feature is no longer being generated, resulting in missing values.

Furthermore, the staging environment of a machine learning model is never completely synonymous with the production environment because the world we live in is always changing. It's because of these constant changes in society that it's so important to use an iterative approach as well. Constantly being vigilant of the health of your dedicated model servers or services deployed is just as important as monitoring the health of your data pipelines that transform data or your entire data infrastructure's key components: data stores, web servers, routers, cluster nodes' system health, and so forth.

Collectively, these model monitoring aspects are referred to as *model observability*, and this step has become an imperative in MLOps best practices. Monitoring the health of your data and models should never be an afterthought; rather, it ought to be a vital part of your model development cycle from the start and should be posted as requirements to the solution, like, for example, how fast the solution needs to react to a change.

Ensuring Efficient ML Model Monitoring

It's important to acknowledge that model validation results during development and training will seldom fully justify your model's performance in a live production environment. This is a key reason why you need to monitor your models after deployment—that is, to make sure they keep performing as well as they're supposed to. Model monitoring will assist you in tracking the model performance shifts that will eventually happen. As a result, you can determine how well the model performs over time, and it will also help you understand how to debug effectively if something goes wrong. The most straightforward way to track the model performance shift is to constantly evaluate model performance on real-world data.

Data quality monitoring is the first line of defense for production machine learning systems. By looking at the data, you can catch many issues before they hit the actual model performance. You can, and should, do that for every model. It is a basic health check, similar to latency or memory monitoring. It is essential both for human- and machine-generated inputs. Each has its own types of errors. Data monitoring also helps reveal abandoned or unreliable data sources.

Organizations often invest significant time and money in developing AI solutions only to find that the business stops using nearly 80 percent of them because they no longer provide value and no one can figure out why that's the case or how to fix them. According to McKinsey (www.mckinsey.com/business-functions/mckinsey-analytics/our-insights/scaling-ai-like-a-tech-native-the-ceos-role), recent figures from the software industry show that companies using comprehensive MLOps practices scrap 30 percent fewer models and increase the value they realize from their AI work by as much as 60 percent. Implementing proper MLOps practices obviously comes with a significant reward in terms of improved ROI.

One way they're able to do this is by integrating continuous monitoring and efficacy testing of models into their workflows, instead of bolting them on afterward, which is common and often futile, leading to additional costs before the model is ultimately abandoned. Data integrity and the business context for certain analytics can change quickly with unintended consequences, making this work essential to create real-time AI systems. When setting up a monitoring team, organizations should, where possible, make sure this team is independent from the teams that build the models, to ensure independent validation of results.

In an example from a pharmaceutical company, a company put a cross-functional monitoring team in place to ensure stable and reliable deployment of its AI applications. The team included engineers specializing in site reliability, DevOps, machine learning, and cloud, along with data scientists and data engineers. The team had broad responsibility for managing the health of models in production, from detecting and solving basic issues, such as model downtime, to complex issues, such as model drift. By automating key monitoring and management workflows and instituting a clear process for triaging and fixing model issues, the team could rapidly detect and resolve issues and easily embed learnings across the application life cycle to improve over time.

As a result, nearly a year after deployment at the pharmaceutical company, model performance remained high, and business users continued to trust and leverage model insights daily. Moreover, by moving monitoring and management to a specialized operations team, the company reduced the burden on those developing new AI solutions so that they could maintain a laser focus on developing new AI capabilities.

Model Scoring in Production

One of the main reasons AI models are built is for them to be used in production to support expert decision making in various ways across different use cases. This is true if your business is deciding what content your customers should be getting in emails or determining a product recommendation for a web page. AI models running in production have the ability to provide relevance and context to customers that drives your business forward.

For healthcare applications, this could mean recommending a patient to consult a health adviser for preventive care to avoid hospitalization. For retail, this could mean triggering inventory decisions ahead of peaks in demand. For financial applications, this may indicate a trading decision on a forecast on some market index. The list goes on. Nearly every vertical comes with tons of use cases where AI/ML can be efficiently used in production.

But how can you guarantee that a model built and trained in a lab will perform accordingly in production? A lot of trust is to be put on the performance of an AI model, so much that an entire company's reputation could be at stake. That's why you need ML model scoring in production.

A plethora of metrics can be used to evaluate ML models, and identifying the right metric to use is a crucial step for accurately assessing your model's performance and whether its predictions are trustworthy. One of the major challenges is that a model could simply memorize the data it is being trained with and consequently perform poorly on new, unseen samples. This is known as *overfitting* your model. In the case of classification, a model could also favor one class over another because the training dataset used contained an imbalanced number of samples from each class. Examples like these demonstrate why choosing the right metrics to evaluate ML models comprehensively is essential.

Evaluation metrics are designed to score different aspects of model performance for many diverse use cases. Remember, however, that evaluation metrics aren't universal and need to be tailored for your specific use cases. For example, in the context of airport security and threat detection, reducing the number of false negative predictions made by a model would be a huge improvement. Identifying a possible threat as passive could cause much more damage than incorrectly identifying something passive as threatening.

Let's suppose someone claims to have constructed a machine learning model that could identify threats boarding U.S. flights with 99 percent accuracy (the ratio of correct predictions over the total number of samples). This seems like a near-perfectly performing model, but is it trustworthy? Given (approximately) the 800 million passengers on U.S. flights per year, and respectively the negligible number of threats that boarded U.S. flights during the years 2000–2017, the model could simply be constructed to label all passengers as nonthreatening, achieving a high accuracy score. This case is an example of how imbalanced data can affect how a model's performance is incorrectly perceived when the wrong metric is chosen for performance evaluation. Rather than only reporting accuracy, reporting recall would be more insightful because it describes the model's ability to find all relevant samples in a given dataset. Even though the threat detection model in this example gives a near-perfect accuracy score, its recall would be 0, because it could not identify any relevant threats.

Assume a new model is designed to identify all passengers as threats. This would produce a perfect recall score of 1. However, the model would not be particularly useful (all passengers would have to be banned), but the way to conduct AI model scoring is to calculate the model's precision. Precision scores the model's ability to identify relevant samples only. In the case of the threat detection model, precision quantifies the ratio of correctly identified threats over all possible threats predicted (correctly and incorrectly).

In AI model scoring, some real-world scenarios require maximizing one metric at the expense of the other. In the case of preliminary disease screenings of patients, it would be ideal to achieve a near-perfect recall score (all patients who truly have the disease), at the expense of precision (the screening can be rerun to identify false positives). However, for cases where precision and recall need to be balanced, the F1 score (harmonic mean between precision and recall) can be used.

AI/ML processes in production works by "scoring" models on data in real-time or batch mode to make decisions. Decisions could be as follows:

- **Binary class:** Decide yes or no. Example: Spam or No Spam, Fraud or No Fraud, Buy or No Buy.
- **Multiclass:** Choose between A, B, C, D, . . . categories. Example: Recommend Product A, B, C, or D.
- **Numeric estimate:** Forecast or estimate a numeric value to act on. Example: Sales Forecast for Store X, this weekend.

Real-time scoring is excellent if you want millisecond response time in making decisions—for example, a retailer is offering recommendations to your users on a website dynamically. Real-time scoring is also instrumental in detecting and flagging fraud or for security when interactions are in flight. You can even think of real-time scoring in a healthcare environment to detect and alert when medical attention is required. In general, real-time scoring is used where your expert system should react and trigger downstream processes to mitigate something urgent, something that cannot wait.

Batch scoring, on the other hand, is useful when doing things like credit risk models and data drift is minimal in transactions arriving in your data lake or warehouse, and scores are considered stationary over a decent period. An example of this is when sending an email or triggering a customer service call to promote, up-sell, inform, or solicit more information from your customer.

The trade-offs in the scoring environment are also determined by how complex your final model is, like what algorithms were decided to use in scoring and the feature engineering effort to transform the incoming data before it's handed off to the algorithms in the pipeline.

Remember that model scoring can't happen without training. You should establish a training setup to support discovering new features, and do ultra-fast training with continuous or full learning as new data arrives, without overfitting your models. Models are expected to be scored with the best possible SLA given the trade-offs of training complexity and feature engineering involved, both real time and batch.

Monitoring loops start beyond software monitoring and logging, and depending on the problem, feedback loops can range from seconds to months (for example, in applications such as fraud detection). The choice of metrics will depend heavily on the context of the business problem and is subject to restrictions (i.e., if you want feedback in seconds but data is slower). Therefore, there are several metrics that you can use to monitor an ML model, and the metric(s) you choose depends on various factors:

- Is it a regression or classification task?
- What is the business objective (e.g., precision vs. recall)?
- What is the distribution of the target variable?

The following metrics are commonly used in ML model monitoring:

Type 1 Error   Also known as a *false positive*, this is an outcome where the model incorrectly predicts the positive class—for example, a pregnancy test with a positive outcome when you aren't pregnant is an example of a type 1 error.

Type 2 Error   Also known as a *false negative*, this is an outcome where the model incorrectly predicts the negative class. An example of this is when a result says that you don't have high blood pressure when you actually do.

Accuracy   Accuracy is defined as the percentage of correct predictions. It can be calculated easily by dividing the number of correct predictions by the number of total predictions.

Precision   Precision attempts to answer "What proportion of positive identifications was actually correct?" The precision is the ratio tp / (tp + fp), where tp is the number of true positives and fp the number of false positives. The precision is intuitively the ability of the classifier not to label as positive a sample that is negative. The best value is 1 and the worst value is 0.

Recall   Recall attempts to answer "What proportion of actual positives was identified correctly?" The recall is the ratio tp / (tp + fn), where tp is the number of true positives and fn the number of false negatives. The recall is intuitively the ability of the classifier to find all the positive samples. The best value is 1 and the worst value is 0.

F1 Score   The F1 score is a measure of a test's accuracy and the balance between precision and recall. It can have a maximum score of 1 (perfect precision and recall) and a minimum of 0. Overall, it is a measure of the preciseness and robustness of your model. The F1 score is 2 * ((precision * recall) / (precision + recall)). It is also called the F score or the F measure.

R-Squared (R^2) R-squared is a measurement that tells you to what extent the proportion of variance in the dependent variable is explained by the variance in the independent variables. In simpler terms, while the coefficients estimate trends, R-squared represents the scatter around the line of best fit.

For example, if the R^2 is 0.80, then 80 percent of the variation can be explained by the model's inputs.
If the R^2 is 1.0 or 100 percent, that means that all movements of the dependent variable can be entirely explained by the movements of the independent variables.

Adjusted R-Squared (adj R^2)   Every additional independent variable added to a model always increases the R^2 value; therefore, a model with several independent variables may seem to be a better fit even if it isn't. This is where adjusted R^2 comes in. The adjusted R^2 compensates for each additional independent variable and only increases if each given variable improves the model above what is possible by probability.

Mean Absolute Error (MAE)   The absolute error is the difference between the predicted values and the actual values. Thus, the mean absolute error is the average of the absolute error.

Mean Squared Error (MSE)   The mean squared error (MSE) is similar to the MAE, except you take the average of the squared differences between the predicted values and the actual values. Because the differences are squared, larger errors are weighted more highly, and so this should be used over the MAE when you want to minimize large errors.

Overall, the metrics that you choose to monitor ultimately depend on the task at hand and the business context that you're working in. For example, it's common knowledge in the data science world that accuracy metrics are irrelevant when it comes to fraud detection models because the percentage of fraudulent transactions is usually less than 1 percent. Therefore, even if a fraudulent detection model has an accuracy of 99 percent because it classifies all transactions as nonfraudulent, that doesn't help to determine whether the model is effective.

Another example is that the severity of a false negative classification when it comes to health screening tests is much worse than a false positive classification. Saying that a patient with high blood pressure doesn't have high blood pressure can ultimately lead to further health complications. This is much worse than saying that a patient has high blood pressure and conducting further tests, only to realize that the patient does not have high blood pressure.

Retraining in Production Using Continuous Training

One of the biggest mistakes data scientists make with machine learning is that they assume their models will keep working properly forever after deployment. But what about the data, which will inevitably keep changing? A model deployed in production and left to itself won't be able to adapt to changes in data by itself.

While MLOps does adapt two concepts from DevOps—continuous integration (CI) and continuous delivery (CD)—it also then needs a further pillar to account for the differences between development and machine learning. This is known as *continuous training* (CT) and it allows for both testing and retraining of models, giving us the *CI/CD/CT* approach. By appreciating the subtle differences and by adopting CI/CD/CT, teams can realize significant improvements with MLOps.

Continuous training is an aspect of machine learning operations that automatically and continuously retrains machine learning models to adapt to changes in the data before it is redeployed. The trigger for a rebuild can be data change, model change, code change, or reduced accuracy according to any of the metrics mentioned in the previous section.

But why is continuous training so important and why do you still need to change your model in production after spending so much time training and deploying it in the first place? Well, the simple answer is that in most cases *machine learning models get stale with time.* As soon as you deploy your machine learning model in production, the performance of your model starts to degrade. This is because your model is sensitive to changes in the real world, and user behavior keeps changing with time. Although all machine learning models decay, the speed of decay varies with time. This is mostly caused by data drift, concept drift, or both. As shown in Figure 5.1, model retraining is triggered when model performance decay reaches the predefined performance threshold.

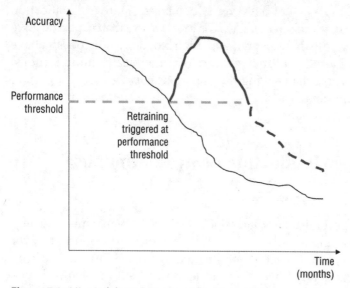

Figure 5.1: ML model retraining in production

It's important to understand your business use cases before retraining a machine learning model. Some use cases have a high requirement for when and how often you need to retrain your model. Business use cases like fraud detection and search engine ranking algorithms need frequent retraining, just like ML models trained on behavioral data, because behavioral data is dynamic. Manufacturing use cases, on the other hand, need less frequent retraining since manufactured data is more static.

There are four approaches to choosing a retraining schedule:

Retraining Based on Interval   Periodic training is the most intuitive and straightforward approach to retraining your model. By choosing an interval for retraining your model, you have an idea of when your retraining pipeline will be triggered—daily, weekly, monthly, or even yearly. Remember that retraining your model based on an interval only makes sense if it aligns with your business use case. Otherwise, the selection of a random period could lead to complexities and might even give you a worse model than the previous model.

Retraining Triggered by Model Performance   After deploying your model in production, you need to determine your baseline metric score. In this approach, the trigger for a rebuild depends on model performance degradation in production. If your model performance falls below the defined threshold, which is the *ground truth*, this automatically triggers the retraining pipeline. Remember that this approach assumes that you have implemented a sophisticated monitoring system in production. The drawback with relying on the performance of a model in production is that it takes time to get the ground truth. In cases of a loan/credit model, for example, it may take 30–90 days to obtain ground truth. What this means is that you need to wait until you get your result before triggering a retraining job and that might come with a business impact. However, this approach is very good for use cases that don't take long to get the ground truth. Figure 5.2 shows how retraining is triggered based on ML model performance degradation.

You can see that the performance of a machine learning model deployed in September keeps dipping with time and retraining is triggered (based on continuous performance monitoring) when performance hits the predefined threshold.

Retraining Triggered Based on Data Changes   By monitoring your upstream data in production, you can identify changes in the distribution of the data that feeds your model. This data monitoring can give you an indication of whether the model is running in a very dynamic environment, and when the model is starting to be outdated. However, remember that retraining should be triggered prior to reaching the performance threshold so that a new model is good to go before hitting the minimal acceptable level for the model. It will take some time to train and test the new model before

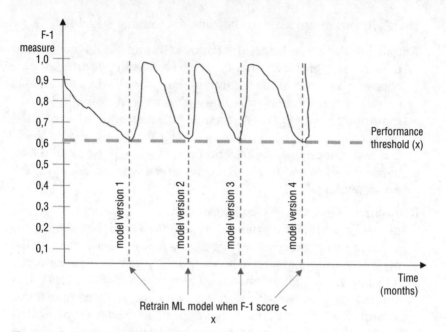

Figure 5.2: Retraining triggered by ML model decay monitoring

shifting over. Furthermore, it's wise to consider whether it's difficult or taking too much time to get ground truth from your model in production. It's also possible to combine this approach with the performance-based trigger approach. Data drift is a major reason your model performance dips in production, and in any case it might also lead to model performance falling below the accepted performance threshold. This approach will then automatically trigger a build for model retraining.

Retraining on Demand   This is a manual way of retraining your models and usually employs traditional techniques to retraining your models. However, retraining could also be scheduled (for example, every night) depending on data access and what type of use case it is. Most AI startups employ this technique in retraining their models, since it's a heuristic approach that might improve your model performance, but it's not the best approach. Remember that in an efficient ML production environment, your machine learning operations should be automated and proactive, not manual and reactive.

Data Aspects Related to Model Retraining

It's important not only to choose the right model retraining schedule depending on your business use case and context but also to know how to select the right data for retraining your models and whether or not to drop the old data.

In general, there are three things to consider when choosing the right size of data for retraining your models:

- What is the size of your data?
- Is your data drifting?
- How often do you get new data?

These three questions can help guide you in selecting one of three proposed approaches to getting the right data scope for retraining your model:

Fixed Window   This is a straightforward approach to selecting the training data for retraining the model. The approach will assist you in understanding whether your training data is too large to fit, and it helps you avoid retraining your model on historical data. By selecting data from x months to retrain your model, it's important to bear in mind the needed frequency of retraining your model. To succeed using this approach, it's vital to select the right window size, because if the window size is too large, you may introduce noise into the data. If it's too narrow, it might lead to underfitting. For example, if you've decided to retrain your model periodically based on your business use case, you should select data before your retraining interval. Hence, this approach is a simple heuristic approach that will work well in some cases but might be less suited in a dynamic environment where data patterns are unpredictable and constantly changing.

Dynamic Window   This is an alternative to the fixed window size approach. This approach helps you determine how much historical data should be used to retrain your model by iterating through the window size to determine the optimal window size to use. Consider this approach if your data is large and you also get new data frequently. Let's use an example to explain this.

Imagine that you trained your model on 100,000 records and now you have 5,000 new records available to you. You can make these 5,000 new records your test data and a part or all of the old dataset can be your training data depending on the best model performance on the test data after doing a grid search to select the right window size. In the future, a different window can be selected for retraining depending on the performance after comparing it with the test data.

However, although the dynamic window size approach eliminates the challenge of what window size to select from and is more data-driven, it also gives more priority to new data like the fixed window size approach. It's compute-intensive and takes a lot of time to arrive at the perfect window size.

Representative Subsample   This approach uses training data that is similar to the production data, which is the basic idea of retraining machine learning models. In order to achieve this, you need to first do a thorough analysis of your production data and exclude data indicating the presence of drift. Then you can select a sample of data that's representative of the population and similar to the statistical distribution of the original data.

Understanding Different Retraining Techniques

Let's assume that you deployed your model in production and also built a monitoring system to detect model drift in real time. After observing model performance degradation, you selected a retraining strategy based on your business use case and decided on a data scope for retraining. Now you're left with selecting tactics for retraining. There are different approaches to retraining your model, and the best approach depends (again) on your use case.

Continual learning is also called *lifelong learning*. This type of learning algorithm tries to mimic humans' ability to continually acquire, fine-tune, and transfer knowledge and skills throughout their lifespan. Continual learning is the ability of a model to learn continually from a stream of data. In practice, this means supporting the ability of a model to autonomously learn and adapt in production as new data comes in. A machine learning algorithm is applied to a dataset to produce a model without considering any previously learned knowledge, and as new data is made available, the continual learning algorithm makes small consistent updates to the ML model over time.

In order to better illustrate this concept, let's consider a use case where you're building a recommendation system for Spotify that recommends what kind of songs users are interested in listening to. In order to recommend new songs based on new interests, you need to retrain your model periodically because user behavior keeps changing with time.

Transfer learning is a machine learning technique that reuses an existing model as a basis for retraining a new model. It's basically a method where the learning happens through transfer of learning from a related task that has already been learned. A major advantage of transfer learning is the ability of a model to be retrained without rebuilding from scratch. It's an optimization technique that allows models to be trained incrementally and is widely used for deep learning algorithms. There are several pros and cons with using transfer learning versus continual learning in your retraining:

Transfer Learning

- Pros
  - Transfer of knowledge is an efficient approach. The model can be trained on a new task/concept.
  - It saves retraining time.
- Cons
  - This method is susceptible to data drift.
  - It has somewhat limited applicability, since transfer learning works well only when the initial problem is relevant to the new problem the model is trying to solve.

Continual Learning

- Pros
  - It retains knowledge after training.
  - It saves training time.
  - It makes the model auto-adaptive.
  - It continuously improves model performance.
- Con
  - This method is susceptible to concept drift.

There are also other retraining aspects you should consider—for example, if retraining should happen offline or online. *Offline learning* is also known as *batch learning*. You're probably already familiar with this type of learning technique but may not know it by name. It's the standard approach to building machine learning models. Basically, you get a training dataset and build the model on the dataset at once. An offline learning system is incapable of incremental learning. Once a model is deployed in production, it applies what it has learned and runs without learning anymore. Retraining your model with offline learning means building a new system from scratch with updated data. This approach is easy and straightforward, but you need to consider a retraining strategy, and coming up with one requires a clear understanding of the business objectives.

Online learning is also known as *incremental learning*. In online learning, you retrain the system incrementally by passing data instances sequentially. This means you're retraining your model as the data comes in. This type of learning makes it easier to retrain and makes no assumption about how the data is distributed. It takes no account of the varying customer behavior. It's also great for systems that receive data continuously, and it's cost-effective. In cases when your data is too large to fit, online learning is an acceptable trade-off. Online learning helps your machine learning model avoid data drift. If your application works on a real-time streaming data feed, then online learning is the method you should choose. However, it's important to be aware of the pros and cons with offline versus online training:

Offline Learning

- Pros

  - It's an easy and straightforward approach.

  - If the training data is properly selected depending on your use case, there is little or no room for data drift.

- Con

  - It takes a lot of time to retrain the model from scratch.

Online Learning

- Pros

  - It saves a lot of training time.

  - It doesn't require a lot of computing power.

  - It's cost effective.

- Cons

  - This approach is susceptible to concept drift.

  - It takes time for the model to converge to minimum compared to offline learning.

Deployment after Retraining

Even though you have retrained your model and the performance metrics look great, there's still a big risk that the updated model will perform worse than the previous model even after retraining. Therefore, it's a good idea to leave the old model for a specific window or until the model has served a particular number of requests. Then you can serve the new model the same data and get the predictions. This way, you can compare both models' predictions to learn which of them is performing better.

If you're satisfied with the new model's performance after that test, you can start using it confidently. This is a typical example of A/B testing, which ensures that your model is validated on upstream data.

Furthermore, it's best practice to automate the deployment of your models after retraining. For more on methods for model deployment in production, see Chapter 4, "Deployment with AI Operations in Mind."

Disadvantages of Retraining Models Frequently

Can frequent retraining be bad? Before considering retraining your models, you should be clear on the business use case and the retraining strategy. Remember that the right strategy won't necessarily mean frequent model retraining.

Retraining your model frequently can lead to complexities or hidden costs in the system, and it can also be error-prone. So, there should be a balance between retraining cost and the business objectives. Some of the complexities or costs that are associated with retraining your models are:

Computational Costs Training models on cloud solutions can be very expensive and can take a lot of time. If your strategy is to retrain your model daily on cloud GPUs, it will probably incur unnecessary costs, especially since retraining a model doesn't necessarily result in improved model performance.

Labor Costs Different teams are involved in a life cycle of machine learning model development, not just the data science team. Before a new model is deployed, it may require the approval of business stakeholders; then machine learning engineers have to worry about deploying it in production. This will be repeated every time a model has been retrained and needs to be redeployed and may cause delay or friction, particularly if your MLOps setup isn't as automated as possible.

Architecture Costs   If you retrain your models rarely, then it's easy to use a simple system architecture. But if you retrain your models frequently, you have to design a more complex system. You need to design a pipeline that retrains, evaluates, and deploys your model to production with high levels of automation and as little human intervention as possible.

Remember that in order to gain the most out of *continuous training* and *continuous monitoring* in production, it's important to apply the MLOps mindset in this phase. The end-to-end ML pipeline should follow the principles of automation, reusability, reproducibility, and manageability (see Figure 5.3). By applying these principles, you will be well equipped to protect your models from undesired performance decline and ensure that the quality of your model in production is up to date.

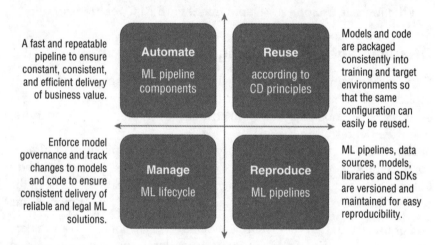

Figure 5.3: Four cornerstones for ML in production

By automating your ML life cycle to build, train, deploy, and monitor your ML models, you are better equipped to deliver your ML applications and the expected business value. Although innovation in this space is far from finished and will continue to see the creation of new tools and ideas for many years to come, MLOps has been able to introduce some particularly useful real-world concepts and technological developments in recent years. These include:

- Using well-established historic cases of fraudulent and legitimate transactions to ensure that the algorithm continues to correctly detect them in back testing while still learning.

- Building effective monitoring metrics that can have appropriately defined Red, Amber, and Green warning flags—for example, we may expect to have either 0.1 percent of all transactions being fraudulent or expect an approximate order of magnitude of 100 transactions per day being flagged. So, setting an Amber warning at 250 transactions per day or 0.5 percent would be a good start, and if fraudulent transactions exceed 10 percent of all transactions, the antifraud algorithm should be pulled into a fail-safe mode.

- Building models that have a training process embedded into them that potentially can be triggered by the monitoring tools.

- Continuous training as an additional part of the continuous integration, continuous deployment loop is a critical part of ensuring that models have longer-term sustainability and continue to deliver business value.

- Adopting containers for ML applications to simplify pipelines and deployment processes, while giving additional advantages such as automating scaling up.

- Increasing awareness of the importance of data pipelines for ML models, which means many organizations are now moving toward embedding data quality monitoring as part of their pipeline.

Diagnosing and Managing Model Performance Issues in Operations

Input data quality is the most crucial component of a machine learning system. Whether or not you have an immediate feedback loop, getting frequent feedback on how your model is performing in production is at the core of model monitoring.

In general, there are two types of data issues in an operational environment for your model that need constant monitoring:

- Something goes wrong with the data itself.
- The data changes because the environment changes.

Unfortunately, data problems are common issues that cause models to underperform or that even break the model entirely. Therefore, monitoring and managing data-related issues in production is vital to achieve good results from your AI solution in an operational environment. The following section describes common data-related problems, how to diagnose them, and how to address them efficiently.

Issues with Data Processing

A machine learning application usually relies on upstream systems to provide inputs. The simplest but unfortunately a quite common problem is when the production model does not receive the data. Or it receives corrupted or limited data, all because of some data pipeline issues. The problem is simple enough; it is detecting it that is the tricky part, eventually boiling down to the importance of knowing and understanding your data.

Let's use an example to explain this further. The data science team in a bank developed a mighty machine learning system to personalize promotion offers, which were distributed to their clients each month. The AI system they built used data from an internal customer database, clickstream logs from the Internet banking and mobile app, and call center logs. Also, the marketing team manually maintained a spreadsheet where they added each month's promo options.

All the data streams were then merged and stored in a data warehouse. When the model ran, it calculated the necessary features on top of the joint table. The model then ranked the offers for each client based on the likelihood of acceptance and split the result.

This means that the data pipeline used multiple data sources, with different functional owners maintaining each one of them. This is not an ideal situation and problems may result, such as the following:

▪ **Using the wrong data source.** The data pipeline points to an older version of the data table, or there could be an unresolved version conflict.

▪ **Access to the data is lost.** Someone moved the table to a new location but did not update the permissions.

▪ **Insufficient SQL usage.** Whatever is used to query your data, the JOINS and SELECTS might work well as long as the query follows the normal process. But let's say that a user is added from a different time zone and makes an action stating "tomorrow"? With such a query, it might not work.

▪ **Infrastructure changes.** A new version of a database is made available and some automated cleaning is initiated. Spaces are replaced with underscores; all column names are adjusted to using lowercase. All looks fine until your model wants to calculate its regular feature as "Last month income/Total income." With the hard-coded column titles, this becomes a mess.

■ **Feature code is broken.** To be honest, the data science code is not always production-grade. For instance, if the promo discounts were never more than 50 percent during model training and the marketing team suddenly decides to introduce a "free" offer and types 100 percent for the first time, some of the dependent feature code suddenly makes no sense and returns negative numbers.

When data processing goes bad, the model code can simply crash and the model stops working entirely, with potentially severe consequences—but at least, you'll learn about the issue fast.

The marketing promo example has batch inference, which is less dramatic. In that scenario you have some room for error. If you catch the pipeline issue in time, you can simply repeat the model run.

However, remember that in high-load streaming AI models, the data processing problems multiply, for example in models used for e-commerce, gaming, or bank transactions.

Issues with Data Schema Change

In other cases, data processing works just fine. But then all of a sudden, a valid change happens at the data source. Whatever the reason, new data formats, data types, and data schemas are rarely good news for the model. It's also not uncommon that the one making the change is completely unaware of the impact it has on various AI solutions, or even that models depend on that specific data source. Let's use the previous case to exemplify this further.

One day, the call center's operational team decides to tidy up the CRM system and enrich the information they collect after each customer call. The intention is to introduce better, more granular categories to classify calls by the type of issue. They also ask each client which communication channel they prefer, and start to log this in a new field. And since updates are already happening, they decide to rename and change the order of fields to make it more intuitive for new users.

It's important to understand that that this is an example of really poor data management culture and a severe violation against master data management. It wouldn't just destroy the AI models, but all SQL queries using the tables would be void too.

As you can see in the example in Figure 5.4, it looks much better after the change, but did anyone consider the impact on the model(s) and other systems using this data?

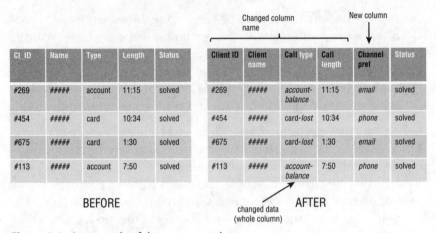

Cl_ID	Name	Type	Length	Status
#269	#####	account	11:15	solved
#454	#####	card	10:34	solved
#675	#####	card	1:30	solved
#113	#####	account	7:50	solved

Client ID	Client name	Call type	Call length	Channel pref	Status
#269	#####	account-balance	11:15	email	solved
#454	#####	card-lost	10:34	phone	solved
#675	#####	card-lost	1:30	email	solved
#113	#####	account-balance	7:50	phone	solved

BEFORE   AFTER

changed data
(whole column)

Figure 5.4: An example of data source updates

In technical terms, this means a lost signal. Unless explicitly told so, the model will not match new categories with the old ones or process extra features. If there is no data completeness check, it will generate the response based on partial input it knows how to handle.

This problem is usually well known to anyone who deals with catalogs. For example, in demand forecasting or e-commerce recommendations, there are often complex features based on category type, like, for example, "laptop" or "mobile phone" is in "electronics." They would be categorized as being expensive. That could turn into a feature. However, "phone case" is in "accessories," and falls under "cheap," which becomes another feature. All good and fine, but then, someone reorganizes the catalog. Now, "mobile phone" and "phone case" are both under "mobile." A whole different category, with a different interpretation. The model will need to learn it all over again or wait until someone explains what happened.

There's no magic going on here, and this is a common problem. However, if catalog updates occur often, it's vital that the data science team factors that into the model design or that the data science team simply tells them to stop changing it. It is important that the catalog team also understands that their actions may result in extra workload on the data science team, which is already swamped with work. Remember that team collaboration and sharing information is key. Furthermore, it's important to educate the business users and on a continuous basis keep track of sudden changes.

Let's look at some more examples:

- An update in the original business system leads to a change of unit of measurement (think Celsius to Fahrenheit) or dates formats (DD/MM/YY or MM/DD/YY).

- New product features in the application add the telemetry that the model never trained on.

- There is a new third-party data provider or API, or an announced change in the format.

The irony is, domain experts can perceive the data source change as operational improvement. For example, a new sensor allows you to capture high granularity data at a millisecond rate. Much better! But the model is trained on the aggregates and expects to calculate them the usual way.

Remember that a lack of clear data ownership and documentation makes data source updates even harder. There might be no easy way to trace or know who to inform about an upcoming data update inside an organization. Therefore, data quality monitoring becomes the only way to capture the change.

Data Loss at the Source

Unfortunately, that's not only the problem with data changes—data can also be lost due to some failure at the very source. For example, the application clickstream data could be lost due to a bug in logging; the physical sensor breaks and the temperature is no longer known; the external API is not available; and so on. It's vital to catch these issues early since they often mean the irreversible loss of future retraining data.

It's worth noticing, however, that such data outages may affect only a subset of the data—for instance, users in one geographical location or for a specific operating system. This makes these data losses even more difficult to detect. Unless another (properly monitored!) system relies on the same data source, the failure can unfortunately go unnoticed.

However, there's an even worse scenario, where a corrupted source might still provide the data, but the *wrong* data. For example, a broken temperature sensor could return the last measurement as a constant value. That is hard to spot unless you keep track of "unusual" numbers and patterns. Furthermore, it is even worse if this data finds its way into the training dataset and an updated model uses it. Then the updated model will also be garbage and continue to be so for a while even if the problem is located and corrected.

As with physical failures, you can't always resolve the issue immediately. But catching it in time helps you quickly assess the damage and take action. If needed, it's possible to update, replace, or pause the model.

Models Are Broken Upstream

In more complex setups, you usually have several models that depend on each other, meaning that one model's output is another model's input. It's also referred to as *nested models*. It also means that if one model's prediction is broken, another model's feature is corrupted.

Let's use an example of a content or product recommendation engine to further explain what this means. In such an example, a model might first predict the popularity of a given product or item. Then, it makes recommendations to different users, taking into account the estimated popularity. These would be separate models, basically looped into each other. Once the item is recommended to the user, it is more likely to be clicked on, and thus more likely to be seen as "popular" by the first model.

Let's use a more technical example, such as a navigation system of a car (see Figure 5.5). First, the system constructs possible routes. Then, a model predicts the expected time of arrival for each of them. Next, another model ranks the options and decides on the optimal route—which could influence the actual traffic jams. Once cars follow the suggested routes, this creates a new road situation.

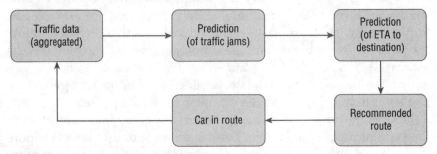

Figure 5.5: An example of nested models

The issue described in Figure 5.5 is also common in logistics, routing, and delivery services. These linked systems with nested models bear an obvious risk that if something is wrong with one of the models, you get an interconnected loop of problems.

Monitoring Data Quality and Integrity

As previously described, many things can go wrong with the input data for machine learning models. Of course, you never want these things to happen, but let's be realistic—they will happen anyway. So, make it your goal to catch them in time instead.

When it comes to data reliability and consistency, it usually falls under data engineering, as described in Chapter 2, "Data Engineering Focused on AI." But how do you set up your monitoring system? To start with, you might have some checks or monitoring systems at the database level. But is there anything else you need to keep an eye on?

The deal with ML systems is that it's not the overall data quality that is most important. Instead, you want to track a particular data subset consumed by a given model, sometimes even exclusively. It does not matter that 99 percent of data in the warehouse is correct; you want to check your specific piece. Furthermore, feature processing code is also a separate moving piece to monitor, which requires a custom setup.

So, on the data quality and integrity side, MLOps meets DataOps, and based on that, what are the things to monitor in production? Let's go through them one by one.

Monitoring the Model Calls

The first question to answer is whether the model even works. For that, look at the number of model responses. It is a basic but useful check to add on top of software monitoring. Why? The service itself might be operational, but not the model. Or, you might rely on a fallback mechanism, like a business rule, more often than planned.

However, if your model is used more seldom, this is less useful, but if there is a "normal" usage pattern, it is a great sanity check. For example, if your model is deployed on the e-commerce website and is fed every day with new sales data, you'll know then what consumption to expect. As shown in Figure 5.6, looking at the number of model calls is an easy way to catch when something has gone very wrong.

As you can see in Figure 5.6, the number of model calls fell to zero overnight and it's easy to understand that something has gone very wrong. Perhaps the service went down? However, depending on the model environment, you might want to check requests and responses separately. For example, was the model not asked (e.g., because a recommendation widget crashed) or did it fail to answer (e.g., the model timed out and you had to use a static recommendation instead)? The answer would point to where you should start debugging.

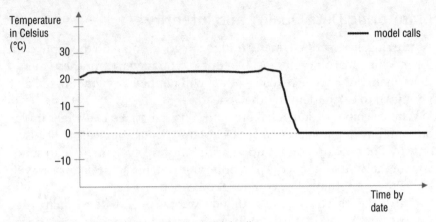

Figure 5.6: An example of monitoring model calls

Monitoring the Data Schema

As previously discussed, data schemas might change. It might be due to bad practices or best intentions; whatever the reason, you want to detect it in time. The goal is to understand when features get dropped, added, or changed. This is best approached by performing a feature-by-feature check and investigating the following:

- **If the feature set remains the same.** In the case of tabular data, how many columns are there? Is anything missing, or is anything new?

- **If the feature data types match.** Did you get categorical values instead of numerical somewhere? For example, you had numerical features ranging from 1 to 10 at a given column. Now when you query it, you see values like "low," "medium," and "high." It must be possible to detect this, and it is oftentimes the result of poor data management practices.

Remember that what you are striving for is a quick summary view that the incoming dataset is shaped as expected.

Detecting Any Missing Data

As part of your monitoring setup, you also want to be able to detect any missing data. Often, however, there is some acceptable share of missing values. It's too cumbersome and time-consuming to react at each empty entry. But what you want to do is to be able to compare whether the level of missing data stays within the "normal" range, both for the whole dataset and individual features. This should help you determine whether any critical features are lost.

Furthermore, it's important to keep in mind that missing values can come in many flavors. Sometimes they are empty, and sometimes they are "unknown." If you do a simple check for the absent features, you might miss those other ones. It's best to scan for standard expressions of missing data, such as "N/A," "NaN," and "undefined." Having an occasional audit with your own eyes is not a bad idea, either. If you have a limited number of features, you might visualize them all in a single plot.

Another way to approach this is to set a data validation threshold to define when to pause the model or use a fallback when, for example, too many features are missing. The definition of "too many," of course, depends on your use case and the model's cost of error.

Validating the Feature Values

It's important to remember that just because the data is there, it does not mean it is correct. And if you're not monitoring the quality of your features, your model output may be corrupted. Let's use a couple of examples to explain:

- After a slip in Excel crunching, the "age" column has values ranging from 0,18 to 0,8 instead of 18 to 80.

- A physical sensor breaks and shows some constant value for a week.

- Someone dropped a minus sign during the feature calculation, and you now see only negative sales numbers.

It's worth noting that the error generated through faulty Excel crunching is the type of error that may manifest itself months or even years after it is first introduced. And these are some of the trickiest problems to solve, since they were not a part of the latest changes. However, in all the preceding examples, the model still works and the data is available—but it is corrupted. To detect these types of problems, you need to monitor the feature statistics and distribution. This is most efficiently done by comparing the production distribution with the distribution during training, as shown in Figure 5.7.

So, how do you monitor the feature value range? For numerical features, check if the values stay within a reasonable range. For categorical attributes, define a list of possible values and keep an eye out for novelties. This can be done by directly defining your expectations (min-max

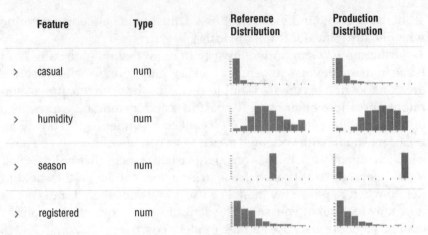

Feature	Type	Reference Distribution	Production Distribution
> casual	num		
> humidity	num		
> season	num		
> registered	num		

Figure 5.7: Monitoring the feature value distribution

ranges, or possible values at a given column) by looking at the training distribution. Another way of doing this is to rely on common sense, for example, that you know the possible values for "age" or the "outside temperature." Additionally, if there is more context, you can involve domain experts to define the normal distribution for the specific input. It also helps to explicitly state when nulls are allowed.

Then you need to monitor statistics for key features. For numerical features, you can look at the average, mean, min-max ratio, and quantiles. The latter would help catch the cases like the broken temperature sensor. Formally, it stays within the range, but the measurement is completely static, indicating that something is wrong since the temperature seldom stays exactly the same over time.

For categorical inputs, you can check the frequencies. If you work with texts, the equivalent might be a percentage of the vocabulary words, for example. The goal is then to monitor the live dataset for compliance and validate the data at the input. This way, you can catch when there is a range violation, unusual values, or a shift in statistics.

Monitor the Feature Processing

One more aspect to consider is where to run your data validation checks. When the data is wrong, the first question is usually, why is it wrong? In an ideal world, you want to locate the error as soon as you detect it. Broken joins or feature code can be a reason. In one example, the source data might be okay, but something happens during its transformation into model features.

It's also worth considering to validate the inputs and outputs separately for each step in the pipeline, simply because it's a faster way to locate the problem and debug it.

Let's use an example where customer churn is predicted for a mobile operator. Marketing data comes from one source. Purchase logs are joined with product plans that keep on changing. You then merge usage logs with external data on technical connection quality. Feature transformation takes several steps.

Of course, you could simply validate the output of your last calculation, but the drawback with that approach is that if you then notice some features make no sense, you'd have to retrace each step, which is very time-consuming. If pipelines are complex, separate checks might therefore save you some detective work.

Model Monitoring for Stakeholders

Who are the stakeholders who should care about machine learning monitoring? Well, anyone who wants to know about a certain model's impact on the business results. Yes, data scientists are the first role that comes to mind, but remember that once an ML model leaves the lab environment, it should be seen as a part of a company's assets. This is true whether it's intended to become part of a commercial portfolio or a part of the internal operational model. It's no longer just a technical artifact, but an asset that should concern a variety of business stakeholders who rely on it to deliver business results.

Various data science roles, users, and stakeholders have different interest in securing continuous ML model monitoring since both data and business teams need to track and interpret model behavior once it is deployed in production. Here are some examples of what different stakeholders need to understand:

- **Data scientist:** Does the model drift because of changes in the data?
- **Data engineer:** Is the model getting the right data?
- **Operational support:** Does the rapid model performance degradation mean that the model is broken and needs to be retrained or even replaced?
- **Product owner:** Is life cycle management of the model working?
- **Legal:** Is the model following applicable regulations?

- **Business user:** Can I trust the model prediction?
- **Business stakeholders:** Is the model delivering the expected business value?

For the data science team, it's about efficiency and impact. You want your models to make the right call and the business to adopt them. You also want the maintenance to be as smooth as possible. It's a fact that with sufficient model monitoring, you can quickly detect, resolve, and prevent incidents, as well as retrain the model as needed. Remember that leveraging capable observability tools will help you keep this under control and free up time to build new things.

For business stakeholders and domain experts, it ultimately boils down to trust. When you act on model predictions, you need a reason to believe they are right. You might want to explore specific outcomes or get a general sense of the model's weak spots. You also need clarity on the ongoing model value and peace of mind that risks are under control. Remember that the compliance team will scrutinize the models for bias and vulnerabilities, and since models are dynamic, it is not a one-and-done sort of test. You have to be prepared to continuously run checks on the live data to see how each model keeps up.

In order to stay in control over time and avoid becoming reactive in production, you'll need a complete view of the production model. That means you won't gain control just by monitoring your model; you need to ensure that you are monitoring the right aspect needed by the various stakeholders throughout the enterprise, even including customers.

The more complex AI solutions that are being put into production, the more the need to understand what's going on inside each model is growing, and it's understandable. If your customers are buying a service from you that used to be managed by people but is now to a large degree replaced with a highly capable AI solution, of course they would want some transparency into the solution. However, it's a tricky balance between being open and transparent about what's going on inside the solution without revealing company secrets. You can read more about explainable AI and handling intellectual property (IP) rights for AI models in Chapter 6, "AI Is All About Trust."

In order for your customers to trust your solution, they too want access to some form of monitoring capabilities. This could vary a lot, of course, from a simple dashboard showing model performance levels with live updates, to perhaps access to a digital twin of your operational AI solution, showing them exactly what issues and decisions that your models are managing on a continuous basis. With a proper model monitoring setup, this service can be provided and provide each party with the right metrics, visualizations, and insights.

Ensuring Stakeholder Collaboration for Model Success

AI adoption on an enterprise level can be a pain, and it usually gets worse after model deployment. But you're not alone; there are reasons this is particularly hard. In an ideal world, you can translate all your business objectives into an optimization problem and reach the model accuracy that makes human intervention obsolete. However, in practice, apart from inflated expectations, you often get a hybrid system and a bunch of other criteria to deal with: data access, ethics, fairness, explainability, user experience, or performance on special (nongeneric) cases. You can't simply blend them all in your error minimization goal. They need ongoing oversight.

We all know that regardless how fantastic the sandbox accuracy is, it makes no difference if the model never makes it to production or if the accuracy in production is terrible. It's vital to go beyond the proof-of-concepts or pilots that are needed in the beginning. You need to be able to show the business value with tangible results. For that, you require transparency, stakeholder engagement, and the right collaboration tools.

Remember that model visibility is key and will increase adoption levels as well as stakeholder trust, even customer trust. It will also be useful when the model performance is off track. For example, let's suppose that a model returns a "weird" response. The domain experts are the ones to help you define if you can or can't dismiss it. Or say your model fails on a specific population. Together you can brainstorm on new features to address this issue. Or suppose you want to dig into emerging data drift, adjust the classifier decision threshold, or figure out how to compensate for model flaws by tweaking product features. All of this requires stakeholder collaboration, and such engagement is only possible when the whole team has access to relevant insights. A model should not be an obscure black box system. Instead, you treat it as a machine learning product that you can audit and supervise in action. When done right, model monitoring is more than just technical bug tracking. It serves the needs of many teams and stakeholders and helps them collaborate on model usage, support, and risk mitigation.

However, in reality, there is a painful mismatch in the industry where research shows that companies monitor only one-third of their models. Unfortunately, this is the case with AI in production. The business value of monitoring models in production is not widely understood yet. Instead, a data scientist usually babysits the model and immediately after deployment, the feedback is collected and the data scientists iterate on the details, which keeps them occupied. Then, when the model is deemed fully operational, its creator leaves for a new model development activity and the model monitoring duty is left hanging in the air.

Furthermore, though some data science teams routinely revisit the models in production for a basic health check, they completely miss everything that happens in between these checks. Other teams are completely reactive and only discover issues from their users and then rush to put out a fire. Unfortunately, the solutions are customized, manual, and only partially covering the needed scope.

For the most important models, however, you might find a dedicated homegrown dashboard. These often become a monster of custom checks based on each consecutive failure the team encounters. If someone on a business team asks for a deeper model insight, this would mean custom scripts and time-consuming analytical work, so often, the request is simply written off.

It is hard to imagine critical software that relies on spot-checking and manual review. But these disjointed, piecemeal solutions are surprisingly common in the modern data science world. How can it be so different for models in production between software engineering and data science still? One reason could be the lack of clear responsibility for the deployed models. In a traditional enterprise setting, you have a DevOps team that takes care of any new software. With machine learning, this is unfortunately still a gray zone, but there are ways to combat these things through strong engineering principles and best practices.

Sure, IT could do some monitoring, but when the input data changes, whose turf is that? Some aspects concern data engineering, whereas others are closer to operations or product teams. The problem is that everybody's business is nobody's business. The data science team usually takes up the monitoring burden, but since they juggle way too many things already and rarely have incentives to put maintenance first, in the end the ball is often dropped.

So, what should be done to improve the situation with the lack of model monitoring of AI in production? Here are some proposals:

- Start applying production-focused tools and practices in your company. As applications grow in number, holistic model monitoring becomes critical. You can handhold one model, but not a dozen.

- Keep the data science team accountable. Machine learning models are deployed to deliver business value; to prove that value you need a structured way to show it clearly in production! This will also help you bring awareness to the costs of downtime and the importance of the operational support and the continuous improvement work also needed after deployment.

- Apply MLOps practices to improve how experiments are logged and deployments are managed as a vital part of the ML pipeline.

- Apply ML model monitoring as soon as your first model gets shipped. When a senior leader asks you how the AI project is doing, you don't want to take a day to respond. Nor do you want to be the last one to know about a model failure. Seamless production, visible gains, and happy users, business stakeholders, and customers are key for machine learning to scale with the business.

Toolsets for Model Monitoring in Production

Obviously, depending on what you want to monitor, your needs will vary. You might not even be interested in a full-blown ML model monitoring tool, or rather just some monitoring capabilities to integrate with your own code. In that case it could be worth checking out what's available in GitHub from Databricks, for example, where they have shared a Python library with model assertions for this purpose.

Whichever direction you decide to take, you should consider whether the selected path fits with your current system environment—for example, can you use Google Cloud Platform (GCP) tools to monitor your pipeline in Microsoft Azure or should you use something from Azure? Also remember that many tools come and go over time, and even if this new cool framework promises a lot of nice stuff, you need to ask yourself if you can count on it being around three years from now when your customers are asking you to troubleshoot their evolved (through time and retraining) models.

However, if you are interested in finding a capable ML model monitoring tool, there are some basic functionalities you should definitely consider. Here are some of these aspects:

- **Ease of integration:** How easy is it to connect the monitoring tool to your model training and deployment tools?

- **Flexibility and expressiveness:** Can you log and see what you want and how you want it?

- **Workload:** How much overhead does the logging add to your model training and deployment infrastructure?

- **Monitoring functionality:** Can you monitor drift related to data, features, concepts, and models? Can you compare multiple models that are running at the same time using, for example, A/B testing?

- **Alerts:** Does the monitoring tool provide automated alerts when the performance or input deviates from target or hits minimum thresholds?

Although the following is not an exhaustive list of ML monitoring tools, it will give you an idea of what's available in the industry as well as what can be expected from these types of tools:

Arize AI   In 2021, Arize AI was claimed to be one of the most promising AI tools by Forbes. This is an ML model monitoring platform that is capable of boosting the observability of your project and helping you with troubleshooting production AI. If the ML team is working without a sufficient observability and real-time analytics tool, engineers can waste days trying to identify potential problems. This tool makes it easy to pinpoint what went wrong so that software engineers can immediately find and fix a problem.

Moreover, it allows ML engineers to robustly update the existing models. Functionality includes simple integration, strong observability of any model in any environment, pre-launch and post-launch validation checks, and automatic and proactive monitoring capabilities with easy-to-customize dashboards.

Prometheus   Prometheus (and Grafana) is a popular combination of open source ML model monitoring tools that was originally developed by SoundCloud to collect multidimensional data and queries. The main advantages of Prometheus are related to the tight integration with Kubernetes and many of the available exporters and client libraries, as well as a fast query language. Prometheus is also Docker compatible and available on the Docker Hub.

Furthermore, the Prometheus server has its own self-contained unit that does not depend on network storage or external services, meaning that it doesn't require a lot of work to deploy additional infrastructure or software. The server reads targets at an interval that you define to collect metrics and stores them in a time-series database. You set the targets and the time interval for reading the metrics. You query the Prometheus time-series database for where metrics are stored using the PromQL query language.

Grafana Grafana allows you to visualize monitoring metrics and specializes in time-series analytics. It can visualize the results of monitoring work in the form of line graphs, heat maps, and histograms. Instead of writing PromQL queries directly to the Prometheus server, you use Grafana GUI boards to request metrics from the Prometheus server and render them in the Grafana dashboard. Key features of Grafana are alerts, dashboard templates, automation, and annotations.

Evidently Evidently is an open source ML model monitoring system. It helps analyze machine learning models during development, validation, and production monitoring. The tool generates interactive reports from the pandas DataFrame. Monitoring functionality includes data drift, numerical target drift (detects changes in the numerical target and feature behavior), categorical target drift, regression model performance and model errors, classification model performance and model errors, and probabilistic classification model performance and model errors (works both for binary and multiclass models).

Qualdo Qualdo is a machine learning model performance monitoring tool in Azure, Google, and AWS. The tool has some nice, basic features that allow you to observe your models throughout their entire life cycle. With Qualdo, you can gain insights from production ML input/predictions data, logs, and application data to watch and improve your model performance. It offers model deployment and automatic monitoring of data drifts and data anomalies; you can see quality metrics and visualizations. It also offers tools to monitor ML pipeline performance in TensorFlow and leverages TensorFlow's data validation and model evaluation capabilities. Additionally, it integrates with many AI, machine learning, and communication tools to improve your workflow and make collaboration easier. However, it's a rather simple tool and doesn't offer many advanced features.

Amazon SageMaker Model Monitor Amazon SageMaker Model Monitor is one of the Amazon SageMaker tools. It automatically detects and alerts on inaccurate predictions from models deployed in production so that you can maintain the accuracy of models. Model monitoring capabilities include customizable data collection and monitoring (i.e., you can select the data you want to monitor and analyze without the need to write any code); built-in analysis in the form of statistical rules, to detect drifts in data and model quality; and you can write custom rules and specify thresholds for each rule, and the rules can then be used to analyze model performance. It enables visualization of monitoring metrics and lets you run ad hoc analysis in a SageMaker notebook instance. It supports model prediction and lets you schedule monitoring jobs. Furthermore, the tool is integrated with Amazon SageMaker Clarify, so you can identify potential bias in your ML models as well. Finally, when used with other tools for ML, AWS SageMaker Model Monitor gives you full control of your experiments.

Neptune   Neptune is a metadata store for MLOps built for research and production teams that run a lot of experiments. You can log and display pretty much any ML metadata, from metrics and losses, prediction images, and hardware metrics to interactive visualizations. It's mostly used for model training, evaluation, testing, hardware metrics display, logging of performance metrics from production jobs, and viewing of metadata from ML CI/CD pipelines. Furthermore, it has a flexible metadata structure that allows you to organize training and production metadata the way you want to. You can think of Neptune as a dictionary or a folder structure that you create in code and display in the UI. You can build dashboards that display the performance and hardware metrics you want to see to better organize your model monitoring information. You can compare metrics between models and runs to see how a model update changed performance or hardware consumption and whether you should abort live model training because it just won't beat the baseline. You can log metadata you want to monitor via an API, and Neptune has available integrations with tools from the ML ecosystem.

Seldon Core   Seldon Core is an open source platform for deploying machine learning models on Kubernetes. It's an MLOps framework that lets you package, deploy, monitor, and manage thousands of production machine learning models. It lets you run on any cloud and on-premises, is framework agnostic, and supports top ML libraries, toolkits, and languages. Also, it converts your ML models (e.g., TensorFlow, PyTorch, H2O.ai), or language wrappers (Python,

Java) into production REST/gRPC microservices. Basically, Seldon Core has all the necessary functions to scale a high number of ML models. You can expect features like advanced metrics, outlier detectors, canaries, rich inference graphs made out of predictors, transformers, routers, or combiners, and more.

WhyLabs   WhyLabs is a model monitoring and observability tool that helps ML teams with monitoring data pipelines and ML applications. Monitoring the performance of the deployed model is critical to proactively addressing this issue. You can determine the appropriate time and frequency for retraining and updating the model. WhyLabs helps with detecting data quality degradation, data drift, and data bias. It has quickly become quite popular among developers since it can easily be used in mixed teams where seasoned developers work side by side with junior employees. The tool enables you to automatically monitor model performance with out-of-the box or tailored metrics and detect overall model performance degradation and successfully identify issues causing it. It allows you to perform easy integrations with other tools while maintaining high privacy-preserving standards via their open source data logging library called *whylogs*. You can use popular libraries and frameworks like MLFlow, Spark, and SageMaker to make WhyLabs adoption go smoothly. Furthermore, you can debug data and model issues easily with built-in tools and set up the tool in seconds with an easy-to-use zero-configuration setup and be notified about the current workflow via the channel that you prefer such as Slack or SMS.

One of the biggest advantages of WhyLabs for model monitoring is that it eliminates the need for manual problem solving and, consequently, saves money and time. You can use this tool to work with both structured and unstructured data, regardless of the scale.

CHAPTER 6

AI Is All About Trust

What does it mean to build trustworthy AI solutions and to operate your AI solutions in a reliable and legal manner? Despite the fact that the industry has made substantial investments in improving AI governance over the last couple of years, many companies still lack needed visibility into the potential risks their AI models pose. This includes taking control over how to mitigate the risks. This is a serious problem, given the increasingly critical role AI models play in supporting daily decision making, the ramp-up of regulatory frameworks, and the weight of reputational, operational, and financial damage companies face when AI systems malfunction, expose personal data, or include biases.

However, by leveraging MLOps practices in your company, you are taking a step in the right direction. It's important to understand that MLOps practices actually include comprehensive risk mitigation measures into the AI application life cycle by, for example, reducing manual errors through automated and continuous testing. Well-documented and reusable components also reduce the probability of errors and facilitate component updates. For example, companies using MLOps practices are starting to document, validate, and audit deployed models to understand how many models are in use, how those models were built, what data they depend on, how personal data is protected, and how they are governed. This provides risk management teams with an auditable trail to show regulators which models might be sensitive to a particular risk and how it's being corrected or monitored in order to mitigate the risk, enabling companies to avoid heavy penalties and reputational damage.

Anonymizing Data

Data anonymization is a technique to process data by encrypting, removing, or modifying data in such a way that personal information cannot be found in a dataset. This then results in anonymized data that cannot be used to identify a specific individual. The main purpose of data anonymization is to protect an individual's or company's private and personal activities. However, data anonymization cannot just happen. In order to maintain the integrity of the data gathered, there are various data anonymization techniques available to use depending on the specific need. Benefits and drawbacks with these techniques will be explained in the next section. Data anonymization is also known as *data masking*.

Data anonymization is carried out by most industries that deal with sensitive information such as the healthcare, financial, and digital media industries while promoting the integrity of data sharing. Data anonymization reduces the risk of unintended disclosure when sharing data between countries, industries, and even departments within the same company. It also reduces opportunities for identify theft to occur.

As an example, a hospital sharing confidential data on its patients to a medical research lab or pharmaceutical company would be able to do so ethically if it keeps its patients anonymous. This can be done by removing the names, Social Security numbers, dates of birth, and addresses of its patients from the shared list while leaving the important components required for medical research like age, previous illnesses, height, weight, and gender.

The flow of data anonymization shown in Figure 6.1 starts with the collection of the raw data from an external data source where the company collecting the data does not own the data being collected. Then, depending on the type of data that is being collected and the company policy for that specific type of data, an appropriate anonymization technique is applied on the data. (For more information about different techniques for data anonymization, see the following section.) Once the data is anonymized, the dataset can be safely stored and shared with appropriate stakeholders.

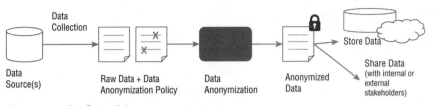

Figure 6.1: The flow of data anonymization

Data anonymization is one of the most commonly used techniques that organizations can apply to adhere to data privacy regulations. Data anonymization removes the personally identifiable information (PII) captured in things such as health reports, contact information, and financial details. However, even though the personal identifiers are cleared, attackers can sometimes use deanonymization techniques to retrace the procedure of data anonymization. It's important to be aware of that since data typically moves through several sources, some of which might be open to the public, and deanonymization methods could cross-reference sources and expose personal information.

Here are some typical cases where data anonymization is needed:

- **Research**—Researchers in areas such as healthcare may need to examine data related to, say, the spread of a disease among a certain population would use data anonymization.

- **Marketing**—Online retailers may seek to improve when and through which channels they best reach their customers, via digital advertisement, social media, emails, or their website. Digital agencies then use insights gained to meet the increasing need for personalized user experience and to refine their services. Anonymization enables them to leverage consumer data while remaining compliant toward data privacy regulation.

- **Software or AI development**—Data scientists need to use real data to train the models to deal with real-life challenges. This data should be anonymized for two reasons: 1) development environments are not as secure as production environments, and if they are breached, sensitive personal data would not be compromised; and 2) even though the data is used for AI model development purposes, data may still have to be anonymized to stay compliant with data privacy regulation.

- **Enterprise performance**—Companies often collect and analyze employee-related information with the motivation that it's needed in order to increase productivity and optimize business performance.

However, by using data anonymization, organizations can access valuable information without causing employees to feel monitored or exploited.

It's worth noting that in the European Union, the General Data Protection Regulation (GDPR) recently changed the definition of personal data. Where previous legislation défined personal data as "any kind of information directly or indirectly attributable to a natural person" (`https://gdpr.eu/eu-gdpr-personal-data`), GDPR now extends this definition to include information that is not in itself sufficient to identify an individual but that can do so in combination with other pieces of information.

"Personal data means any information relating to an identified or identifiable natural person. It is crucial that the task, individually or in combination with other data, can be tied to a living person" (`https://gdpr.eu/eu-gdpr-personal-data`). Therefore, what is considered to be personal data under GDPR becomes a matter of what other information the organization might hold, since it is the theoretical combination that determines whether or not it is personal data.

This brings additional complexity to data anonymization, since it means that you have to extend the scope of what needs to be anonymized beyond obvious data types. GDPR has therefore also adjusted the definition of data source. Where previous legislation focused on databases, GDPR applies to any source of information that can be searched. This includes, of course, databases, but also *unstructured data* such as files and emails, and even analog filing cabinets where the information is sorted in such a way that search is possible.

However, it's important to remember that GDPR does not contain any prohibition for the processing of personal data. Instead, it sets specific requirements on how and when personal data may be handled. In short, it requires organizations to

- Know where the personal data is located
- Provide access to the personal data through permissions and similar techniques
- Know and document what the legal ground is for processing the personal data

If these main rules are followed, there are no obstacles to processing personal data. It may seem like an overwhelming task for major companies to figure out where personal data is stored, not only as a onetime inventory but on an ongoing basis, but there are companies that specialize in this. For example, Aigine offers an AI-based software to help companies stay legal by identifying and managing personal data in both structured and unstructured data.

Data Anonymization Techniques

Not all datasets need to be anonymized. The data architect, in collaboration with the data engineer, should identify which datasets need to be made anonymous and which data can safely remain in its original form. Choosing which datasets to anonymize may seem like a straightforward task; however, "sensitive data" is a subjective idea that changes according to the individual and the sector, what the data will be used for, and in what detail the data will be exposed. For example, contact information could be seen as impersonal to a marketing agency's manager, whereas it may be viewed as highly sensitive by security personnel.

Most compliance standards and organizational policies agree that PII should be treated as sensitive data and stored safely. Therefore, such information should be seen as a perfect candidate for anonymization, but unfortunately this still leaves some room for interpretation. The main reason is that PII might mean different things in different industries, and there is also debate about the legal definition of PII in different places in the world.

The positive aspect here, though, is that there is a broad consensus about certain data being PII, regardless of legal or industry influence. Data types that always need to be anonymized include the following:

- **Name of an individual**—Regardless of context, a person's name is the most significant key identifier in any dataset. If this information is obtained by a cybercriminal, they can easily trace the source of a dataset.

- **Credit card information**—Credit card information (such as credit card numbers, expiration date, and CVV codes) and credit card tokens are very sensitive information. This data is also regarded as highly personal, is unique to an individual, and can have financial implications for an individual if compromised.

- **Phone numbers**—Remember that if a cybercriminal gains access to a phone number, they could also gain access to other, more sensitive data about an individual.

- **Photos**—With the image recognition techniques available today through AI, photographs are the perfect means of identification. Nowadays, photos are used for a variety of use cases where you need to verify a person's identity and to ensure security.

- **Any type of password**—A cybercriminal can more easily than you think gain access to personal data by compromising the password. In any backend structure created to store passwords, you should encrypt and protect your passwords end to end.

- **Security questions**—It's also possible to use personal security questions that different companies store as key identifiers. Many software services and web applications use these questions as a step toward granting user access.

Other data types that you need to anonymize (when applicable) are biometric data, political views, ethnic or racial data, and sexual orientation.

Remember that in order to establish trust with your customers and end users, you might need to go further than the actual legal requirements that apply in your specific country. Depending on what line of business you are in, brand reputation might be more important than cutting cost or being faster than competition. Perhaps the winning concept for your business is to be seen as conducting the most *trustworthy business*.

Once you have established what PII means for your company and line of business, you can use some common techniques to anonymize sensitive data:

Generalizing Your Data Involves intentionally excluding some data details to make it less sensitive. For example, data may be modified into a series of ranges where the house number at an address may be deleted. But make sure the name of the lane does not get deleted. The overall purpose is to remove some of the personal identifiers while maintaining the accuracy and integrity of the data.

Masking Data Refers to the exposure of data with purposely modified values. Data anonymization is performed by creating a mirror image of a database and implementing alteration strategies, such as character shuffling, encryption, term, or character substitution. For example, a value character may be replaced by a symbol such as * or x. It makes identification or reverse engineering difficult.

Pseudonymization Is a data deidentification technique that substitutes personal identifiers with false identifiers or pseudonyms. This can be done by swapping the identifier for one person for the identifier for another person. Using the method maintains statistical precision and data confidentiality, and allows changed data to be used for creation, training, testing, and analysis, while at the same time maintaining data privacy.

Data Perturbation   Modifies the initial dataset marginally by applying round numbering and adding random noise to the dataset. Remember that the set of values must be proportional to the disturbance you are creating. A small base can contribute to poor anonymization, whereas a broad base can reduce a dataset's utility. For example, a base of 5 should be used for rounding values like age or house number.

Data Swapping   Is also known as data shuffling and refers to rearranging the dataset attribute values so that they do not fit the original information. Switching attributes such as date of birth can make a huge impact on anonymization.

Using Synthetic Data   Refers to using algorithmically generated information with no relation to any actual case. The data is used to construct artificial datasets instead of modifying or utilizing the original dataset. The synthetic data method includes the construction of mathematical models based on patterns contained in the original dataset to produce synthetic results.

Pros and Cons of Data Anonymization

Obviously, there are many positive aspects of anonymizing data in order to protect individuals' personal information. However, it's worth reflecting on that from an analytical perspective; anonymizing data may hinder or limit what type of insights can be drawn from the data. But let's start by specifying the positive aspects:

Pros of Data Anonymization

It protects against the possible loss of market share and trust.   Data anonymization is a method of ensuring that the company understands and enforces its duty to secure sensitive, personal, and confidential data in a world of highly complex data protection mandates that can vary depending on where the business and the customers are based. Thus, it protects companies against the possible loss of market share and trust.

It safeguards against data misuse and insider exploitation risks.   Data anonymization is a safeguard against data misuse and insider exploitation risks that result in the failure of regulatory compliance.

It provides increased governance and consistency of results.   Data anonymization improves the quality of the data governance, as well as consistency of results. Clean, accurate data allows you to leverage apps and services and preserve data integrity and privacy in performing analytics and applying AI. It fuels digital transformation by providing protected data for use in generating new market value.

Cons of Data Anonymization

It restricts the ability to extract meaningful insights from data. The regulatory compliances require websites to receive permission from users to gather personal information, such as cookies, IP addresses, and computer IDs. Gathering anonymous data and removing identities restricts the ability to extract meaningful information from the results for many end user–oriented use cases applying analytics and AI. For example, anonymized data cannot be used for targeting purposes or personalizing the user experience.

It could cause overreliance in how resilient the data anonymization is.   According to research published in Science Daily (www .sciencedaily.com/releases/2019/07/190723110523.htm), it's easier than most companies understand to apply reverse engineering using machine learning to re-identify individuals in anonymized datasets, despite which anonymization techniques have been applied. This could result in sensitive information about personally identified individuals being exposed. The research demonstrates how easily and accurately this can be done—even for incomplete datasets.

However, even if data anonymization isn't 100% secure, it's what's legally required to ensure protection of privacy and it's still better than doing nothing. Remember that data anonymization is a way to demonstrate that your company recognizes and enforces its responsibility for protecting sensitive, personal, and confidential data in a world of increasingly complex data privacy mandates that may vary based on where you and your global customers are located.

An industry survey by PricewaterhouseCoopers in 2022 found that 85 percent of consumers will not do business with a company if they have concerns about its security practices (www.pwc.com/us/en/

services/consulting/cybersecurity-risk-regulatory/library/global-digital-trust-insights.html). And those customers who do entrust their sensitive data to companies will consider a breach of that data as a serious breach of their trust as well, consequently taking their business elsewhere as a result. Furthermore, it's also worth noting that the same report claims that only 25 percent of respondents believe most companies handle their PII responsibly.

In addition to protecting companies against potential loss of trust and market share, data anonymization is a defense against data breach and insider abuse. It's worth noting that the fine for a GDPR violation, for example, can be up to $24.1 million, or 2–4 percent of global annual turnover, whichever is greater for a large company. Even a single complaint can trigger a costly and time-consuming audit, so even if data anonymization might seem cumbersome, slow, and costly, the alternative could be a lot worse.

Explainable AI

AI has the power to automate decisions, and those decisions have business impacts, both positive and negative. Much like hiring decision makers in the organization, it's important to understand how AI makes decisions. A lot of organizations want to leverage AI but are not comfortable with letting the AI model make more impactful decisions because they do not yet trust the model. So, how do we achieve AI model transparency while harnessing the efficiencies AI brings? This is where the field of explainable AI can help.

Explainable AI (XAI) refers to methods and techniques used to explain to a human how an AI solution works. XAI is the opposite of the concept of the "black box" in AI, where even the data scientists that developed the models cannot explain why an AI solution arrived at a specific decision. XAI is relevant and important even if there is no legal right or regulatory requirement for it. Since we allow an AI solution to make decisions on behalf of humans, understanding how decisions were made ultimately becomes a question of trust. For example, XAI can improve the user experience of a product or service or assist potential customers in trusting that the AI solution is making good decisions.

XAI and interpretable machine learning (IML) are important and exciting new fields that are moving AI development toward more transparent modeling. They bring accountability and transparency to the black box problem.

Remember that one of the biggest challenges usually isn't building the right model; it's getting stakeholders to buy in that the model makes a better decision than a human. A better decision is not the same as higher accuracy scores. It's using the right inputs to derive a good answer. Usually the decision maker wants to understand the decision. Decision makers need to see how the model reasoned in order to be comfortable with allowing the model to make the decision in their place.

Complex AI Models Are Harder to Understand

Some ML models are quite easy to understand, where you know how changing the inputs will affect the predicted outcome and you can make justification for each prediction. However, with the recent advances in machine learning and artificial intelligence, models have in some cases become very complex, including deep neural networks and ensembles of different models. These models are referred to as *black box models*.

Unfortunately, the complexity that gives extraordinary predictive abilities to black box models also makes them difficult to understand and trust. The algorithms inside the black box models do not expose their secrets. They don't, in general, provide a clear explanation of why they made a certain prediction. They just give you a probability, and they are opaque and hard to interpret.

Sometimes there are thousands (or even millions) of model parameters and often combinations of multiple models using many parameters affecting the prediction. Some of these models also need enormous amounts of data to achieve high model accuracy. It's therefore sometimes hard to figure out what the models learned from the datasets and which of the data points had more impact on the outcome.

But what happens if the models learn the wrong thing? What happens if they are not ready for deployment? There is a risk of misrepresentation, oversimplification, or overfitting. Thus, you need to be careful when using them, and you'd better understand how those models work.

In machine learning, accuracy is measured by comparing the output of a machine learning model to the known actual values from the input dataset. A model can achieve high accuracy by memorizing the unimportant features or patterns in your dataset. If there is a bias in your input dataset, this will also affect your model. In addition, the data in the training environment may not be a good representation of the data in the production environment in which the model is deployed. Even if it is sufficiently representative initially, it can become outdated quickly, since the data in the production environment constantly changes.

Thus, you cannot rely only on the prediction accuracy achieved for a specific dataset. You need to demystify the black box machine learning models and improve transparency and interpretability in order to make them more trustworthy and reliable.

What Is Interpretability?

Interpretability means giving explanations to the end users for a particular decision or process. More specifically, it includes aspects such as these:

- Understanding the main tasks that affect the outcomes
- Explaining the decisions that are made by an algorithm
- Finding out the patterns, rules, and features that are learned by an algorithm
- Being critical about the results
- Exploring the unknown unknowns for your algorithm

Remember, interoperability is not about understanding every detail about how a model works for each data point in the training data; it's about grasping the bigger picture and being able to understand, as well as explain to others, how the model works in general, rather than for each specific case.

Furthermore, it's worth noting that interpretability is important to different stakeholders for different reasons. For example:

- *Data scientists* want to build models with high accuracy. They want to understand the details to find out how they can pick the best model and improve that model. A data scientist also wants to get insights from the model so that the findings can be communicated to the target audience.

- *End users* want to know why a model gives a certain prediction. They want to know how they will be affected by those decisions. End users want to know whether they are being treated fairly or whether they need to object to any decision. Being able to trust a model when they are shopping online, or clicking ads on the web, for example, is important for end users.

- *Regulators and lawmakers* want to make the system fair and transparent. They want to protect consumers. With the inevitable rise of machine learning algorithms, they are becoming more concerned about the decisions made by models.

Although these user groups think interpretability is important for different reasons, on a general level all three user groups want similar things from the black box models. They all want AI solutions to be transparent, trustworthy, and explainable. In this context *transparent* means that the system can explain how it works and/or why it gives certain predictions. *Trustworthy* means that the system can handle different scenarios in the real world without continuous control. And finally, *explainable* means the system can convey useful information about its inner workings for the patterns that it learns and for the results that it gives.

In a typical machine learning pipeline, that means you need to have control over the dataset used to train the model, have control over the model that you use, and have control over how you assess, deploy, and operate those models.

The Need for Interpretability in Different Phases

If you realize that need to improve the level of interpretability for your AI solution, first you must ask yourself why you need it. In which stage of the ML pipeline do you need interpretability? It may not be necessary to understand how a model makes its predictions for every application. However, you may need to know it if those predictions are used for high-stakes decisions. After you define your purpose, you should focus on what techniques you need in which stage of the process. Let's go through each phase:

Interpretability in Data Engineering   Understanding your dataset is very important before you start building models. You can use different exploratory data analysis and visualization techniques to reach a better understanding of your dataset. This can include summarizing the main characteristics of your dataset, finding representative or critical points in your dataset, and finding the relevant features from your dataset. After you have an overall understanding of your dataset, you need to think about which features you are going to use in modeling. If you want to explain the input-output relationship after you do modeling, you should start with meaningful features. While highly engineered features (such as those obtained from methods like distributed stochastic neighbor embedding [t-SNE], random projections, and principal component analysis [PCA]) can boost the accuracy of your model, remember that they will not be interpretable when you put the model to use.

Interpretability in Model Development   In general, you can categorize models as white box (transparent) or black box (opaque) models based on their simplicity, transparency, and explainability. *White box* (transparent) models—like decision trees, rule lists, and regression algorithms—are easy to understand when used with few predictors. They use interpretable transformations and give you more intuition about how things work, which helps you understand what's going on in the model, and it's pretty easy to explain them to a technical audience. But of course, if you have hundreds of features and you build a very deep, large decision tree, things can still become complicated and uninterpretable. For black box (opaque) models, like deep neural networks, random forests, and gradient boosting machines, the situation is a bit different. They usually use many predictors and complex transformations, where some of them have many parameters. It's usually hard to visualize and understand what is going on inside these models and it's a lot harder to communicate to a target audience. However, their prediction accuracy can be much better than other models. Recent research in this area aims to make these models more transparent, since some of that research includes techniques that are part of the training process. Generating explanations in addition to the predictions is one way to improve transparency in these models.

Interpretability in Production   Interpretability in the model predictions in production helps you assess the dynamics between input features and output predictions. Some post-modeling activities are model-specific, whereas others are model-agnostic. Adding interpretability at this phase can help you understand the most important features for a model, how those features affect the predictions in live environments, how each feature contributes to the prediction, and how sensitive your model is to certain features.

There seems to be little debate in the industry that building trust is essential for end users and customers to accept AI-based solutions and decisions made by them. There are, however, significant challenges in developing explainability methods to support this need. One of them is the trade-off between attaining the simplicity of algorithm transparency and impacting the high-performing nature of complex but opaque models. The reason is that when you increase AI model transparency, data privacy and the security of sensitive data come into question.

Another challenge relates to identifying the right information or knowledge needed by the user/customer to experience trust in the solution. Generating a concise (simple but meaningful) explanation on the right level to different stakeholders is a real challenge. Most explainability methods focus on explaining the processes behind an AI decision, which is sometimes agnostic to the context of the application, and then provides unrealistic explanations. This is being addressed in AI research, where the ambition is to integrate knowledge-based systems so that the explanation becomes relevant to each application's context.

Being aware of the importance of explainable AI for the users or customers of your AI solution is important, although there might not be ready-to-go solutions available to solve the problem at the moment. However, keeping the following properties in mind and continuously trying to achieve XAI in your AI solution(s) will help keep you on the right path toward delivering trust:

- **Trustworthiness**—Explain the characteristic and rationale of the AI model output.

- **Transferability**—Increase understanding by transferring (applying) the AI model on another problem.

- **Informativeness**—Inform a user/customer regarding how an AI model works in order to avoid misconception.

- **Confidence**—Ensure that the AI model is robust, stable, and explainable to gain human confidence in deploying an AI solution.

- **Privacy**—Ensure that the AI and XAI methods do not expose personal data.

- **Actionability**—Provide indications on how a user could change an action to yield a different outcome, as well as the rationale for that outcome.

- **Customized explanations**—Tailor explanations of behavior and predictions made by AI-based systems for users and customers based on their roles, goals, and preferences.

Reducing Bias in Practice

AI bias could be described as a phenomenon that occurs when an AI algorithm produces results that are systemically prejudiced due to erroneous assumptions in the machine learning process. Another common reason for replicating AI bias is low quality of data on which AI models are trained.

Societal AI bias occurs when an AI solution behaves in ways that reflect social intolerance or institutional discrimination. At first glance, the algorithms and data themselves may appear unbiased, but their output reinforces societal biases. It's vital to understand that the fundamental principle of bias is that it prevents you from being objective and you therefore need to present factual information and informed assertions that are supported with credible evidence. If you let your personal biases take over, you've missed the whole point.

So, what are the main reasons for bias in AI systems? Machine learning bias generally stems from problems introduced by the individuals who design and/or train the ML systems. These individuals could either create algorithms that reflect unintended cognitive biases or they could introduce real-life prejudices. But if humans are the source of AI bias and risk, how can you reduce the risk of introducing it? It's not easy, but it all starts with creating an awareness of the bias you might introduce. And there are things that can be done to remove or at least reduce the risk of injecting bias into your AI solution. Some of these steps are as follows:

Clearly define and focus the business problem. Trying to solve far too many problems often means you'll need a ton of labels across an unmanageable number of classes. Focusing your problem definition on a smaller scope to start with will help you make sure the model is performing well for the exact reason it was built.

Structure the data collection. There are often multiple valid opinions or labels for a single data point. Gathering those opinions and accounting for legitimate, often subjective, disagreements will make your model more flexible.

Understand the training data properly. Both academic and commercial datasets can have classes and labels that introduce bias into your algorithms. The more you understand and own your data, the less likely you are to be surprised by objectionable labels. Check also that your data represents the full diversity of your end users. Are all of your potential use cases covered in the data you've collected? If not, you may need to find additional data sources.

Secure diversity in the ML team(s). We all bring different experiences and ideas to the workplace. People with diverse characteristics, like gender, age, experience, and culture, will ask different questions and interact with your model in different ways. That can help you catch problems before your model is running in production.

Consider end users of your AI solution.   Likewise, understand that your end users won't simply be like you or your team. Acknowledge the different backgrounds, experiences, and demographics of your end users. Avoid AI bias by learning to anticipate how people who aren't like you will interact with your technology and what problems might arise in them doing so.

Annotate with diversity.   The more spread out the pool of human annotators, the more diverse your viewpoints. That can help reduce bias both at the initial launch and as you continue to retrain your models. One option is to source from a global crowd of annotators, who can not only provide different perspectives but also support a variety of languages, dialects, and geographically specific content.

Design your AI solution with feedback in mind.   Models are almost never static over their lifetime. A common mistake, which could have a large impact on the success of your AI solution, is deploying your model without a way for end users to give feedback on how the model is working in the real world. Opening up a discussion and forum for feedback will continue to ensure that your model is maintaining optimal performance levels for everyone.

Be prepared to update, adjust, and retrain the AI model based on feedback.   It's not only a question of continually reviewing your model using customer feedback, but you also need to be open to other relevant stakeholders and allow for auditing and identifying instances of bias you might've missed, and more. It's also a question of acting upon the feedback by retraining and adjusting the model to improve its performance, constantly iterating toward higher accuracy.

However, even if you actively initiate and enforce all the preceding activities as part of your internal processes, cognitive science research shows that humans have major difficulties in identifying their own biases. And since humans create algorithms, bias blind spots will multiply unless systems are created to shine a light, gauge risks, and systematically eliminate them.

The European Union has defined a framework to help characterize AI risk and bias. The EU Artificial Intelligence Act (EU AIA) is intended to form a blueprint for oversight of AI. The recommendation from EU AIA in how to take control of bias in AI development and operations in a systematic manner includes taking a holistic view, including addressing the following aspects:

Use analytics on AI performance for human oversight. AI systems should empower human beings, allowing them to make informed decisions and foster fundamental rights. At the same time, proper oversight mechanisms are needed through human-in-the-loop, human-on-the-loop, and human-in-command approaches. Human-in-the-loop systems are facilitated by model operationalization (ModelOps). ModelOps tools are like an operating system to algorithms. They manage the process, helping algorithms travel the last mile to be used by the business. ModelOps tools provide human-in-command tools to ensure humans have oversight into how algorithms perform, their historical performance, and their potential bias. Algorithm analytics help humans look inside an algorithm's judgments, decisions, and predictions. By analyzing algorithm metadata (data about AI data), human observers see, in real time, what algorithms are doing. Analytics on model metadata therefore helps put the human in the loop to exercise oversight over AI.

Ensure security and technical robustness.   Since AI systems need to be resilient, safe, and secure, you should have a fallback plan when something goes wrong and the fallback solution should be reliable and reproducible. That is the only way to ensure that both unintentional and intentional harm can be minimized and prevented. AI is deployed in many shapes and forms, and each deployment should include the latest security, authentication, code-signing, and scalable capabilities that any enterprise-class technology typically includes. These include but are not limited to two-factor sign-in, security models, and robust DevOps deployment paradigms. Enforcing sufficient security measures will at least help you to lower the risk of someone entering intentional bias into your AI system.

Establish solid data governance.   AI systems must ensure adequate data governance mechanisms, taking into account the quality and integrity of the data and ensuring legitimized access to data. Agile data fabrics provide secure access to data in any corporate silo to secure data and evaluate the results of the actions taken or recommended by AI models. This data fabric must adhere to data privacy and data protection standards found in regulations such as GDPR in the EU and the California Consumer Privacy Act (CCPA) in California and ISO standards for best practice software development for software vendors. Agile data fabrics help ensure that algorithms provide trusted observations, again minimizing the risk of entering bias into any part of the AI life cycle.

Strive for transparency. Data, systems, and AI models should be transparent, and traceability mechanisms will help you achieve this. Moreover, AI systems and their decisions should be explained in a manner adapted to the stakeholder concerned. Finally, humans must be made aware that they're interacting with an AI system and must be informed of its capabilities and limitations. Transparency is a blend of proper disclosure, documentation, and technology. Technologically, data fabrics, and model operationalization tools track and expose data transparency through change logs and history to trace and play back the actions of AI models. This data and model traceability, combined with proper disclosures and documentation, help make the data used, decisions made, and the implications of those decisions more transparent across the entire organization, including to customers and partners, ultimately assisting in the identification of any unwanted bias.

Prioritize AI model fairness. Unfair bias must be avoided because it could have multiple negative implications, from the marginalization of vulnerable groups to the exacerbation of prejudice and discrimination. To foster diversity, AI systems should be accessible to all, regardless of any disability, and involve relevant stakeholders throughout their entire life circle. Bias mitigation and reducing bias is hard, but the solution is hidden in plain sight: have someone else identify it for you! The collaborative aspects of agile data fabrics and AI model operationalization tools help provide teamwork surrounding AI bias analysis, collaboration, and mitigation and are therefore essential tools to consider for bias mitigation.

Express accountability for AI model outcomes. Self-guided mechanisms should be in place to ensure responsibility and accountability for AI systems and their outcomes. The subject of regulation, oversight, and accountability for AI ethics is massive. Modern data fabrics and model operationalization tools are the technological foundation of a new AI culture to raise awareness of algorithmic risk and bias and in raising the accountability bar.

There is no question that AI comes with a huge number of potential benefits for businesses and the economy, and for tackling challenges in society. But that will only be possible if people trust the AI systems to produce unbiased results. The interesting thing is that AI can actually help humans prevent bias in society—but that won't happen if the bias problem isn't taken seriously, and we as humans must work together to avoid entering our human bias into the AI solutions we build.

Rights to the Data and AI Models

Let's start by clarifying that whenever AI technologies work with information relating to individuals (or natural persons in legal terms), data protection laws will be applicable. Functionalities of AI tools may even work to include data that previously wasn't included—for example, being able to collect and connect data from different data sources that initially isn't referable to a specific person but where the analysis of the data could lead to the identification of an individual.

Developers of AI systems should therefore aim to integrate technical and organizational measures for data protection into the design of a solution. Using AI systems in business operations may additionally require a risk assessment regarding the protection of personal data and trigger an obligation to designate a data protection officer.

GDPR requires a legal basis for any processing of personal data and obliges the data controller to provide transparent information. If, for example, an AI solution is using natural language processing to assist employees of a support hotline in finding possible solutions for the callers, use of such a solution must be made transparent to the person seeking support. This includes providing information on its purpose and the legal basis for the processing. Depending on the nature and extent of the data processing (for example, storing and analyzing the voice of the person making the call in order to enhance the tool), consent by the data subject may have to be obtained.

With regard to using AI-based automated decision making, GDPR gives an individual the right not to be subject to a decision based solely on automated processing, including profiling, which has legal effects for the individual. With regard to AI, a broad range of software agents in sectors like banking and finance, retail, healthcare, insurance, and advertising may be restricted. The regulation applies where an algorithm (rather than a human) decides on the question of whether a certain service, payment method, or rate of interest is offered to the consumer (based on credit scoring, profiles on the consumer's personal preferences, or other data collected about the individual user). So, staying on top of potential data privacy concerns that might potentially be violated by your company's new AI solution, once it's operational, will be vital.

However, automated decision making can be legitimate if it is necessary for entering into a contract with a customer. For example, if a web shop uses an algorithm that collects credit reports from third parties and declines delivery on an account in case the customer does not meet a certain credit score, this may be justified by the shop provider's need to reduce its risks. In any event, the shop provider must inform the customer of the automated decision making and grant them the right to obtain human intervention and to contest the decision. But in a future that is quickly becoming characterized by artificial intelligence, legal challenges such as these will have to be managed more efficiently, but data protection laws should potentially also be more open to AI-driven decision making.

Data Ownership

Another area where companies using AI solutions will have to deal with new legal ground is data ownership. Within the European Union, there is no coherent approach on ownership of data as such. Restrictions on usage and disclosure of data other than personal data mainly stem from contractual relationships. Developers of AI tools and users will have to be clear on what they want to do with the data and what the respective contracts allow. Data ownership should therefore already be an item on the to-do list for any contract manager dealing with AI-related contracts.

An artificial intelligence due diligence will help with assessing risks and ensuring compliance on the one hand but also with gaining an overview of IP assets on the other hand. And it will be necessary with forward-looking contract design to prevent conflicts. An example of copyright problems may be prevented, for example, if co-authors of source code contractually deal with their rights beforehand, specifically if they use AI in developing such code.

The scope of copyrights on AI-generated content is subject to discussions and depends on national regulation rather than the EU legal framework. Starting from the insight that only humans and not machines have legal capacity to be creators of copyrighted works, copyright presupposes a certain level of originality of a human being. Drafting an initial source code that autonomously collects information and enhances its technique leads to the question of whether the result, like a software source code or an artwork, will still be considered a product of human creativity. Where artificial intelligence solutions directly create software code the answer might be "no copyright." Therefore, law firms working with AI are in the process of developing contractual tools to deal with these issues.

However, where no human creator is involved in creating the result, a company may still have IP rights created by their AI solutions. With regard to the technological capacity to structure and analyze information, database rights might apply. In the context of AI business models, data compiled by AI solutions may represent a protected database under this directive.

As the need to deliver value from AI system outputs becomes more urgent, smaller players will see their chance to stake a claim in this multibillion-dollar landscape. More than contractual rights, it's intellectual property (IP) rights that could give smaller companies the winning edge.

Advances in computing and the explosion of accessible, diverse, depersonalized, and valuable datasets are driving the latest AI developments. In turn, existing business models are being disrupted as companies scale up with vast amounts of structured and mature data, as well as unstructured data. One crucial issue is how to share datasets where parties are co-developing common AI ML-related products and services. Through a trained AI model (i.e., where an AI algorithm is fed data to learn), smaller players can control and own their IP rights, as well as claim new business models and seek a financial return.

Since IP rights may exist in the data or software under patents, trade secrets, copyright, and database rights, each of these requires a separate assessment, along with the main purpose of the AI model. An infringement risk analysis can further identify new product features, design workarounds, and more importantly, competitor differentiation.

IP protection should be considered before any disclosure requirements for transparency, explainability, and interpretability. This is because once trade secrets are publicly available, protection is lost. For novel features and functions worthy of patent protection, there may be options to prevent publication in the public domain during the filing process.

However, new business models must also take into account the growing demands of free access to valuable data and use of open source data toolkits. Understanding the legal implications of an AI model requires a collaborative multitalented approach to ensure that robust operational measures are incorporated into the compliance process. This must involve all relevant stakeholders, including development, deployment, and operations teams working together with IP lawyers (see Figure 6.2).

To move from structured learning based on labeled datasets to a system based on unstructured and unlabeled learning (e.g., for automated decisions), businesses must be able to open the black box and explain how the AI model works, what it learns, and how it makes decisions, as well as explain how outputs are generated.

This requires robust levels of scrutiny to be built into the model, such as introducing smarter labeling for datasets, thereby increasing trust in the model's decision making. It's also a good idea to involve a legal team when designing and developing an automated and AI-based

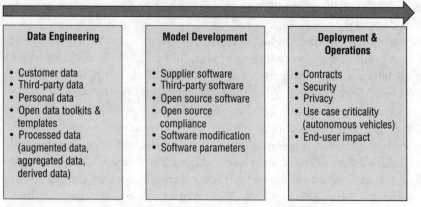

Figure 6.2: Understanding the legal implications of an AI model

decision-making capability. The legal team could then ensure that best practices are captured, making it easy to monitor and manage legal compliance over the life cycle of the AI solution(s).

Who Owns What in a Trained AI Model?

In a business example of ownership division related to an AI model (see Figure 6.3), the datasets needed to train the AI model are owned by Company A and the model is owned by Company B. Company B charges Company A for the use of the AI model, while Company A charges Company B for use of its datasets. These are used to produce a trained model adjusted for the specific context of Company A. Outputs or insights can also be sold to Company A in a business-to-business (B2B) setup or all the way to an end user in a business-to-business-to-customer (B2B2C) commercial model. The trained AI model here refers to the combination of the training data, the developed AI model, the trained AI model, and the generated outputs.

Figure 6.3: Legal entities of an AI model

Any data-related IP rights must be considered at an early stage in order to build an optimal data pipeline and to determine the full scope of the datasets, along with data readiness and data prioritization. Remember that the training data itself needs protecting too! It's vital to consider the following:

- What comprises the core datasets needed in your AI solution?
- Where do these core datasets originate from?
- Who has the rights to those datasets?
- How, and for what, are these datasets used?

The pipeline may include data from numerous sources, including third-party data, open data, text and mining data from research institutes, licensed data, and/or company-owned data. It is therefore crucial to determine some data fundamentals for the data pipeline from the beginning (see Figure 6.4):

- The type of dataset (e.g., real time, near real time, meta, supervised, or unsupervised)
- The category of the data (e.g., raw, aggregated, or derived)
- Third-party (including open) datasets

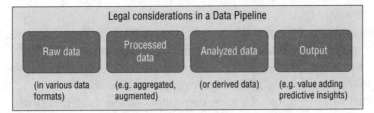

Figure 6.4: Legal considerations related to a data pipeline

Typically, raw data is ingested, preprocessed, tested and retested, curated, and stored in a cloud data lake and/or in open source machine learning software (e.g., API libraries). It is then combined with data from different sources through either aggregation or augmentation.

Derived data or second-generation data (typically owned by the creator) can't usually be reverted to raw data or used to replace it. As such, data input here cannot normally be unlearned.

It's important to know that data protection laws (e.g., GDPR) do not mention "data ownership." Instead, GDPR merely refers to the "data controller" as the party that determines the purposes and means for processing personal data and makes decisions about processing activities. However, data rights holders can carve out rights related to data with robustly drafted contracts, but these are personal rights binding only the contracted parties. Thus, it is crucial to consider IP rights (enforceable against the entire world with full remedial rights) alongside contractual rights. This is important, since there is also a total contrast between IP rights and data protection laws, meaning that maintaining secrecy under trade secrets can come in conflict with disclosure under audit rights.

While most raw data will likely lack novelty (datasets are not patentable per se), new elements or creative combinations may be considered novel and worthy of patent protection. Patents can be used to protect datasets or backroom datasets where data is part of an envisaged product (e.g., patents to software and business processes that manipulate and process data, rather than the actual dataset itself). For example, tens of thousands of patents have been filed worldwide covering data processing and encoding methods.

If patent protection isn't possible, or where it is likely that the datasets can be reverse-engineered, valuable training data should be protected as confidential information, trade secrets, or know-how. Here, company-wide processes and policies are key to show that reasonable steps have been taken to maintain the secrecy of valuable data. Creating a secure and trusted environment where valuable data can be processed and analyzed is crucial.

However, trade secrets in data cannot be shared or fully exploited without fear of copying. In this case, datasets should be prioritized, from sharable to protected trade secrets. Nevertheless, this still carries a risk that datasets may be revealed through reverse engineering.

Before choosing any course of action, data rights holders should ensure that they are able to answer the following:

- Are the raw datasets, derived datasets, or any other components of the AI model best protected as patents or trade secrets?

- Who owns or controls the use of the IP in the data or software (i.e., the data producer, data curator, data user, person producing the output, original software rights holder, or person/machine making modifications)?

- From the perspective of an end user seeking to commercialize data, what is the scope of permitted licensing (i.e., who can exploit what and when) over the life cycle of the trained AI model, given the proliferation of complicated, unclear, inconsistent contracts involved in a data pipeline?

- When balancing the interests of copyright owners in the data pipeline, what constitutes "fair use"? And what constitutes derivative works for outputs?

- What is the IP infringement risk? How can it be detected? Where is the infringement evidence? If the output is publicly available, can it be reverse-engineered (or disassembled)? If the output is stored in backend servers in the cloud, how would you identify the infringer?

- Is it possible to make a copy of the work for the sole purpose of research for noncommercial use? But what is considered commercial use when a company wants to exploit the research-based computational analysis results?

Balancing the IP Approach for AI Models

The AI algorithm normally undergoes swift updates in fast and agile development cycles. As such, it is not a good candidate for patent protection, given that patents are notoriously slow to grant and an application might be published 18 months after filing. Arguably, patent and data protection laws usually require some aspects of the solution being disclosed to prove that it's sufficient or to be more transparent about its capabilities.

Since the heart of an AI investment lies in the algorithms, which are usually kept secret under black box principles, it's vital that competitors be unable to understand how the machine arrives at its decisions during the processing of inputs to generate a specific output. In those situations, the algorithm is best protected under trade secret law.

But when it comes to patents for AI models, the problem is that the lack of disclosure may mean that the software is viewed as a nonpatentable abstract idea. Furthermore, the trained algorithm may not be sufficiently creative or inventive, since both are considered human traits requiring a human actor in the chain of control. Moreover, proving infringement of AI-enabled software patents and the operation of AI can be challenging. Unfortunately, all this can leave some patents seemingly unenforceable against infringers.

However, AI models may be patented where functionality can be protected for novel and inventive ideas. The challenge is to select an appropriate invention for patenting and to draft suitable patent claims, which cannot be reverse-engineered. Typically, it is unlikely that training data for machine learning algorithms will need to be disclosed to show the methodology (removing the black box problem). Nor is it always necessary to disclose how the output was discovered. Furthermore, a human actor is involved since all new inventions build on previous work, so the foundation of human intelligence is arguably always present.

In Europe, AI-enabled software can be patented as a computer-implemented invention. This covers claims involving computers, computer networks, or other programmable apparatus, where at least one feature is realized by means of a program and general methodologies. This does not involve computer programs being claimed as concrete software code, but rather a higher level of abstraction where there is a further technical effect that goes beyond the effects generated by any computer program and that is novel and nonobvious, and that has utility.

In the United States, claims on AI solutions are patent-eligible under US Code Section 101. Claims directed to an abstract idea may still be patent-eligible if the additional claim elements, considered individually or as an ordered combination, amount to significantly more than the abstract idea.

In the UK copyright protection is available under Section 178 of the UK Copyright, Designs, and Patents Act of 1988 for computer-generated works with no human author. The act states that the author of a computer-generated work is the person "by whom the arrangements necessary for the creation of the works are undertaken." The key is to build this into the operational steps of the AI model.

In the United States, a computer program can be protected if it is "an original work of authorship fixed in a tangible medium of expression," according to the US Code Section 101. The work must not be copied from a preexisting source, but it's fine if it only added a minimal degree of creativity and adaption.

The Role of AI Model Training

Let's be honest. IP ownership of a trained AI model is complicated. There are at least two moving parts as a result of the training process:

- Training data and the elements related to the data points
- The parameter settings of the algorithm

For example, a training dataset will train the complex underlying algorithms multiple times while parameters of the algorithm (e.g., the number of layers in a neural network) are adjusted to optimize performance. When training deep learning algorithms, the underlying algorithm is not usually subject to change, despite the fact that the parameters provided to the algorithm change. Here the parameters represent what is learned through training, not the algorithm itself. The algorithm can be used with new parameters to be retrained with new data.

Robust patent claim drafting can capture small modifications of concrete software code (and whether there are any as a result of parameter optimization) under broadly scoped claims for those modifications in the trained model; otherwise, trade secret protection should be maintained for any unique attributes for elements or parameters as the model learns.

If training does not alter the AI algorithm, copyright ownership will usually be retained by the owner or creator of the source code. However, copyright ownership in respective parties related to any software modifications based on the model learning should be considered, especially if they are specific to the model.

Typically, complex algorithms that underpin such AI inventions will lead to patentable technological advancements beyond abstract ideas. Here, patents have been granted for ML models or training methodologies, as well as AI-aided discoveries (e.g., for security operations, workforce management, network strength, call protection, marketing, and controlling social media).

Addressing IP Ownership in AI Results

IP ownership in output and insights, along with any other trends, recommendations, patterns, connections, or predictions, is another important area to address. These insights may come in the form of a decision tree, classification, cluster grouping, a list of prioritized outcomes, or a list of factors. The full scope of permitted use cases for all outputs across different industry sectors should be considered.

It's important to understand that copyright ownership can be claimed in outputs where there is a human such as a developer, user, or employer. Where there is no human element or it is difficult to identify the creator of the specific AI result, contractual provisions should identify who performed the work.

In the United States, the owner of a copyright prepares adaptations or derivative works based on copyrighted works. However, it's key to ask if the output is a derivative work of the input—that is, does the work recast, transform, or adapt a preexisting work? Anyone who violates the exclusive right related to derivative works is infringing the copyright.

In the UK, obtaining a copy of any copyrightable output, or making an adaptation, requires authorization from the copyright holder; otherwise, it constitutes infringement.

Legal Aspects of AI Techniques

We're already experiencing a world of data, and the expansion of computational power through AI will drastically alter the landscape of data privacy. A connected life through IoT devices and smart cities, fueled by AI, promises a wealth of potential benefits, including more dynamic use of resources, increased efficiency, and a higher standard of living. The possibilities that AI technology could provide in, for example, healthcare, manufacturing, transportation systems, the justice system, and government services are immense. Yet, as with many technologies before it, AI presents social, technological, and legal challenges to how we understand and protect data privacy.

However, while the long-held principles of data privacy may need to be reconceptualized, the emergence of AI does not mean that privacy will cease to matter or exist. Privacy provides an important framework for making ethical choices about how we develop, use, and regulate new technologies. It will also continue to be integral to how we mediate our identities, develop a sense of self, and realize other important rights, including freedom of speech and association. Answering the privacy questions raised by AI will be essential to the long-term success of artificial intelligence.

Moving forward, our understanding of AI and data privacy may see a shift in focus from the collection aspect toward emphasizing that the data is handled ethically and responsibly once it is obtained. Attempts to control or limit collection of data are likely to become increasingly difficult as data-collecting technology will be present everywhere. This would require a genuine commitment to transparency and accountability through good data governance practices.

Governments around the world have an important role to play in creating an environment in which a commitment to developing safe and fair AI can be balanced with technological progress. The right balance requires a consultative, interdisciplinary approach, as excessive, inappropriate, or misplaced regulation could slow the adoption of AI or fail to address its true challenges. Leveraging existing data privacy frameworks, as well as reimagining traditional concepts, will be a key component in building, using, and regulating AI in a relevant and efficient manner.

Different AI techniques also pose different challenges related to how decisions generated by AI models can be understood and explained. AI models in use today are referred to as *narrow AI*. This means that the models have been deliberately programmed to be capable in one specific area. It is sometimes also referred to as *augmented intelligence* to highlight its ability to enhance (but not necessarily replace) human intelligence. For example, a computer developed by IBM in the 1980s called Deep Blue can play chess at a level superior to human beings—a feat of huge importance in the timeline of AI development. However, although Deep Blue exhibits an above-human ability in chess, its intelligence ends there.

In contrast, the concept of *artificial general intelligence (AGI)* refers to a level of intelligence across multiple fields. The distinction between narrow and general intelligence is already apparent in the natural world. For example, that bees know how to build beehives and ants know how to build a nest are examples of intelligence in a narrow sense. However, this intelligence is specific to a certain domain, since bees can't build a nest and ants cannot build a hive. Humans, on the other hand, have the capacity to be intelligent across a range of areas and can learn intelligence in new fields through experience and observation.

Building on the idea of AGI, *artificial superintelligence* is generally regarded as AI that both is general and exceeds human levels of intelligence. In the book *Superintelligence: Paths, Dangers, Strategies* (Oxford University Press, 2014), author Nick Bostrom defines superintelligence as "an intellect that is much smarter than the best human brains in practically every field, including scientific creativity, general wisdom and social skills."

It's a fact that different AI techniques used today (within the narrow AI category) pose different challenges when it comes to explainability and transparency for both the data scientist and the end user of the AI model. One example of this is deep learning, which is a subset of machine learning and most commonly used to refer to deep neural networks. In generalist terms, a neural network processes data through a layered approach, where each successive layer takes its input from the output of the layer before it. The term "deep" refers to the number of layers in the neural network.

As the output of each layer becomes the input of the next in deep learning, it can become increasingly difficult to understand the decisions and inferences made at each level. The process of going through each layer can create what is referred to as the black box effect, making it challenging to truly understand and describe the steps that lead to a particular outcome. The nature of this process presents challenges for transparency of decisions, as the logic can become increasingly unclear to the human eye with each layer of processing.

However, as you might already know, deep learning is an extremely powerful technique, and many credit it for the recent explosion of AI. It has given computers the ability to recognize spoken words almost as well as a human, transformed computer vision, and dramatically improved machine translation—capabilities that are far too complex to code into machines by hand. When selecting AI techniques for your AI solution, however, it's worth considering whether a more traditional machine learning model could get the job done with a similar result. Not only is it more difficult to understand how a deep learning model arrives at an output, but as mentioned earlier, deep learning models are usually more expensive to train and also require an insane amount of data.

Operational Governance of Data and AI

In order to understand how to govern data and AI in an operational setting, as well as the role of intellectual property, it's fundamental to understand how the black box works and how training occurs in that context.

As you already know, neural networks (or deep-learning algorithms) are typically used for image processing or natural language processing, and they can be trained in at least two ways:

- *Supervised learning* involves teaching machines by providing them with labeled datasets and is predominantly based on structured datasets (e.g., learning a function that maps an input to an output based on examples of correctly labeled input-output pairs, before models can be used for inference).

- *Unsupervised learning* involves teaching machines to learn for themselves so that they can make their own decisions. Machines can then act autonomously or augment human decision making, where the target label or output is unavailable, and the learning involves, for example, clustering or segmentation.

While IP rights can be used to protect the supervised learning model provided that some transparency is built in, it is less straightforward in the case of unsupervised learning, especially for automated decision making. Contractual provisions are key when labeling is unavailable and where the human element necessary for IP protection is absent.

However, new interpretable or explainability models are being used in unstructured learning to ensure that the logic of the model can be inspected, audited, and trusted, and further to explain algorithmic outputs. In this way, it is possible to train the neural networks (see Figure 6.5) by introducing intermediary steps or extra outputs into the neural networks as cross-checks and key stepping-stones or operational workflows along the way.

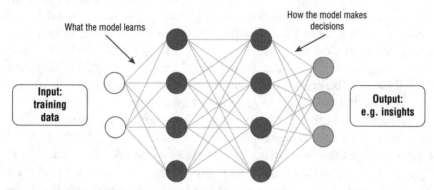

Figure 6.5: Explainability in a neural network

The key here is to determine what the neurons learn in the model and the decision-making process (i.e., how the algorithm makes decisions) before then translating this language (so-called *neuralese*) into English so that the output can be read by a human, thus building in a human element.

The role of IP law will depend on the operational steps implemented in the development of human-centric AI while tracking ownership in the data pipeline. That includes activities such as these:

- Identifying all human roles involved in training the AI model.
- Detailing of data flow activities during the life cycle of the model, including, for example, who owns the data, what is the source data, and where the data is sourced).
- Tracking data ownership (including third-party data).
- Identifying who the last human was to touch the model, for example, in review or validation of the output. If no human can be identified, was the data scientist the only person involved?
- Assigning and training reviewers to review machine decisions in order to determine what logic was involved in automated decisions and to assign needed authority.

- Monitoring the AI model during operations in production to understand and review model ways of working.

- Allowing interventions (including right to object) in real time by monitoring AI decisions. This can be done by using audit trails for explainability with rules on when and how the AI solution would augment or override human decision making.

Let's use an example to explain how to apply the licensing model in an AI operational setting. In this example, Company A owns the datasets and Company B owns the algorithm. Company A and Company B therefore have cross-license rights. Typically, Company B will have invested heavily in the algorithm (and its modifications) and has full ownership. It will base its business model on licensing the algorithm to multiple users. In exchange, Company A has full ownership of the outputs.

As shown in Figure 6.6, Company A is granted a perpetual, royalty-free right to use the AI algorithm and any modifications. All third-party rights (including open source) must also be considered. Meanwhile, Company B is granted perpetual rights to use the datasets in relation to the trained model. The scope of the license regards permitted use (including datasets), duration, sublicensing, any grant-backs, and rights to outputs.

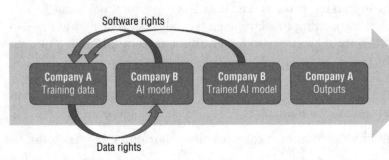

Figure 6.6: Cross-licensing AI and data

Let's use another example to explain how to apply an ownership model in a data and AI operational setting. In this example, Company A owns the trained AI model except for any underlying IP rights. This may avoid complex joint ownership issues given that property laws usually set high bars. In the UK, these include that the interests of all co-owners must arise at the same time (unity of time); be identical in nature, duration, and extent; and arise from the same document; and that each co-owner must have an equal right to occupy or possess the entire property.

In the United States, joint work is defined as prepared by two or more authors with the intention that their contributions will be merged into inseparable or interdependent parts of a unitary whole. Where Company A pays in full a onetime fee for custom, exclusively created software provided by Company B, it may be entitled to full ownership of the trained model with free, perpetual rights to any underlying IP. In this case, Company A may look for contractual provisions excluding competitors from use.

A trained AI model licensing scope includes the following:

- The source data
- The model purpose
- Usage scope
- Geographical limitations
- Internal usage scenarios (or sublicensing)
- Any particular exclusivity (or nonexclusivity)
- Irrevocable model aspects (or model revocability)
- Any tope of grant-back rights
- Handling of post-term rights (perpetual)
- The post-term duration of confidentiality
- Rights to commercial (or noncommercial) use

Remember that data protection laws do not address data ownership. Robust contracting for securing rights related to data is therefore key. IP rights are important because they are enforceable against the entire world (not just the contracting parties) and aren't limited to contractual breaches only.

Finally, it's quite obvious that a trained AI model and its components are best protected under database rights, copyright, patents, and trade secrets. Remember that data and its optimized elements may be valuable as confidential information, so IP protection should be considered before disclosure of any requirements.

In the absence of patenting, it is critical to show which reasonable steps have been implemented in-house to protect valuable confidential information and trade secrets and to carve out contractual confidentiality provisions that survive contract termination.

As AI solutions gets better at producing their own outputs (using automated decision making), it will blur the lines between human- and machine-created work.

Succeeding with your AI investment with regard to legal aspects of data and AI will be critical going forward and will most probably be easier for smaller, more agile players. The winners will be companies that are able to maneuver through the constantly shifting areas of IP, data protection, new data laws, new data governance laws, and new regulations that will appear. Intellectual property is a fundamental part of this and must be taken into consideration early and include all aspects of the AI decision-making pipeline, from data engineering, to model development and deployment, to full operation of the AI model in production.

Achieving Business Value from AI

As AI continues to capture the attention of the business community, some predict that this technology will foster the greatest period of transformation since the Industrial Revolution. Until now, a lot of the innovation around AI has been driven and commercialized by companies such as Google, Amazon, and Facebook. But that has begun to change.

As adoption of AI increases and spreads across various industries, companies can no longer afford to sit on the sidelines. As businesses from every sector start ramping up their efforts to integrate AI into their operational model, as well as their commercial offerings, companies must invest immediately in AI solutions or risk falling behind.

However, not all companies will be able to develop their own AI solution in-house, so to catch up with the tech giants, many smaller companies will need to seek technology partners to set up the least expensive, most effective way to harness the business value from AI. But as more and more AI models are put into production and used to make critical business decisions, the primary challenge of leveraging value from AI will change. The next major challenge will become operation and management of *multiple models in production*, and MLOps is the technical response to that issue.

Remember that MLOps practices are intended to improve the speed and success rate with which models are deployed into production and operated over time. Since model deployment into production is how machine learning creates economic value, MLOps practices is a means of achieving greater economic return from AI. MLOps practices will make sure that you are not only gaining value today, but that your company is positioned to manage the challenges of tomorrow, to continue harnessing the value of AI going forward.

The Challenge of Leveraging Value from AI

To understand the business impact of a balanced AI investment and end-to-end MLOps, it is helpful to view the potential business impact from four perspectives: productivity, reliability, risk, and people. Inefficiencies in any of these areas can significantly hamper an organization's ability to achieve scale and ultimately run into difficulties in leveraging the business value from AI. Let's walk through these aspects one by one.

Productivity

Unfortunately, it's not uncommon that companies say that moving AI solutions from concept to deployment (not even to running in production) takes nine months to more than a year, depending on industry. That is way too slow! The slow pace is also making it difficult for companies to account for changing market dynamics impacting the ongoing implementations. When it comes to managing updates and retraining models in production, it's even more important, with efficient pipelines and ways of working to secure productivity.

Even after years of investment in AI, it seems that companies implementing AI still aren't moving any faster. In contrast, companies applying MLOps can go from idea to a live solution in just 2–12 weeks without increasing head count or technical debt, thus reducing time to value and freeing teams to scale AI faster. It might sound like it's too good to be true, but it's achievable with MLOps. What you need is higher productivity and speed, which requires streamlining and automating processes, as well as building reusable assets and components. AI implementation also needs to be managed closely in terms of quality and risk so that engineers spend more time putting components together instead of building everything from scratch.

To achieve this desired productivity and speed, it's vital that companies invest in many different types of reusable assets and components. This makes it much faster and easier for teams to leverage data across multiple current and future use cases (internal as well as commercial), which is especially crucial when scaling AI within a specific domain where AI teams often rely on similar data.

An Asian financial services company, for example, was able to reduce the time to develop new AI applications by more than 50 percent. This was achieved by creating a common data model layer on top of source systems that delivered high-quality, ready-to-use data products for use in numerous products and customer-centric AI applications. The company also standardized supporting data management tooling and processes to create a sustainable data pipeline, and it created assets to standardize and automate time-consuming steps such as data labeling and data lineage tracking. This was a huge difference from the company's previous approach, where teams structured and cleaned raw data from source systems using different processes and tools every time an AI application was being developed, which contributed to a lengthy AI development cycle.

Another critical element to achieve higher productivity in AI is developing modular components, such as data pipelines and generic models that are easily configurable for use across different AI projects. To achieve that, you need to be prepared to invest in new operating models, talent, and technologies. Some companies solve this by setting up an AI center of excellence, hiring MLOps engineers, and then focusing on standardizing and automating model development to create "model production pipelines."

Reliability

It's a sad fact that companies tend to invest significant time and money in developing AI solutions only to find that either models are never deployed in production or the business stops using nearly 80 percent of them because they no longer provide value. It also seems difficult for companies to figure out why that's the case or how to fix the AI solutions.

However, based on statistics from McKinsey, it seems that companies that are using comprehensive MLOps practices discard around 30 percent fewer models than companies that haven't applied MLOps (www .mckinsey.com/business-functions/mckinsey-analytics/our-insights/ scaling-ai-like-a-tech-native-the-ceos-role?cid=eml-web). Furthermore, it also seems that companies using MLOps practices are able to increase the value they realize from their AI work by as much as 60 percent, according to the McKinsey report. How is this possible? Can it be so that applying MLOps practices is the answer companies are looking for when it comes to realizing the value of AI? Maybe MLOps isn't the only answer, but it's a fact that MLOps practices have been developed as a response to the challenges most businesses face in leveraging the expected value from AI.

One way MLOps practices can enable increased business value is by integrating continuous monitoring and A/B testing in production of models into the workflows instead of bolting them on as an afterthought. Data integrity and the business context for certain analytics can change quickly with unintended consequences, making this work essential to create real-time responsive AI systems. Therefore, when setting up a model monitoring team, organizations should, where possible, make certain this team is independent from the teams that build the models to ensure independent validation of results.

By automating key monitoring and management workflows and instituting a clear process for fixing model issues, teams can rapidly detect and resolve issues and easily embed learnings across the application life cycle to improve over time. As a result, model performance will remain high, and business users will continue to trust and leverage model insights daily. Moreover, by moving monitoring and management to a specialized operations team, you can free up time for those developing new AI solutions, leaving them to focus on bringing new AI capabilities to the market.

Risk

Despite many companies' substantial investments in data and AI governance, a majority of organizations still lack visibility into the risks their AI models pose, including which steps (if any) have been taken to mitigate the risks. This is a major problem, given the increasingly critical role AI models play in supporting daily decision making and business operations; the ramp-up of regulatory scrutiny; and the weight of reputational, operational, and financial damage companies face if AI systems malfunction or contain inherent biases.

While a robust risk management program should be a key part of any AI program, many of the measures for managing these risks rely solely on the practices used by AI teams. MLOps, for example, includes comprehensive risk mitigation measures in the AI application life cycle by reducing manual errors through automated and continuous testing, as one example. Furthermore, MLOps practices demand reusable components, with full documentation on their structure, use, and risk considerations, which significantly limits the probability of errors.

MLOps practices also enforce documentation, validation, and audits of deployed models to understand how many models are in use, how those models are built, what data they depend on, and how they are governed. This consequently provides the risk management teams with an auditable trail to show regulators which models might be sensitive to a particular risk and how they're correcting for this, ultimately enabling them to avoid potential penalties and reputational damage.

People

In many companies, the availability of technical talent is one of the biggest bottlenecks for scaling AI and thereby leveraging its business value. However, when deployed well, MLOps can function as part of a company's value proposition to attract and retain critical talent. Most technical talent get excited about doing cutting-edge work with the best tools that allow them to focus on challenging business problems and seeing the impact of their AI solutions live in production.

So, it's worth considering that in this competitive situation related to AI talent that exists in the industry today, attracting key talent is no longer only a question of the right salary level, access to data, a solid tech stack, or even interesting AI use cases. Without robust MLOps practices in place in your company, top tech talent will quickly become frustrated by working on transactional tasks (for instance, data cleansing and data integrity) and not seeing that their work has a tangible business impact.

Top Management and AI Business Realization

The much sought after, but very elusive, ability to capture the expected value of AI continues to be a challenge for many companies. However, company executives are starting to realize the importance of not getting stuck in endless loops of running AI experiments and proofs of concept. It's vital to understand that capturing lasting value at scale from AI requires a conscious decision to be taken, without fear of the fundamental transformation it will require both from an organizational and a business perspective.

A critical ingredient in leveraging the value of AI is investing in strong foundations. Building a strong foundation in AI includes many things, but the key is aligning AI across core areas of the business, such as the following:

- Embracing important cultural, organizational, financial, commercial, and operational shifts needed
- Investing in new kinds of technology and related data and system architectures
- Identifying and establishing new data science roles and competences (including the important operational roles)
- Investing in data science–related training for various stakeholders
- Scoping and designing end-to-end processes for developing, deploying, and operating AI
- Establishing production-like AI practices like MLOps for speed and efficiency, and securing successful data and model life cycle management, including development, deployment, and operation

More and more organizations are starting to adopt these basic practices, and those that do are also the ones that tend to report the highest bottom-line impact from AI. But successful organizations don't just behave differently; they are also thinking differently about AI. In companies that are leveraging business value from AI, there's usually a collective mindset in place where expressions like "AI first" or "We are AI enabled" are common. This is different from seeing AI as "Let's try and see what it means for our line of business" or "Here's a use case where AI can potentially add value."

Embracing AI fully through this type of mindset means deeply internalizing the long-term competitive benefits of augmenting human decision making and having the competence to do so in place. It means processing data from many sources at a massive scale and enormous speed, as well as continuously adapting business models and operational strategies based on patterns or deviations identified in the data.

This approach means prioritizing collaboration and continuous learning over individual knowledge and experience. It means encouraging employees to seek out new data, skills, workflows, and technologies for driving continuous performance improvements. This mindset also embraces end-to-end thinking and consistent architectural principles over siloed solutions when combining new technologies and tools with existing infrastructure.

It is worth stressing that the change this shift requires should not be underestimated. Company top management must lead the way, and all leaders must reorient their own thinking and then change every mindset in the organization. Getting all leaders to support this shift is imperative. The most successful companies' leadership teams are the ones who lay the groundwork for strong support up front. Such leaders take time to explore and share examples of AI-enabled companies inside and outside their industry and hire AI-experienced senior talent to fill the leadership positions required or to act as advisers on a very senior level to help drive the change—that is, if the talent doesn't already exist in the organization.

Successful companies also actively work to reduce hierarchy, make AI education a priority, and consistently communicate at every level the strategic nature of these changes. Flattening organizational hierarchies means restructuring the organization and enables frontline teams to own the responsibility to act on new AI insights. This type of built-in independence is key in building a strong AI foundation. It gives employees the confidence needed to widen their scope from identifying, for example, which customers are churning, to taking actions that bring the company closer to its customers. This can in turn potentially open a new wave of opportunities.

Leaders at AI-enabled companies also use a systematic approach to this shift, focusing on indicators of long-term ability to add value to the company. This requires company leaders to agree that the purpose of AI is to fundamentally transform the way the business conducts its day-to-day operations and ultimately its entire operational model. In practice, that means using AI in the end-to-end process of capturing every event or data point from customers, products, services, processes, and/or machines (a click, transaction, milestone, indicator, or sensor) to ensure that consequent actions, decisions, and interactions are more focused and effective—in other words, applying MLOps practices as part of the company foundation.

Truly embracing MLOps requires a significant cultural change and breaking apart siloed ways of working. It's vital to get teams focused on creating a factory-like and streamlined environment for AI development and operations. Building an MLOps capability will materially change how data scientists, engineers, and developers work as they move from customized builds to a more industrialized production approach. As a result, company top management will play a critical role in the business realization of AI in mainly four key areas:

Set the right expectations. As in any technology transformation, company management can break down organizational barriers by vocalizing company values and their expectations so that teams can rapidly develop, deliver, and maintain systems that generate sustainable value. Top management should be clear that AI systems operate at the same level as other business-critical systems that must run 24/7 and drive business value daily. While vision setting is critical, it's vital to be specific on what's expected and what will be measured.

Be clear on accountability. Clearly communicate that goals are shared within the company and that the ambition is joint accountability among business, AI, data, and IT teams. One of the fundamental checkpoints for impact is the degree to which goals are shared across business leaders and the respective AI, data, and IT teams. Ideally, the majority of goals for AI and data teams should be in service of business leaders' goals. Consequently, business leaders should be able to articulate what value they expect from AI and how it should be realized.

Invest in AI talent. The role of data scientists is changing. While they might previously have depended on low-level coding, they must now possess knowledge of software engineering to assemble models from modular components and build production-ready AI applications from the start, as part of applying an operational mindset. Newer roles needed on AI teams have emerged as well. One is that of the machine learning engineer who is skilled in turning AI models into enterprise-grade production systems that run reliably.

Address key technology investments with flexibility. Another vital aspect is the level of collaboration around strategic technology investments to provision tooling, technologies, and platforms that optimize AI workflows. With the rapid pace of technological change, IT often struggles to balance the need for new AI tooling and technologies supporting the rapid evolution in AI with concerns that short-term fixes increase technology costs over the long term. Comprehensive MLOps practices ensure a road map to reduce both complexity and technical debt when integrating new technologies. Most AI leaders usually spend significant time building strong relationships with their IT counterparts to gain the support they need, but when top management actively encourages these partnerships, it accelerates their development considerably.

It's vital to realize that AI is no longer just a frontier for exploration. It has so much more potential for businesses. However, while organizations increasingly realize value from AI applications, many fail to scale up because they lack the right operational practices, tools, and teams. As demand for AI has grown, so has the pace of technological innovations that can automate and simplify building and maintaining AI systems. MLOps can help companies incorporate these tools with proven software engineering practices to accelerate the development of reliable AI systems. With knowledge of what good MLOps can do and what levers to pull, company leadership can facilitate the shift to more systematic AI development and operations, ultimately enabling more business value to be gained from the AI investment.

Measuring AI Business Value

As enterprises from every industry pour money into AI, it's important to remember that this is still an early adopter market, and the business impacts of many of these implementations are still very much in the "wait and see" phase. But even as organizations rush to implement AI strategies to align with their own digital transformation journeys, it's important to shift the conversation around AI from simply "Everyone needs it" to focusing on how to truly derive value from and measure the success of these initiatives.

Measuring the business success of AI is a complex question. For some companies, these solutions are a labor and cost savings measure and should be analyzed accordingly. Other implementations are tied to revenue generation, whereas some might not fit so nicely into "hard" metrics. So how can companies really know if things are working or, if they're just starting out, how can they at least tell if they're heading in the right direction? As you might understand, there's no silver bullet to this question, but before diving into how to identify relevant AI business metrics for your company, I would urge you to ask yourself three high-level questions when evaluating whether your AI initiative will be worthwhile:

Will your AI solution increase productivity through the automation of routine decisions and augmentation of decision making? Automating routine decisions that fall under fairly rigid, established parameters is a perfect use case for AI. Imagine how powerful it would be if, rather than having to manually run data analysis, employees were given access to tools that automatically present them with simple, reliable, and machine-accurate recommendations of the next business actions they should take, as well as having tools augmenting them to do more complex tasks.

Will incorporating AI into your business model lead to a reduction of errors and biases?   Humans, no matter how intelligent, are prone to error and bias when it comes to data analysis, as we discussed in Chapter 6, "AI Is All About Trust." Fortunately, AI is ideal for cutting down on servicing mistakes, human-driven interpretation errors, and incorrect financial projections. Machines are getting better at extracting insights from complex data than humans are.

Can you leverage AI to deepen your customer relationships with new products?   Incorporating AI into your business model can benefit your customers in ways that facilitate a better customer experience and better relationships, and can create opportunities for new revenue streams. And if those three things are happening, your AI program is already a success.

If your AI initiative addresses one or several of the preceding questions, it's a good starting point. However, it's not uncommon that business cases for AI initiatives sometimes tend to become unrealistic and difficult to measure. That is not good. Everyone involved in leading or financing a companywide AI initiative must be able to understand its potential in more detail, as well as set clear objectives related to the company ambition. In short, each company should know the real status of its processes, activities, and routines, and the right way to know it is to use measurements.

As you know, there are many methods and approaches for quantifying incomes and results, profits and costs, customer satisfaction, and so on, but what about AI? How can you understand and measure the impact of AI on your business? Well, in order to evaluate the impact, you will need to define some business metrics that are valid for your company. First, let's start with some general metrics related to the actual transformation activity needed to introduce AI in your company:

- **Measurable results**—Transformation project results should be measurable. This is important both for assignment and technical specifications but also for proving the business value that AI brings. The project should have clear success and failure criteria. A good starting point is to combine AI and automation initiatives, since most automation initiatives should be in line with what's needed for AI already.

- **Progress reporting**—Make sure to stay informed on how the project is progressing. Is it in the right direction or not? Remember that AI initiatives can have many right directions. The project development team should know the applicable metrics. A specific feature of AI initiatives is that the impact on business results can be hard to identify. However, once that is identified and agreed upon, make sure to track the project metrics continuously.

▪ **Business value**—It's vital to fully understand the expected value from the AI initiative, especially for business planning and for managing expectations. Remember that the real value from your AI investment won't be understood until it's finally tested on real data, in a live production environment. Therefore, it's worth spending some extra time to investigate, calculate, and estimate the real impact on your business from AI.

So, how should you identify and specify the right metrics for measuring the business value of your AI initiative? Well, calculating the impact on the company's profit is a generic and very high-level starting point for AI measurement (valid for most companies) that is used in the example that follows. Of course, there could be other relevant starting points depending on what line of business your company is in and what the main purpose of adopting AI in your business is. Nevertheless, increased profit is the main objective in the following example, which explains the high-level steps you need to take to identify and specify the right AI metrics for your company:

1. Decide how the impact on your business will be assessed.
   The impact can be represented as time or resource (materials, money, etc.) savings for employees or manufacturing processes, as an increase in the number of clients, as direct additional profit or savings, and so on.

2. Select the level of impact that you expect to get.
   The level should be based on measurements and adjusted for your business specifics. You can use information from other successful AI initiatives and you should choose two scenarios for the assessment: low impact level and high impact level. In general, the difference between the two assessments should be within 20–25 percent. This limitation will help you to be more careful in your prognosis.

3. Turn your impact levels into cash.
   In other words, calculate the profit that the AI initiative should help you earn. It will show a real impact on your business, help adjust the project budget, and help you make the final decision on project implementation. Remember that the preliminary results can be confusing and that the project may require some adjustments after deployment. However, the metric(s) you have decided on will help you avoid such confusion.

Let's look at an example using a metric for an investment firm that has a department that helps make investments for private investors. The department has two databases with many millions of rows each: one investor (client) database and one investment package database. The AI solution will be built to match potential clients from one database with the most optimal investment package from the other database. The main source of profit is the percentage of profit from a successful investment. A major success factor is the compliance of an investment package with a client's expectations and capabilities. Before introducing AI in this investment firm, all compliance checks were done manually. The baseline prior to applying AI was as follows:

- Rate of successful cases: 90 percent
- Margin from a successful case: $10,000
- Loss from an unsuccessful case: $2,000
- The average number of cases: 100 per month

The objective of applying AI in the investment firm was to use AI to maximize the percentage of successful cases and thereby increase profits. By applying the aforementioned generic steps in this specific example, it would look like this:

1. The source of the impact is the percentage of successful cases.

2. AI should help increase the percentage up to 93–98 percent (low-impact and high-impact assessments).

3. Calculations (see Table 7.1).

Table 7.1: Calculation of business impact (example)

CALCULATION CRITERIA	LOW-IMPACT ESTIMATION	HIGH-IMPACT ESTIMATION
Increase in % of successful cases	6%	8%
Savings on unsuccessful cases	12,000 USD /month	16,000 USD/month
Profit from additional successful cases	60,000 USD/month	80,000 USD/month
Total profit increase	**72,000 USD/month**	**96,000 USD/month**

As you can see, the profit from implementing an AI solution in the investment firm should be between 72,000 and 96,000 USD/month. Hence, the value is quite significant and it would be wise to make the investment in AI, since it would pay off in a month.

Remember that in the data science team, the most important figure to focus on is the increase in the success rate of 6–8 percent. This metric will allow progress follow-up with a direct relation to their impact on company profits. It will also allow for a baseline for different versions of improvements. For example, maybe the data science team reaches 95.5 percent in a shorter time and that will be enough for the company targets. Or maybe the team finds a way to reach 99 percent success rate with more time. However, remember that the cost of the solution needs to be put against the gain as well; if the 95.5 percent solution costs 5,000 USD/month and the 99 percent costs 25,000 USD/month, you will be better off if you stay with 95.5 percent (if no other factors apply). It all depends on what's most important in your company, but with these types of metrics you can elaborate on different scenarios to make the right decisions, since you have measured the AI business value in money.

Measuring AI Value in Nonrevenue Terms

If you want to complement your monetary metrics with more performance-related measurements that are easier to assign and apply across the organization and the teams, there are quite a lot of relevant ones to pick from. Just remember to make sure that the metrics you select can be connected to your overall ambition with your AI initiative so that these specific metrics don't start driving behavior in the wrong direction. Table 7.2 includes examples of performance-related AI metrics that can be valuable to use to complement your financial metrics.

The metrics listed in Table 7.2 are just examples of what could be useful to apply as complementary targets. But the importance of detailing metrics as subtargets contributing to the overall ambition with the AI initiative should not be underestimated. Experience shows that if company targets are set too high-level, employees have a tendency to feel disconnected from the objective. It simply gets too difficult to see how the individual contribution connects to the overall target.

Ideally, the goals should be shared across business leaders and the respective AI, data, and IT teams. Meanwhile, company leadership must be clear on what value they expect from AI, where they need to make the investments, and how business realization should be approached. Furthermore, it's important to be patient when it comes to tangible

Table 7.2: AI performance-related metrics

TARGET GROUP FOR METRICS	PERFORMANCE OBJECTIVE	METRICS (EXAMPLES)
Data science team	Cost (development per use case)	▪ Cost for data collection, transfer, and processing ▪ Cost for data and AI tools ▪ Cost for architectural changes, etc.
	Speed of deployment (per use case)	▪ Time from concept to running in production ▪ Number of deployments (to production) per month, week, day ▪ Number of use cases in parallel (with required quality)
	Managing change (identification and implementation)	▪ Number of A/B tests per month ▪ Time to implement learning-induced changes ▪ Time for retraining and redeployment initiated from production
	Reuse of assets per use case (data, models, code, pipelines, architectures, etc.)	▪ Percentage of assets reused ▪ Percentage of code reuse
Management	AI (data science) strategy	▪ Number of AI targets on unit scorecard (for shared accountability) ▪ Frequency of AI communication to employees (for priority) ▪ Number of AI use cases in manager's unit planned and executed ▪ Frequency of AI topics on the company leadership agenda
Employees	AI training	▪ Average number of AI training courses completed per employee
	AI toolsets and solutions	▪ Number of active users per AI tool and month ▪ Percentage of decisions made using an AI solution/tool ▪ Number of ML scenarios run each week
	AI use cases	▪ Number of new data and new AI use case proposals submitted per month ▪ Number of AI use cases/initiatives completed

business results from AI. To fully realize the overall AI objectives, 12 to 24 months is to be expected. However, with full focus on applying MLOps practices, significant progress toward those goals could be achieved in just two to three months.

Operating Different AI Business Models

Every day we read about some new AI breakthrough. AI is ever-present in our everyday lives whether we use mobile devices, wearables, or voice assistants, or stream our favorite series and films. Enterprises control the focal point of the AI economy and drive the innovation through a new trajectory, attracting investors through perfectly timed innovations and promises of enormous business growth. A forecast from IDC Worldwide predicts the AI market will have worldwide revenues surpassing $400 billion already in 2022 for AI software, hardware, and services, and the market is expected to break the $500 billion mark in 2023 (`www.idc.com/ getdoc.jsp?containerId=prUS48881422`).

Artificial intelligence is revolutionizing the market. Machine learning creates new business models that were not even conceivable a few years ago. Anyone who, at the turn of the last century, predicted that a company would soon offer virtual customers to other companies and even earn money on that would have been ridiculed. But this has become reality today. The structure of a new "AI economy" is beginning to emerge. The question, however, is will your company be able to leverage this value through relevant AI business models?

As AI enables companies to use new forms of networked communication with customers and with each other, it is important to note that every company is a provider of products, services, and information, but at the same time it also consumes data and knowledge. Today, the business success of every market participant is heavily dependent on the availability of data and the processing quality of the same. Here are examples of ways to leverage AI in the business:

Evaluation of Data   Artificial intelligence optimizes the evaluation of data. It makes data sources, whose analysis was difficult or impossible with previous methods, accessible, understandable, and usable. More data leads to improved and refined results.

Productivity   Employee productivity improves with access to AI tools. This enables the targeted use of employees for truly innovative tasks.

Technology   AI software can provide a competitive edge through the efficient use of machine learning. In addition, existing hardware becomes more powerful through intelligent programming.

Customer Dialogue   AI makes communication with customers easier, more efficient, and less expensive. Chatbots can be used for standardized requests. If things get complicated, a person intervenes and attends to the customer. In this communication, the person also supplies the algorithm with new information.

Efficiency   The use of AI is rapidly replacing experts. This makes products with previously high secondary costs more affordable.

But what about the operational aspects of different AI business models? As you can imagine, there are significant operational differences between AI offerings that run on a public cloud environment and a private cloud environment, or between running an AI solution on the cloud and running in an on-premises setup. However, the largest difference, and maybe the most interesting one, can be found between running an *artificial intelligence–as-a-service (AIaaS)* solution on the cloud and running an AI-embedded solution in a device on the edge. Regardless of which business model and AI solution setup is valid for your company, there are vital AI operational aspects you must consider. The following sections explain this topic in more detail.

Operating Artificial Intelligence as a Service

Leveraging AIaaS is a way to help organizations incorporate AI functionality without needing to have in-depth expertise in all areas. Usually, AIaaS services are built on cloud-based providers like Amazon AWS, Google Cloud, Microsoft Azure, and IBM Cloud. The AI service, framework, and workflows built on these infrastructures are offered to final customers for various use cases, such as inventory management services and manufacturing optimizations. AIaaS allows businesses to experiment with artificial intelligence in a low-risk environment and without a significant up-front investment.

AIaaS is a more recent addition to a suite of "as a service" products that help businesses maintain a focus on their core operations, and it's somewhat connected to the cloud SaaS (software-as-a-service) model. To understand this industry, it's important to understand its various layers. Just as SaaS is built on top of a platform-as-a-service (PaaS) and an infrastructure-as-a-service (IaaS) setup, AIaaS is built on top of a cloud infrastructure that works as the basis for the service itself.

As shown in Figure 7.1, the main business models in the top application layer are *SaaS* (software as a service) and AIaaS, and in some cases even MLOps. SaaS providers sell access to application software and databases. SaaS customers are end users who typically access the software through a web browser or client program. They don't see the underlying infrastructure or platform it's built on, because SaaS providers take care of all the necessary hardware and coding. SaaS is easily the most popular form of cloud computing. Gmail, Slack, and Microsoft Office 365 are all commonly used SaaS products. Customer relationship management (CRM) systems are also SaaS-based, as are many customer service and support solutions.

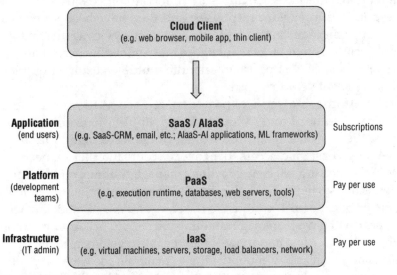

Figure 7.1: The infrastructure of "as a service" business models

When it comes to AIaaS there are an increasing amount of "as a service" AI solutions, and many more are in development for specific industries and use cases. By using pretrained models, companies can use out-of-the-box ML algorithms to find patterns in data and make predictions. Businesses can customize these predictions to continually improve products, services, and processes. For example, Amazon has made the AI-based recommendation engine they are using on their own retail site available as an AIaaS to other retailers.

There are also many AIaaS solutions available for computer vision and natural language processing, meaning that if your company wants to start analyzing large volumes of text, images, or video streams, you can simply start with these AIaaS solutions, which are delivered via the cloud. All you need to do is upload or stream your data to the cloud and subscribe to the AIaaS to get started.

AIaaS also enables cloud-based data integration. The AIaaS vendors offer application programming interfaces (APIs) to enable communication between two pieces of software. AIaaS allows users to upload and stream data, run cutting-edge models, and analyze data using a cloud platform.

Another example of AIaaS is chatbots, which are now offered as simple plug-and-play tools. Using natural language processing (NLP) and machine learning, chatbots use AI to simulate human conversation through online interfaces. Chatbots are trained to process user queries and respond with relevant responses, and they have been shown to improve customer satisfaction and save customer service agents time so they can focus on other tasks that require human intelligence. Chatbots can also provide 24/7 support and handle multiple customer queries simultaneously at very low costs.

PaaS (platform-as-a-service) providers sell access to everything a customer would need to develop their own applications on top. You purchase the resources you need from a cloud service provider on a pay-as-you-go basis and access them over a secure Internet connection. Unlike in the IaaS model, PaaS providers manage runtime, middleware, and operating systems. However, PaaS customers still get to manage data and applications, in contrast to the SaaS and AIaaS model, where customers don't have to manage anything but should of course monitor ongoing activities. Most importantly, PaaS enables customers to develop, test, and launch an app without having to maintain the necessary software or invest in any new infrastructure. Examples of PaaS products include AWS Elastic Beanstalk, Google App Engine, and Adobe Magento Commerce.

IaaS (infrastructure-as-a-service) is a type of cloud computing service that offers essential compute, storage, and networking resources on demand, on a pay-as-you-go basis. IaaS providers sell access to virtualized resources, including servers, networks, and storage. Enterprise customers typically purchase these compute resources as needed, which is more cost-effective than buying hardware outright. Unlike SaaS users, IaaS customers must manage the applications, runtime, middleware, operating systems, and data they access. The IaaS providers, meanwhile, manage the servers, hard drives, networking, virtualization, and storage. Amazon Web Services, Microsoft Azure, and Google Compute Engine are the three biggest IaaS providers.

The as-a-service models are sometimes referred to as the second wave of Web 2.0. Indeed, the idea with these types of business models is to offer a capable solution to the end customer quickly, without having to host it on-premises. On-premises solutions come with complex implementations; are slow and costly, usually with a large overhead; and lack the flexibility to easily and quickly scale up and down. Yet while IaaS targets IT administrators, PaaS is skewed toward development teams. SaaS and AIaaS, on the other hand, have wider applications toward end users, also in nontechnical departments (see Figure 7.2).

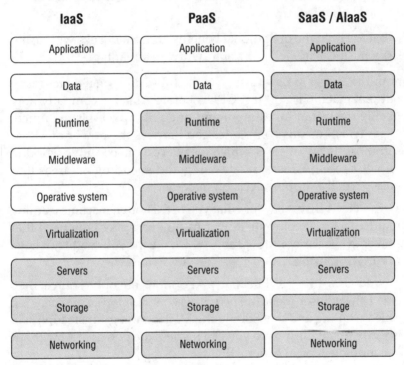

Figure 7.2: The different "as-a-service" layers

AIaaS is also a relatively broad term that can be divided into distinct types:

- **Cognitive computing APIs** is where an application programming interface (API) developer can utilize API calls to incorporate artificial intelligence into applications. This encompasses a range of services, including computer vision, knowledge graphs, and natural language processing (NLP). Each has the ability to generate business value from unstructured information.

- **Bots and digital assistants** are a very popular form of AIaaS offerings, including automated email services, chatbots, and digital customer service agents.

- **Fully managed machine learning services** are ideally suited to nontechnological organizations that desire a fully managed approach or a complete AI solution offering a specific service with built-in AI capabilities.

- **Machine learning frameworks** are frameworks that allow organizations to build custom models that will only handle a small amount of data.

So, what are then the operational benefits and drawbacks with using AIaaS as a business model? Let's start with the advantages:

Computing Power at Low Cost   Successful AI and ML requires many parallel machines and fast GPUs. Before AIaaS, a company may decide the initial investment and ongoing upkeep is too much. Now, AIaaS means companies can harness the power of ML at significantly lower costs, which means you can continue working on your core business, not training and spending on areas that only partially support decision making.

Charging Flexibility   Pay for what you use. Though machine learning requires a lot of compute power to run, you may only need that power in short amounts of time, which means you might not have to run AI nonstop.

Improved Usability   While many AI options are open source, they aren't always user-friendly. This means your developers are spending time installing and developing the ML technology. Instead, AIaaS is ready out of the box, so you can harness the power of AI without becoming technical experts first.

Scalability   AIaaS enables you to start with smaller projects to learn if it's the right fit for your needs. As you gain experience with your own data, you can tweak your service and scale up or down as project demands change. To be successful, however, you still have to follow the principles outlined in this book to be able to move from experimentation to production, since it still allows for the same pitfalls.

Now let's have a look at some of the drawbacks with offering and operating your AI solution using the AIaaS business model:

Reduced Security   AI and machine learning depend on significant amounts of data, which means your company must in one sense share that data with third-party vendors. Although data storage, access, and transit to servers are usually strictly regulated in contracts, it's important to ensure the data isn't improperly accessed, shared, or tampered with.

Reliance Issues   Because you're working with one or more third parties, you're relying on them to provide the data you need. This isn't inherently a problem, but it creates dependencies that can lead to delays or other issues if any problems arise.

Reduced Transparency   In AIaaS, a customer is buying the service but not the access. Some view an as-a-service offering, particularly those in ML, like a black box. In other words, you know the input and the output, but you don't understand the inner workings, like which algorithms are being used, whether the algorithms are updated, and which versions apply to which data. This may lead to confusion or miscommunication regarding the stability of your data or the output generated from your AI solution.

Data Laws and Regulations   Government laws and regulations related to countries or various industries may limit whether or not data can be transferred out of a country to the country of the cloud servers. It can also regulate if and for how long data can be stored on the cloud. Remember that you need to be acutely aware of how the data is handled by the as-a-service provider, since the main servers might be located in your country but for redundancy handling some data might be replicated to servers in other countries. This may prohibit your company from launching an AIaaS solution running on a public cloud, taking advantage of certain types of AIaaS solutions, or even using certain AIaaS providers.

So, how do you monetize AIaaS? AIaaS gets monetized in the form of subscriptions, which include managing, running, and monitoring the AI/ML models that are used as the foundation for the provided service. Imagine the specific case of a company providing AI models for improving manufacturing processes. The AIaaS company will work on cleaning the data from the customer, plugging that into its AI models to generate reports, monitoring, and workflows for process optimization.

Part of AI services will also require maintenance and retraining of models. In these cases, they can be part of the AIaaS package or charged separately on a pay-per-consumption basis as MLOps. As a rapidly growing field, AIaaS has plenty of benefits that bring early adopters to the table. While there may be bumps in the road when developing AIaaS, it's likely to be as important as other "as a service" offerings. Taking these valuable services out of the hands of the few means that many more organizations can harness the value and power of AI and ML in their business.

Operating Embedded AI Solutions

So, it's obvious that modern cloud computing infrastructures provide on-demand access to large amounts of computing resources and are therefore the primary choice for running sophisticated AI applications, like autonomous driving and large-scale fraud detection. In several cases, AI/ML applications are also hosted on private clouds such as on-premises data centers. Nevertheless, executing AI in the cloud is not always the best option, especially for applications that require low latency and must be run close to the end users. Specifically, cloud-based AI requires the transfer of large amounts of data from the place where they are produced to cloud data centers, a process that consumes significant network bandwidth and incurs high latency. Furthermore, such data transfers can be susceptible to privacy leaks, especially in applications that manage sensitive data. Moreover, the use of GPUs and tensor processing units (TPUs) in the cloud is associated with a significant carbon dioxide emission, which raises environmental performance concerns.

The benefits of running AI closer to the users are experienced on a daily basis by millions of consumers who execute deep learning applications in their smartphones, including popular applications like Siri, Google Assistant, and Apple FaceID. These applications take advantage of ML/DL models that are (pre)trained in the cloud but that run in applications closer to the user. Furthermore, they illustrate the possibility of training models in the cloud and executing them in devices with less powerful computing capabilities.

In the case of smartphones, it is also possible to execute machine learning models on all sorts of embedded devices, ranging from networked and mobile embedded systems to small-scale microcontrollers. The latter operates based on a general principle that ML models like neural networks are trained on computing clusters or on the cloud, whereas inference operations and the execution of the models take place on the embedded devices. Contrary to what most people believe, it turns out that once a model is trained, the operations of deep learning models can be effectively executed on CPU-constrained devices or even tiny (e.g., 16- or 32-bit) microcontrollers. Specific chipsets are also being introduced with devices either stand-alone or integrated in the CPU, like for example how Apple's bionic chip introduced cores for neural networks, and how IBM introduced neuromorphic chipsets.

Over the past several years, an important shift in focus has occurred from cloud-level to device-level (on the edge) processing of AI tasks, data, and results. *Embedded AI*, or *edge AI*, is the direct result of this important shift. Embedded AI unlocks the potential of processing data within the hundreds of billions of ubiquitous microprocessors, sensors, and embedded controllers, which are available in a variety of settings such as industrial plants, manufacturing shopfloors, smart buildings, and residential environments. In this way, embedded AI also facilitates the processing of the data produced by embedded devices (e.g., Internet of Things [IoT] devices), most of which are currently unexploited. As shown in Figure 7.3, a key operational difference between running an AIaaS model on the cloud and running an embedded AI solution on the edge is related to where the model inference happens.

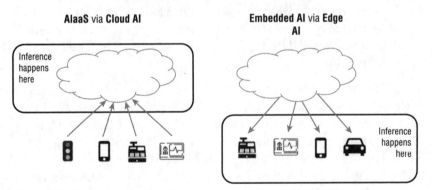

Figure 7.3: Operational difference between AIaaS and embedded AI

However, this difference in terms of where the AI model inference happens has its pros and cons. The execution of AI models on embedded devices (edge AI) comes with several benefits over conventional cloud-based AI:

- **Low latency**—Embedded machine learning is much more efficient than cloud AI in cases where execution of low-latency operations close to the field is required. This is because there is no need to transfer large amounts of data to the cloud, which can incur considerable network latency. As such, embedded machine learning is an excellent choice when it comes to supporting real-time use cases like field actuation and control in industrial environments.

- **Reduced power consumption**—Many embedded systems such as microcontrollers are power-efficient and can operate for a long time without being charged.

- **Improved environmental performance**—Cloud AI results in too many carbon dioxide emissions and has very poor environmental performance. In contrast, machine learning on embedded devices has a significantly lower carbon footprint, which yields better sustainability.

- **Network bandwidth efficiency**—The execution of machine learning models on embedded devices enables the extraction of insights at the source of the data. This eliminates the need for transferring raw data to edge or cloud servers, which saves bandwidth and network resources.

- **Strong privacy management**—Embedded machine learning removes the need for transferring and storing data on cloud servers. This reduces the risks of data breaches and privacy leaks, which is particularly important for applications that process sensitive data like personal data, intellectual property (IP) data, and business-sensitive data.

Based on these benefits, embedded AI (or edge AI) can sometimes be a much better choice than conventional cloud-based AI, especially in use cases that require real-time, low-latency, and low-overhead interactions. For instance, enterprise maintenance and intelligent asset management in various industrial sectors can greatly benefit from embedded AI. The latter can enable the extraction of real-time insights on potential machine failures and production defects by processing data inside the asset (e.g., within the machine). As another example, precision agriculture applications can benefit from instant discovery of crop problems, based on the direct processing of sensor data from field sensors (e.g., images and temperature data). The latter processing is usually much faster than cloud data processing.

Nevertheless, embedded AI must not be seen as a replacement for cloud-based AI. In most cases, embedded AI complements cloud-based applications with value-added functionalities such as real-time control operations and privacy management for sensitive datasets.

Embedded AI applications run on different types of embedded devices, based on tools and techniques that enable the development and deployment of AI models on resource-constrained nodes. Hence, the embedded AI ecosystem includes device vendors, notably the original equipment manufacturers (OEMs), where AI models are deployed and executed. Moreover, it also extends the global AI ecosystem with tools and techniques for developing, deploying, and operating AI applications on embedded devices, including IoT devices. In the latter case, the AI applications are conveniently called AIoT (artificial intelligence on IoT) devices.

Embedded AI (edge AI) provides a wealth of innovation opportunities for enterprises that wish to apply AI and make the best possible use of their data. It empowers enterprises to exploit unused datasets, while optimizing the bandwidth, storage, and latency of AI solutions in need of that. In this context, it also boosts the development of value-added applications like, for example, real-time monitoring in IoT-based production environments.

Operating a Hybrid AI Business Model

Even though embedded AI (which is realized through edge AI) and AIaaS (which is realized through cloud AI) are both quite different, neither hinders the other, and edge computing was not developed as a means of replacing cloud computing. For the processing of information that isn't time sensitive, cloud computing is a great option, but for applications that require real-time processing of data or enhanced privacy, edge computing is the fittest for the job. This depicts one of the differences between embedded AI/edge AI and AIaaS/cloud AI.

As shown in Figure 7.4, differences between edge AI and cloud AI show that edge AI allows AI algorithms to run in real time with increased privacy and security and the instantaneous processing of data through a decentralized architecture. With AI models in the cloud, there is support for knowledge sharing, large AI models, and a reduction of factors that obstruct implementation. Edge AI and cloud AI are both advantageous and not without their shortcomings as well. Combining the advantages of both of them, with seamless and secure data flow across the whole computing environment, is probably a good way forward.

The computational power and large amount of data that AI models require explains why the resources of a centralized cloud are used to train them. The trained models are then distributed to edge devices or set up in a centralized cloud.

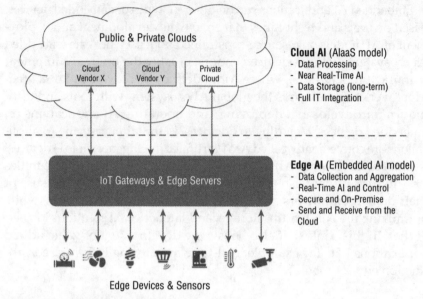

Cloud AI (AIaaS model)
- Data Processing
- Near Real-Time AI
- Data Storage (long-term)
- Full IT Integration

Edge AI (Embedded AI model)
- Data Collection and Aggregation
- Real-Time AI and Control
- Secure and On-Premise
- Send and Receive from the Cloud

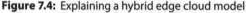

Figure 7.4: Explaining a hybrid edge cloud model

Cloud AI and edge AI are not supposed to be seen as opposing elements, but rather as complementing architectures, as is evident in cases where edge AI devices make use of cloud resources. However, there is an ever-increasing need for more edge AI implementations because of issues with bandwidth, privacy, latency, security, and autonomy that are present in cloud models (which offer scale and simplicity).

Looking ahead, it's not going to be a discussion of edge AI *or* cloud AI; instead, it will in many cases be a case of edge AI *and* cloud AI, since the cost of data transport, latency issues, and security/data privacy concerns hinder applying cloud AI to everything.

Likewise, the raw data processing power at the edge, along with the inability to do deeper exploration of the edge data over longer periods of time for better insights, means edge AI alone is not a solution either. Instead, an operationally optimized AI solution must allow for the right processing at the right level, and this definitely calls for more hybrid edge cloud architectures going forward.

Index